INTRODUCTION TO RESIDENTIAL LAYOUT

Mike Biddulph

ELSEVIER

Amsterdam • Boston • Heidelberg • London • New York • Oxford
Paris • San Diego • San Francisco • Singapore • Sydney • Tokyo
Butterworth-Heinemann is an imprint of Elsevier

Butterworth-Heinemann is an imprint of Elsevier Ltd
Linacre House, Jordan Hill, Oxford OX2 8DP
30 Corporate Road, Burlington, MA 01803

First edition 2007

British Library Cataloging in Publication Data
A catalog record for this book is available from the British Library

Library of Congress Cataloging in Publication Data
A catalog record for this book is available from the Library of Congress

ISBN 13: 978-0-75-066205-5
ISBN 10: 0-75-066205-0

For information on all Butterworth-Heinemann publications visit our website at
www.books.elsevier.com

Typeset by Macmillan, India
Printed and bound in Great Britain

Working together to grow
libraries in developing countries

www.elsevier.com | www.bookaid.org | www.sabre.org

ELSEVIER   BOOK AID
            International   Sabre Foundation

Contents

Preface

I have always felt that the design of residential areas offers more potential than any other aspect of urban design, but that this potential is rarely reflected in practice. Where they are well done, residential areas are some of the most diverse and stimulating environments that have been created, but too often they are simply dull and one-dimensional; offering few opportunities for the people that live there. As a result, I have set out to draw together the whole range of themes and issues that might be considered in the design of a residential scheme, and tried to provide advice about the ways in which designs might be influenced by them.

A number of books exist on the design of residential areas. This book is different because I have tried to offer a comprehensive discussion about a whole range of design perspectives and issues, and I have tried to base design ideas firmly within existing theories about how to design, as well as the evidence from the schemes that I have visited. This approach is supplemented by links to other authors who have guided me in my thinking, and which could be used as a starting point in any further reading on the topics discussed here.

In travelling around looking at and thinking about housing schemes I have been struck by their diversity, and that the schemes often 'work' well in certain respects. In general, I would suggest that this book reflects upon three design traditions: north American, northern European and British. I don't distinguish between these traditions within the book, but instead I suggest that there is something to learn from all of them. The theory helps us to decipher what we might find interesting about any of these schemes, and I have used a wide range of illustrations to help the reader understand what makes these schemes interesting, as well as providing ideas for how we might design in the future.

When writing this book I have always been conscious about the different types of jargon used to discuss features of a housing scheme. In general, the UK jargon is used, although at times I have, for example, referred to *pavements* as *sidewalks*. I have tried to write for a wide audience, partly as I feel that each country has something to teach us all about this subject, but I am sorry if the language reflects my own heritage.

Mike Biddulph

Acknowledgements

I would like to thank Mr Paul Talbot and his colleagues at Crest Nicholson for advising on the costs discussed in Chapter 2. Thanks to Dr. Stephen Marshall for his permission to redraw Figure 5.45. Thanks to Prof. Bill Hillier for his permission to redraw Figure 6.10. Finally, thanks to the Ordnance Survey for permission to use their map base data in Figures 2.10, 3.3, 3.4, 3.10, 7.23 and 8.5.

Photographic Sources

Austria

Am Hirschenfeld Bruenner Strasse/Empergergasse, Vienna: 3.29, 3.34 (top), 8.49 (bottom left), 9.18

Aspern an der Sonne, Wulzendorfstrasse, Vienna: 5.34 (bottom left)

Siedlung Wienerberg, Vienna: 5.35, 6.38 (bottom), 9.27

Trondheimgasse / Stavangergasse, Vienna: 5.17

Wulzendorf (West), Bergengasse, Vienna: 7.41

Germany

Beethovenstrasse, Cologne: 3.24, 5.34 (top right), 8.49 (top right)

Franzoesisches Viertel, Tuebingen: 4.16, 4.28, 5.34 (bottom right), 5.72, 5.74, 6.26, 9.6, 9.32 (bottom left)

Heinrich Boell Strasse, Berlin: 4.33

Kirchsteigfeld, Potsdam-Drewitz: 3.2 (top left), 3.20, 7.12, 7.30

Kreuzviertel, Dortmund: 9.26

Kupferstrasse, Luenen: 4.9

Marzahn, Berlin: 9.14;

Neu Karow, Berlin: 6.14

Rauchstrasse, Berlin: 6.8 (left)

Rieselfeld, Freiburg: 4.10, 4.17, 4.49, 6.37 (top), 6.38 (top), 7.29, 9.11 (top right), 9.25

Rummelsburger Bucht Wasserstadt, Berlin: 4.32, 4.48

Siedlung Arkadien, Asperg: 5.48, 5.55, 5.64, 9.21, 9.33 (middle)

Spandau, Berlin: 4.29

Vauban, Freiburg: 1.14, 3.17, 4.31 (left), 5.34 (top left), 8.6 (third down), 9.11 (bottom left), 9.22, 9.33 (bottom)

Netherlands

Alphen aan den Rijn: 9.11 (bottom right), 9.20

Borneo Sporenburg, Amsterdam: 7.19, 8.6 (top)

De Aker, Amsterdam: 3.27, 5.46 (left), 6.23, 7.39, 9.17

De Dijk, Rijswilk, The Hague: 7.26, 9.33 (top)

Delft: 1.15

Ecolonia, Alphen aan den Rijn: 4.34, 5.46 (right), 8.45 (bottom right)

KNSM Island, Amsterdam: 9.32 (top right)

Nieuwland, Amersfoort: 1.10, 4.36

Rijswilk, The Hague: 5.22

Vondel Park, Amsterdam: 3.13

Ypenburg, Delft: 7.18, 8.6 (second down), 8.44 (middle), 9.11 (top left)

Sweden

Bo01, Western Harbour, Malmo: 3.2 (middle left), 4.30, 4.37, 5.54 (right), 7.20, 8.39, 9.32 (top middle)

UK
Abode, Newhall, Harlow: 2.41, 8.49 (top left)
Acorn Televillage, Crickhowell, Monmouthshire: 2.13, 3.2 (middle right), 8.44 (bottom)
Bishop's Castle, Shropshire: 4.39
Caerphilly, S. Wales: 1.13, 7.34
Cardiff Bay, Cardiff: 2.23
Castlefields, Runcorn, Cheshire: 5.21
Chancellor Park, Chelmsford, Essex: 2.9, 7.15, 7.45 (top), 8.40
Crickhowell, Monmouthshire: 2.39
Eldonians, Liverpool: 2.20
Field Farm, Shepton Mallet, Somerset: 2.17
Gallowgate, Glasgow: 3.7, 5.70
Garston, Liverpool: 2.24
Gorbals, Glasgow: 5.54 (left)
Homes for Change, Hulme, Manchester: 6.25
Ingress Park, Greenhithe, Kent: 3.2 (top right), 3.14, 4.8, 7.2, 8.2
Kew Riverside, Kew, London: 1.8, 2.18, 2.22, 2.32, 2.35, 2.45, 9.32 (bottom right)
King's Hill, West Malling, Kent: 2.21 (top), 3.11, 3.34 (middle), 8.43, 9.32 (top left)
Llanedeyrn, Cardiff: 4.6, 7.40, 9.3
Millennium Village, Greenwich, London: 2.14, 2.21 (bottom), 6.24, 8.45 (bottom left), 9.13
Newhall, Harlow: 2.26, 8.45 (top right)
Polperro, Cornwall: 8.7
Pontprennau, Cardiff: 1.5, 1.7, 3.16, 4.7, 4.15, 4.26, 5.56, 6.20, 7.31, 8.1
Port Marine, Portishead, Somerset: 2.25, 7.6
Poundbury, Dorchester, Dorset: 3.2 (bottom right), 5.6, 5.49, 6.30, 7.35, 9.19
St James' Park, Surbiton, Surrey: 7.33
St Mary's Island, Chatham: 2.36, 5.32, 7.45 (bottom), 8.6 (bottom), 8.45 (top left)
Staith's South Bank, Dunston, Gateshead, Tyneside: 2.42, 8.44 (top)
Sturminster Newton, Dorset: 7.36
Thorley Lane, Bishop's Stortford, Hertfordshire: 2.34, 3.34 (second bottom)

USA
Beaufort, South Carolina: 8.51 (top)
Charleston, South Carolina: 8.3
Davis, California: 6.29
Fairview, Portland, Oregon: 3.34 (bottom)
Habersham, Beaufort, South Carolina: 2.33, 4.38
Ion, Charleston, South Carolina: 2.40, 3.2 (bottom left), 6.17, 6.27, 8.49 (bottom right)
Laguna West, Sacramento, California: 1.4, 1.6, 9.2
New Point, Beaufort, South Carolina: 6.8 (right), 6.16, 8.51 (bottom)
North Beach, San Francisco: 7.17
Orenco, Portland, Oregon: 3.32, 3.34 (second top), 4.12, 4.14, 5.12, 6.18, 9.8
Pearl District, Portland, Oregon: 7.5
Rivermark, Santa Clara, California: 7.24, 7.25
Sacramento, California: 1.2, 7.11
Seaside, Florida: 1.12, 2.31, 2.37, 5.53, 6.37 (bottom), 8.46, 9.24
Watercolor, Florida: 2.38

1 Introduction

THE DESIGN OF RESIDENTIAL AREAS

This book aims to bring together current thinking on the design of residential areas to provide a comprehensive source of practical advice for anyone responsible for the layout of a residential scheme. It tries, in particular, to combine current thinking about residential layout with reference to a wide range of examples of good practice from actual schemes. This is done so that the practical value of the ideas presented in this book is always apparent.

Housing environments take up the majority of developed land and we spend long periods of our life within them. As such the way that they are designed can simply make our lives a pleasure, or they can make it hard for us to live our lives the way that we would like. How they are designed can, in particular, open up or reduce opportunities for us. It is important that in planning any residential scheme, designers are conscious of the design choices that are available to them so that these can be either encouraged or rejected through the design process. This book aims, therefore, to suggest that there is a whole range of design options available to us in the design of residential schemes. It also tries to show us what the consequences of the design choices that we might make are, so that, as designers, we are informed in our decision-making.

This book is not about residential architecture, and it won't tell you how to design and construct a house. Instead, it is a book about residential urban design. In this respect the use of the term 'urban' is loose, and merely refers to situations in which a group of buildings come together to form villages, towns or cities. The focus is more specifically on the places that are created as a result of the planning and layout of individual homes–more explicitly the gardens, streets, yards, parks and other attributes that characterise the spaces between our homes. This book points out the problems associated with particular approaches to laying out houses. In particular, it aims to be optimistic and encourage an understanding of the possibilities that are realised when the planning of a housing scheme is undertaken.

In order to do this, however, it has been necessary to focus on a type of residential development. When you think about it, there is a whole range of environments which have been designed for human habitation, and it wouldn't be sensible to try and write a book that would be relevant to all these forms. This book therefore focuses on the types of environment that result from certain densities of development. Rudlin and Falk (1999) illustrate how Kowloon, north of the Hong Kong island, has a density of 1,250 units per hectare, whilst the average net density of Los Angeles is 15 units per hectare (Figure 1.1). This book will be of little interest to you if you are planning schemes at either of these extremes. Instead the book is concerned with the design of residential environments at a medium density of between about 30 and 450 units per hectare. This itself is a wide range, but for anything above 30 units per hectare many of the layout issues in this book become more pertinent, whilst densities of 450 units per hectare, despite being high, reflect common densities achieved, for example, in the centre of London (see Llewelyn Davies, 2000). High quality residential environments are still commonplace at such densities, even if they really do start to restrict the types of layout qualities that you might aspire to achieve.

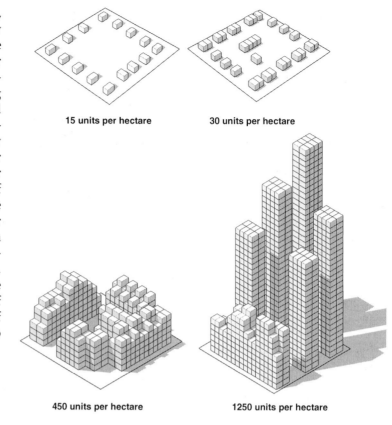

15 units per hectare   **30 units per hectare**

450 units per hectare   **1250 units per hectare**

Figure 1.1   Visualising units per hectare

SUSTAINABLE SCHEMES

This book considers a range of issues associated with residential layout from a variety of perspectives, but all of the content is organised around the principle that the planning and design of new residential areas should create physical conditions where economically, socially and environmentally sustainable lifestyles become possible. Economically, this means that housing should form part of a wider environment that remains popular with not only the initial residents but also subsequent residents, while commercial and community uses should be designed and integrated into any plans so that they remain viable. Socially, this means that the designs should allow residents to have equity of access to housing, the wider environment or facilities and that all residents (whatever their relative affluence) should be able to enjoy a good quality of life. Environmentally, this means that the designs should create conditions where resource consumption can be minimised and biodiversity within or around the residential schemes are sustained or enhanced.

It is possible to design residential areas which favour economic, social or environmental concerns; for example, an exclusive residential area which is economically very successful and socially unmixed and which offers a wide range of facilities, but only for immediate residents. Such schemes would, however, exclude other people who may not have access to similar opportunities elsewhere. Equally, it is also possible to design commercial uses into a scheme that will be extremely viable but dependent exclusively on people who are auto-dependent. Such a plan would exclude residents without access to a car, and the scheme would also have poor environmental credentials. Ultimately it will be your, or your client's, choice as to how you respond to the challenge of creating sustainability, but the objective of this book has been to present an approach in which a whole range of issues are considered in a balanced way. At least then it will be possible to critically appreciate the nature of the choices being made and the range of options available.

DESIGN CHOICES AND LIFESTYLE OPPORTUNITIES

The design of urban spaces won't determine how people will live within the residential area. However, as already suggested, it will create or limit opportunities for people. For example, it is possible to design a residential environment in which it would be difficult or unpleasant to walk (Figure 1.2). Even in situations like these, people may still choose to walk as they adapt quite successfully to their environment, and walking may be the only way they can get around. A better design, however, would have acknowledged the needs of the pedestrian and involved a design that would support that need.

However, maintaining these options involves difficult decisions, and to a certain extent the designers of residential areas must exercise value judgements in deciding which choices should be available to residents. Some choices might be obvious; for example, providing people with the opportunity to walk to local facilities would appear to be an obvious choice. Other choices, in contrast, might have an economic, social or environmental cost attached to them. Making it possible for residents to drive quickly through a residential area may be good for people who choose to drive, but it will encourage car use and probably make the residential area more dangerous. This in turn would limit the extent to which children would be allowed to play in the street, whilst elderly people might feel more insecure outside their home (Figure 1.3). Designers, therefore, must be conscious of the

Figure 1.2   It is possible to design a residential environment in which people might not feel too comfortable about walking

Figure 1.3   Designers need to understand the implications of their design choices

consequences of their design decisions and the fact that creating opportunities for certain types of activity might directly limit the choices of some individuals. Again, this book tries to highlight in what ways design decisions might create or limit choices in how people might choose to live within an area, whilst it also considers the positive and negative consequences of the range of design solutions that are available.

BLAND HOUSING

A common criticism of many residential areas is that they are all fundamentally the same. This is far from the case, but there certainly is a tendency towards a standard form of suburban development in, say the USA and UK, for example.

In the USA and UK, residential development is often dominated, in particular, by detached houses 'strung out' along very standardised roads, and the miles and miles of these roads come to define what we collectively, and sometimes a little dismissively, call 'suburbia' (Figure 1.4).

There is actually a lot of variation within suburbia, and this form of housing remains very popular. It is *not* therefore, the purpose of this book

Figure 1.4   American suburbia

to be 'anti-suburban'. Its purpose is, however, to explore the variety that does exist in the form of both urban and suburban housing to illustrate what is actually possible for the forces of standardisation to be overcome. There are three main forces of standardisation.

Standard house types

Developers design and want to build standard, tried and tested, houses. This is actually quite a good idea. It keeps costs down, and the developers can guarantee the quality of the home to a greater extent. String the same houses unimaginatively out along a road, however, and soon everywhere starts to look and feel the same. It is possible to use either individually designed or standard house types, but to use them in such a way that greater variety in a residential area is achieved (Figure 1.5).

Standard roads

Engineers want to build and maintain a limited number of standard, tried and tested, roads. This is also a good idea. When roads are tried and tested their performance is more predictable. It is necessary to suggest, however, that some engineers may not be aware of the whole range of highway–or even parking–options that exist, or that other colleagues in other places may have adopted a greater variety of layouts (Figure 1.6).

Amenity standards

The third force for standardisation is what we call amenity standards. These are typically quantitative measures which try to ensure that existing and new residents gain adequate levels of light, privacy, and outdoor garden or balcony space (Figure 1.7). Planners and developers like amenity standards. They create certainty for both groups and developers know they will get planning permission quickly if they conform. Often, however, they conform too specifically and so houses are then the same distance apart and gardens are as small as possible. This creates little variation in the qualities of the spaces between buildings. Designers, on the other hand, want to create variation. Many designers would use architectural or landscape designs in order to create both light and privacy, or they would create a whole range of outdoor spaces (not just tiny gardens), if only developers and planners would let them.

Although standard solutions may work on only one level, they–instead of urban design–often tend to be adopted. As a result, residential areas can be quite bland because these stringent standards will have been vigorously adhered to, with its residents being denied the opportunity to live in a residential environment which they may have enjoyed more.

This book illustrates variety in the form of residential layouts that are now emerging. It is also meant to be a source book which highlights the range of design opportunities that exist. It tries not to dogmatically present and defend one particular perspective on how residential areas should be designed. Instead, it highlights the key issues that should be considered, and some of the design ideas that might form possible solutions. This reflects the fact that people are choosing to live in residential areas that, in turn, reflect a greater diversity of lifestyles–and housing developers are starting to be more responsive to this diversity of consumer preference.

Figure 1.5   Standard house types

Figure 1.6   Standardised and excessively wide highways undermine the character of residential areas

Figure 1.7   The inflexible use of amenity standards results in repetitive environments

APPROACHES TO RESIDENTIAL LAYOUT

If you are involved in the designing of a new residential area there are eight major issues that you need to address, and for each issue there are a range of approaches to design that might be considered appropriate.

Is the scheme commercially viable?

Homes are very often built for profit and so it is important that any approach to design reflects consumer aspirations which, in turn, will create a demand for such houses (Figure 1.8). Some costs will relate directly to the price of building the private homes or businesses that people will buy or rent. But other costs will result from building and maintaining structures that the whole community may collectively benefit from–such as roads and footpaths, new facilities for children's play or community buildings that every neighbourhood expects. Taken together, the costs of a design solution must not be so high that a developer will be dissuaded from undertaking the scheme. Therefore, the commercial viability of any scheme needs to be carefully considered, and Chapter 2 explains how this should be done.

Figure 1.8   Creating commercially viable schemes

Building place and defining space

A common complaint against many residential areas is that the housing and its layout are monotonous and dull. This is because house builders often utilize standard house types repeatedly along a road has been planned using the inflexible standards referred to above. The result is 'anywhere' housing–as the same developer could build the same houses along the same form of road anywhere else. Chapter 3 discusses how to lay out housing so that more distinctive places and spaces are both considered and achieved within schemes (Figure 1.9).

Environmentally benign development and design

It is possible to design and build residential neighbourhoods in which residents have the opportunity to live in a way that does less damage to the environment. Chapter 4 therefore provides practical design advice for how this might be achieved. It discusses general approaches to using density when creating urban vitality, and therefore viability for a mixture of uses within a neighbourhood. It considers how existing land, buildings and other resources might be reused. It explores how energy might be generated and conserved, and how water might be used, conserved, treated and reused within schemes. It also looks at how waste might be collected

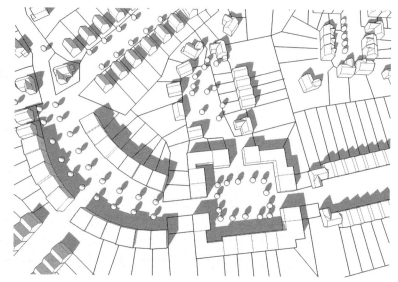

Figure 1.9   Designing distinctive places and spaces

and recycled; and, finally, how biodiversity might be maintained and enhanced (Figure 1.10).

Pedestrian and vehicular access and movement

Chapter Five looks at how to accommodate movement within schemes. How people choose to travel within an urban environment also has environmental implications–but there are so many issues and concepts to consider, and so many design implications that these will be discussed separately from the environmental issues considered in Chapter Four. Chapter Five looks, in particular, at how to support and encourage pedestrian activity within residential areas whilst also accommodating the safe circulation, stopping and parking requirements of cyclists, public transport and cars (Figure 1.11).

Figure 1.10   Creating environmentally benign forms of development

Integrating other uses

Chapter Four will refer to how greater density might be used to support a mixing of uses in residential areas, and Chapter Six will look in more detail at how and why other uses can be accommodated within a layout. Neighbourhoods typically contain shops and services, pubs and restaurants, or religious and other community buildings. In addition, there is an increasing desire to accommodate other spaces for business use and, therefore, located near to where people live, so that they don't have to travel exclusively to remote offices or business parks. These chapters will consider the design concepts, development forms and building configurations that allow this mixture of uses to be achieved (Figure 1.12).

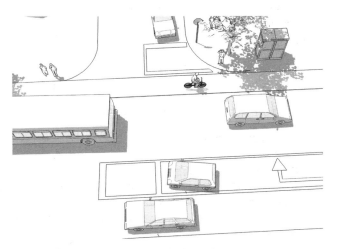

Figure 1.11   Designing for pedestrian and vehicular access and movement

Figure 1.12   Integrating other uses

Safe, and easy to find your way around

Feeling safe where you live would appear to be a fundamental human right. The likelihood that people will be the target of criminal activity is relatively low and typically results from actions shaped by social or economic conditions, rather than anything to do with environmental design. Despite this, however, it is possible to create environments where people *feel* safe or where it may be more difficult to get away with criminal activity. Chapter Seven looks in more detail at how these qualities might be achieved (Figure 1.13).

Figure 1.13   Understanding what makes environments disorientating and feel unsafe

Contemporary residential townscape

There is an important visual dimension to the design of residential areas, and people will enjoy a place if it looks right. Chapter Eight discusses, therefore, how we can compose well-designed housing together into distinctive places, and how we can then detail those places, so that the resulting environment both functions well and is attractive (Figure 1.14).

Figure 1.14   Designing a contemporary residential townscape

Social life in outdoor spaces

Residential areas are places for living, and in this respect the streets and other spaces within the scheme should allow a social and domestic life to flourish. Children need places to play. Youths need places to 'hang out'.

Figure 1.15   Designing for social life in outdoor spaces

Adults–including physically disabled people and the elderly–need attractive and safe outdoor spaces to sit and socialise with friends and neighbours. Chapter Nine will therefore consider how these and other aspects of socialising can be supported within housing schemes (Figure 1.15).

THE STRUCTURE OF EACH CHAPTER

Each chapter is organised roughly into three parts. Initially the theme of the chapter is introduced with reference made to the key concepts and debates surrounding the theme. Following this, a discussion of key design principles is presented and illustrated. It has not been possible to be completely comprehensive within the pages of this book, and on all of the themes covered here there is plenty more that can be found elsewhere. Therefore, at the end of each chapter there is a section of *Further reading* which lists other publications which might also be referred to.

2 Ensuring commercial viability

In this chapter we explore the commercial aspects of housing design and layout. It is really important that designers understand that the buildings and spaces that they design are typically built and sold for profit, and to understand something of how their product will be evaluated in commercial terms. As a result, this chapter outlines a development appraisal known as the *residual valuation technique* and we apply it to a particular development scheme. The point is not to turn designers into quantity surveyors, but instead to inform the mentality of the designer so that their work is not commercially naïve. The residual valuation is a straightforward technique that can be used early in the planning of a simple development scheme, although other, more elaborate and precise techniques will also be used by quantity surveyors working in practice. We will work through a valuation to explore how a design might shape its market potential, and explore how a design can be adjusted to become more profitable. We will also consider how designers can use design to add value to schemes by using layout techniques commonly observed in practice.

COMPLETING A DEVELOPMENT APPRAISAL

The basic equation

In costing a planned residential development it is important to design a scheme where the predicted returns are greater than the costs. The difference between the returns and the costs is known as the *residual*. This residual can be used to determine the value of the land onto which the planned homes will be built.

In preparing a valuation for a scheme the following basic equation should be used:

Development Value − Development Costs = Possible Land Value

Calculating development values

The costing of speculative residential development is relatively straightforward as the value of the property is simply the price that the property is ultimately sold for. In predicting this value it is important to have a clear sense of the local market and how similar homes are selling within that area. It makes sense to be a little conservative with predictions so that values do not become inflated, although there is a tendency for new houses to sell with a slight premium over similar houses that have previously been occupied.

Values will vary significantly according to the location of the home (Figure 2.1), but also–and more specifically–according to the nature of the home and plot. In the UK, homes are sold according to the number of rooms they have, whilst in slightly more refined markets, a total floor area is also compared. The value will also be significantly influenced by the quality of the internal and external design and finish, the size of the garden, the location of parking and the type of house; for example, whether it is detached, semi-detached or terraced.

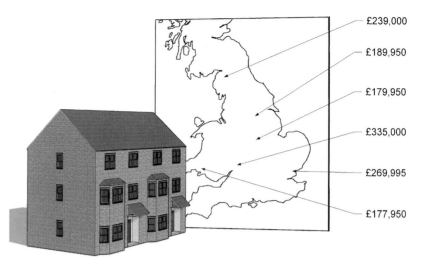

Figure 2.1   Price of the house type Ashbourne across England and Wales in 2006

Values will also vary across the site as certain areas of a scheme may be more desirable than others. This is discussed further below. It is important to refine predicted values relative to judgements about how much demand there will be for properties within a scheme relative to other local areas.

Although housing markets can be very dynamic and predicting sales prices can be imprecise, it is necessary to have a clear sense of the local market using information about previous sales from within the area. However, it is also important to have a sense of how the circumstances surrounding a site might change. For example, the planning of a new road might make the site more accessible and inflate future prices.

In the UK, information about the value of previous residential sales can be obtained from the Land Registry which records details of all sales. They provide national reports of sales trends as well as information for specific post code areas (http://www.landreg.gov.uk). In addition, general information on property market trends can be gathered from reports produced by banks and building societies which are published in the national or regional press releases. As a guide, the average cost of residential land in the UK can also be determined by looking at the *Residential Building Land Figures* published by the Valuation Office Agency (http://www.voa.gov.uk/publications).

More current data on the value of houses can be gathered from the sales prices for properties posted by local estate agents or realtors. Actual sales prices may be a little lower than those posted, but they give a good indication of general expectations. You must judge the value of your scheme relative to similar areas in a locality, taking into account any more specific design and management qualities that might impact on the predicted price.

Calculating costs

The normal costs associated with a development would include the building costs, professional fees, marketing costs, the cost of borrowing, the developer's profit and some form of contingency fund (Figure 2.2).

Figure 2.2   The costs of development

Building costs

The building costs will be determined by a quantity surveyor based on the housing designs and quality of the finish. Standard houses will have a more predictable cost than schemes that are of a bespoke design but organisations will have experience of trying to develop particular types of building and the costs involved.

Using the *Spon's Architects' and Builders' Price Book* (2005) for UK prices we can get a general indication of the costs of some typical building types per square metre.

Housing (prices per square metre)	
Terraced bungalow	£640 – 810
Semi-detached bungalow	£750 – 890
Terraced house	£560 – 690
Three storey terraced house	£580 – 860
Semi-detached house	£620 – 750
Three storey semi-detached house	£600 – 910
Affordable detached house	£560 – 850
High quality detached house	£850 – 1190
Affordable low rise apartments (no lift)	£730 – 910
High quality low rise apartments (no lift)	£1180 – 1400
High quality high rise apartments	£1910 – 2200
Prestige high rise apartments	£2500 – 3310

Source: *Spon's Architects' and Builders' Price Book* (2005)

Other expenses associated with development will include the costs of highways, parking, open space landscaping and boundary treatments. The costs of such features will also be known by quantity surveyors based on previous projects.

Using the *Spon's Architects' and Builders' Price Book* (2005) we can also get a general indication of the costs of some of these features which might be put into a scheme. Although these prices will change, it is useful to have an indication of the relative cost of certain features.

Roads	
6.5m estate road with 2 × 2m pavements	£825 per metre length
5.5m access road with 2 × 2m pavements	£785 per metre length

Parking	
Normal tarmacadam car parking	£55 per square metre
Normal concrete block car parking	£85 per square metre

Parking at ground level under building	£5000 per space
Basement parking under buildings	£20000 per space
Multi-storey car parks	£10000 per space
Garages (prices per unit)	
Single, flat roof	£2184 – 3119
Single, pitched roof	£2156 – 6370
Double, pitched roof	£7137 – 9142

Paving (prices per square metre on prepared ground)

Gravel	£9 – 13
Concrete slabs	£22 – 31
Concrete paviours	£26 – £37
Brick paviours	£56 – 66
Cobblestone paving	£66 – 86
Granite setts	£93 – 100
York stone	£100 – 119

Boundaries (price per metre length)

1.8m close board timber fencing	£30 – 40
1.8m brick screen wall	£219 – 273

Source: *Spon's Architects' and Builders' Price Book* (2005) London: Spon

Using the plan for the scheme the quantity surveyor would add up the costs associated with the design, and might suggest reasonable savings where necessary.

Professional fees

The cost of professional fees will vary according to the nature of the development company. Larger companies may have all professionals 'in house' so they will be able to predict costs relative to salary expenditure. Where external consultants are used, a percentage of the total building cost is used to provide an estimate of likely fees. Isaac (1996) and Cadman and Topping (1995) both suggest estimating the cost of professional fees at 12.5% of the building costs to cover architects, quantity surveyors and engineers, as well as the cost of gaining relevant planning and building regulation approvals. Competitive bidding for work may bring these costs down.

Marketing and sales costs

Sites may be marketed using site boards and hoardings, web sites, marketing brochures, newspaper adverts, show homes and on-site sales offices and staff. The scheme may be marketed by in-house sales staff or external agents might be employed. This costs money and it needs to be accounted. Cadman and Topping (1995) suggest that 2% of the development value should be set aside for this purpose.

The cost of borrowing

Money will be borrowed and tied up within a scheme at different stages during the development process. The land will need to be purchased at the start of development, and for the duration of the project the developer will need to pay interest on any money borrowed to purchase the site. It is then assumed that other costs will be paid gradually over the period of the project. It is important to carefully calculate the time that the project might take to be prepared, planned and built–as once we start to work out the cost of borrowing we learn that time costs money. This explains why developers are often keen to build a more standard type of home, and why typically they will gain planning permission prior to buying the land.

   To work out the cost of borrowing you need to balance the two sides of the basic equation discussed above. Initially it will be necessary to ignore the cost for the land as we are trying to work out how much we might pay for it. Instead, we can calculate the interest paid on the total building costs and fees. The interest rate will be known to the developer, and based on that negotiated with the lender. We will assume that it is a few percent (say 3%) above the national bank base rate. Interest will probably be paid on a quarterly basis so this percentage will need to be compounded.

Compounding Interest Rates: An example

Assume an interest rate of 8% borrowing £100,000 for a year compounded quarterly.

Basic equation: Total Sum + Interest paid = $S(1 + (R/N))^{NY}$

   S = sum borrowed

   R = interest rate

   N = the number of compoundings per year

   Y = the number of years the money is to be borrowed

Total Sum + Interest paid = $£100,000 (1 + (0.08/4))^{4 \times 1}$
Total Sum + Interest paid = $£100,000 (1.02)^4$
Total Sum + Interest paid = $£100,000 \times 1.08243$
Total Sum + Interest paid = £108,243
                   Interest paid = £8243

   As a 'rule of thumb' it is assumed that all building costs and professional fees are divided in half and then the cost of borrowing is calculated on that sum for the whole projected period of the development. As a final stage, once the land value is roughly estimated, it will be necessary to work out the cost of borrowing money to purchase the land. The land will be purchased at the start of the development and so interest should be calculated for the total sum applied over the whole development period.

Developer's profit

Although the value of the developer's profit will vary according to the success of the scheme, it is necessary to add an operating profit to the costing. The developers will know what level of profit they need to continue operating and covering their broader costs, but we will calculate it as 20% of the development value.

Contingency

A contingency sum is typically included in the costing to help account for unforeseen expenses which might result from delay, or additional unforeseen work such as extra site investigation or remediation. We will calculate this as 3% of the summed development costs.

Determining the land value

Once the total development value and costs have been determined it is possible to calculate the potential value of the land for the given development scheme. The costs are subtracted from the values to determine what is left for negotiations. If this sum is too small it will be necessary to adjust the development scheme to either increase the level of development or reduce the necessary costs.

Before this value is to be offered to the land owner it is still necessary to calculate the cost of borrowing this sum for the total duration of the scheme using the 'cost of borrowing' calculation technique discussed above. This should then be added to the development costs to give the complete picture of the scheme, and the cost of this borrowing may force further changes to the scheme or the land price that might be offered.

WORKING THROUGH A THEORETICAL EXAMPLE

A site in its context

A 1.69 hectare development site has been designated in the local development plan produced for Telbury, Gloucestershire in the South West of England (Figure 2.3). The 'Valuation Office Agency' indicates that Gloucestershire has a constant demand for residential land, but that only a limited supply has come on the market over recent years, whilst figures from the same source suggest an average land value of about £2.5 million per hectare might be expected in the county.

Telbury is a beautiful Cotswolds wool town which is famous for its antiques shops and very high quality historic town centre environment. Highgrove House, the home of Prince Charles, is less than two miles away. The Cotswolds countryside is also famous nationally for its outstanding beauty. Local facilities and schools are regarded very highly. Telbury is therefore a very desirable location in which to live.

The site is located on the southern edge of the settlement and abuts existing newer housing to the north and east, although it is not possible to make connections through this

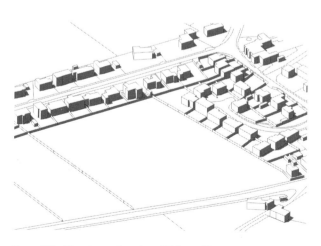

Figure 2.3   The site on the edge of Telbury, Gloucestershire

housing to other parts of the town. Access to the site would therefore be from Bath Road to the south. The site is currently a flat, open green field owned by a local farmer.

The initial scheme

Danning Homes have taken an option on the site. This is a paid for agreement that the farmer will allow the developer to negotiate with the planning authority about the development of the site, and give the developer a chance to purchase the site should the negotiations be successful. Danning prepare an initial scheme using their standard housing range and road types (Figure 2.4). Using this scheme they also prepare an initial valuation as follows:

Figure 2.4   The initial scheme

Development value

13 × 2 bed house (Type 1) @ £194,950	=	£2,534,350
8 × 2 bed house (Type 2) @ £209,950	=	£1,679,600
6 × 3 bed house @ £284,950	=	£1,709,700
14 × 4 bed house @ £325,000	=	£4,550,000
5 × 5 bed house @ £395,000	=	£1,975,000
Development value	=	£12,448,650

Building Costs

3 × 2 bed house (Type 1) @ £63,000	=	£819,000
8 × 2 bed house (Type 2) @ £72,100	=	£576,800
6 × 3 bed house @ £80,500	=	£483,000
14 × 4 bed house @ £107,100	=	£1,499,400
5 × 5 bed house @ £155,200	=	£776,000
Building costs	=	£4,154,200

Professional Fees
(@12.5% of Building Costs)   =   £519,275

Marketing and Sales Costs
(@2% of Development Value)   =   £248,973

Initial Cost of Borrowing
Cost of Borrowing for Building and Fees/2 (4,154,200 + 519,275)/2
(@8% compounded over 2 years)

£2,336737.5 + Interest paid = £2,336737.5 $(1 + (0.08 / 4))^{4 \times 2}$
£2,336737.5 + Interest paid = £2,336737.5 $(1.02)^8$
£2,336737.5 + Interest paid = £2,336737.5 (1.1716593810022656)
£2,336737.5 + Interest Paid = £2,737,860   =   £401,122

Developer's Profit
(20% of Development Value)   =   £2,489,730

Contingency
(3% of summed costs)   =   £234,399

Land Value and Interest Cost

Development value	–	*Development costs*	
£12,448,650	–	£4,154,200	
	–	£519,275	
	–	£248,973	
	–	£401,122	
	–	£2,489,730	
	–	£234,399	= £4,400,951

Interest to be paid over two years on a land purchase price of £3.8 million would be £652,306, suggesting a land value of £3.8 million could be offered on this scheme.

Revising the scheme

Making an offer of £3.8 million for land results in rejection from the farmer, who thinks that this site is worth more than the county average. Following negotiation with the local planners, Danning Homes also learn that their standard houses and roads do not conform to the standard of design expected in the locality. A new scheme must include better quality materials and have a clearer and more distinctive form. In addition, the local authority requires the developer to include a proportion of more affordable homes for young local people within the scheme, in order to meet a recognised local need.

As a result, Danning Homes go to a recognised urban design practice to help them formulate a better scheme. They offer the same range of standard house types but allow the consultants to develop a number of others which might perform a particular layout role. Included are a number of apartments which Danning hopes will offer affordable homes. The plots of these homes are a little smaller, but Danning expect that the improved character of the scheme might be enough to maintain sale values (Figure 2.5). Using this scheme they prepare a revised valuation as follows:

Figure 2.5   The revised scheme

Development value

4 × 2 bed house (Type 1) @ £194,950	=	£779,800
2 × 2 bed house (Type 2) @ £209,950	=	£419,900
4 × 3 bed house (Type 1) @ £284,950	=	£1,139,800
9 × 3 bed house (Type 2) @ £294,000	=	£2,646,000
2 × 3 bed house (Type 3) @ £274,950	=	£549,900
8 × 4 bed house (Type 1) @ £325,000	=	£2,600,000
8 × 4 bed house (Type 2) @ £314,950	=	£2,519,600
3 × 4 bed house (Type 3) @ £339,950	=	£1,019,850
6 × 5 bed house (Type 1) @ £395,000	=	£2,370,000
4 × 5 bed house (Type 2) @ £374,950	=	£1,499,800
10 × 1 bed apartments @ £101,250	=	£1,012,500
10 × 2 bed apartments @ £155,950	=	£1,559,500
Development value	=	**£18,116,650**

Building costs

4 × 2 bed house (Type 1) @ £70,500	=	£282,000
2 × 2 bed house (Type 2) @ £72,400	=	£144,800
4 × 3 bed house (Type 1) @ £85,200	=	£340,800
9 × 3 bed house (Type 2) @ £89,000	=	£801,000
2 × 3 bed house (Type 3) @ £85,700	=	£171,400
8 × 4 bed house (Type 1) @ £120,400	=	£963,200
8 × 4 bed house (Type 2) @ £118,500	=	£948,000

3×4 bed house (Type 3) @ £123,800   =   £371,400
6×5 bed house (Type 1) @ £174,200   = £1,045,200
4×5 bed house (Type 2) @ £162,800   =   £651,200
10×1 bed apartments @ £42,750   =   £427,500
10×2 bed apartments @ £75,750   =   £757,500

Building costs   =   **£6,904,000**

Professional fees
(@12.5% of Development Costs)   =   £863,000

Marketing and sales costs
(@2% of Development Value)   =   £362,333

Initial cost of borrowing
Cost of borrowing for building and fees/2 (6,904,000 + 863,000)/2
(@8% compounded over 2 years)
£3,883,500 + Interest paid = £3,883,500 $(1 + (0.08/4))^{4 \times 2}$
£3,883,500 + Interest paid = £3,883,500 $(1.02)^8$
£3,883,500 + Interest paid = £3,883,500 (1.1716593810022656)
£3,883,500 + Interest Paid = £4,550,139
                                      =   £666,639

Developer's profit
(20% of development value)   =   £3,623,130

Contingency
(3% of Gross Development Costs)   =   £372,573

Land value and interest cost

Development value	–	*Development costs*		
£18,116,650	–	£6,904,000		
	–	£863,000		
	–	£362,333		
	–	£666,639		
	–	£3,623,130		
	–	£372,573	=	**£5,324,975**

Interest to be paid over two years on a land purchase price of £4.5 million would be £772,467, suggesting that a land value of £4.5 million could be offered on the revised scheme.

The impact of a longer development period

Such a scheme might take slightly longer to build, however, and it is interesting and important to note that increasing the build time to 3 years would increase the cost of borrowing as well as the contingency costs. For this scheme the impact on the land value is as given below.

Initial cost of borrowing

Cost of borrowing for building and fees/2 $(6,904,000 + 863,000)/2$
(@8% compounded over 3 years)

£3,883,500 + Interest paid = £3,883,500 $(1 + (0.08/4))^{4 \times 3}$

£3,883,500 + Interest paid = £3,883,500 $(1.02)^{12}$

£3,883,500 + Interest paid = £3,883,500 (1.26824179456255)

£3,883,500 + Interest Paid = £4,925,217   =   £1,041,717

Land value and interest cost

Development value	–	*Development costs*
£18,116,650	–	£6,904,000
	–	£863,000
	–	£362,333
	–	£1,041,717
	–	£3,623,130
	–	£383,825
	=	**£4,938,645**

Interest to be paid over three years on a land purchase price of £3.8 million would be £1,019,319, suggesting that a land value of £3.8 million would be offered on the revised scheme. Such a sum is the same as that produced by the initial, unacceptable scheme. To reduce the cost of borrowing the developer may therefore need to pursue one of five options:

1. Guarantee a quicker build to reduce the loan repayment period
2. Reduce the company's profits and allow some of the freed up money to contribute to the cost of the land
3. Try to negotiate the additional planning requirements out of the scheme by arguing that they are uneconomic
4. Try and convince the farmer that given the planning constraints this is the best deal that can be obtained
5. Build the scheme in phases and use value released from selling the initial phases to reduce the borrowing requirement for subsequent work. For a large scheme this is the most likely option that will be pursued.

Phasing the development

The phasing of a scheme would be planned to allow successful marketing, to protect new residents' amenities and to bring the units most in demand to sale first. Some house builders would plan a marketing suite of homes into a scheme. These would typically be built at the entrance to the scheme, so that home buyers can look at model house types whilst the scheme behind is being built. A future double garage could be used as the marketing office. The first phase would then be selected in a location where future building would not disturb new residents. In this respect, the back of the site might be selected so that construction vehicles did not need to constantly drive past the new homes. Finally, houses which sell the quickest might be selected so that some confidence in the scheme can be achieved, whilst some of the profits from the early phases can be used to fund subsequent work.

Valuing the phased scheme

Danning Homes prepare a phased valuation for their scheme, splitting the work up into three phases. A rough summary of the costing is below to show the impact on the land value.

Phase One

Twenty-two houses built along the northern boundary of the site (Figure 2.6).

Development value:	£7,001,400
Building costs:	−£2,595,900
Professional fees:	−£324,488
Marketing and sales:	−£140,028
Initial borrowing @ 8% compounded four times over 1 year:	−£120,366
Developer's profit	−£1,400,280
Contingency	−£137,432
Phase One Surplus =	£2,282,906

Phase Two

Twenty-nine houses built in the second cul-de-sac (Figure 2.7).

Development value	£5,466,650
Building costs:	−£2,349,800
Professional fees:	−£293,725
Marketing and sales:	−£109,333
Developer's profit	−£1,093,330
Contingency	−£115,386
Phase One Surplus	+£2,282,906
Phase Two Surplus =	£3,787,982

Phase Three

Nineteen houses built at the front of the site (Figure 2.8).

Development value:	£5,648,600
Building costs:	−£1,958,300
Professional fees:	−£244,788
Marketing and sales:	−£112,972
Developer's profit	−£1,129,720
Contingency	−£103,373
Phase Two Surplus	+£3,787,982
Phase Three Surplus =	£5,887,429

Note: over a 3 year period the values used will vary as a result of interest rates influencing the surplus values and inflation affecting costs, although this hasn't been reflected here.

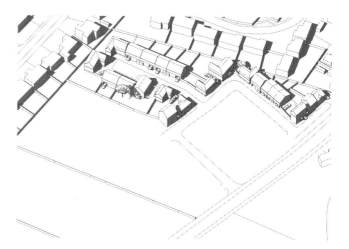

Figure 2.6   Phase one

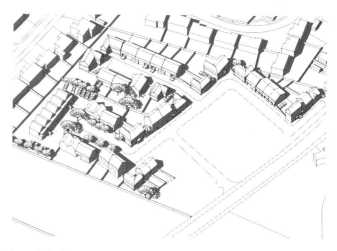

Figure 2.7   Phases one and two

Figure 2.8   The completed scheme

Phase one includes a borrowing element incurring a cost of £120,366, but the surplus value from phases one and two can be used in the second and third phases to cover the cost of building and professional fees. This results in a final phase three surplus value of £5,887,429. As the land needs to be bought at the start it will still be necessary to pay interest on the land purchase loan. At 8% over three years this would be £1,233,912 on a land value offer of £4.6 million. Phasing the development and the costs therefore allows the developer to reduce the cost of borrowing and this value can be transferred into a higher land purchase offer if necessary.

THE VALUE OF DESIGN

England's *Commission for Architecture and the Built Environment* tried to explore the extent to which people were prepared to pay a premium to live in a better designed scheme (CABE, 2003). They found that people would pay more to live in schemes where a distinctive 'sense of place' had been achieved and that such schemes would help to make specific locations, and therefore the land on which they are built, far more desirable and valuable (Figure 2.9). However, this is not just restricted to one site:

> Neighbouring developers and landowners also benefit. Commercial developments of high quality on a large scale have pushed up neighbouring land values for both commercial and residential development… Other developers on nearby sites may well be benefiting from the sense of place that these schemes have provided for the location (*CABE, 2003, p. 46*)

CONSUMER PREFERENCES

What types of residential environment do people like to live in? When asked to express a preference, UK housing consumers indicate a variety of answers, although a number of common themes do tend to emerge:

Facilities: Residents want a range of facilities, shops and services. They would like them to be accessible on foot, but for many this isn't necessary (Figure 2.10).

Schools: People buy houses in areas which form the catchments for schools which have a good reputation (Figure 2.11).

Public transport: People who use public transport to commute to work are drawn to locations close to the necessary transit stops and stations. Many people don't feel that they

Figure 2.9   CABE research found that well designed housing in Chelmsford, Essex achieved 10.3% greater residual value than a comparable standardised scheme in a similar location

Figure 2.10   New housing in the centre of Bakewell, Derbyshire is in walking distance of many facilities, shops and services

Figure 2.11   People try to buy homes within the catchments of good schools

Figure 2.12   People who commute by bus like to be close to public transport stops

rely on public transport, however, and so they are more flexible with their location (Figure 2.12).

Countryside and village: There is a general aspiration to live in the countryside, or to have views of the countryside, and a village type environment is often referred to as the ideal. Having said this, there is evidence that people think that some urban areas have recently become better places to live, whilst urban residents find living there both more convenient and more exciting (Figure 2.13).

Open space: If they can't live in the countryside, then people would like to live within the vicinity of a significant open space (Figure 2.14).

Figure 2.13   Housing in villages and close to the countryside remains popular

Figure 2.14   If people can't live in the countryside they like to live within the vicinity of a significant open space

Parking: One of the main frustrations that cause concern are areas that lack car parking, so people want to live where there is a generous amount of parking to meet their needs (Figure 2.15).

Good street lighting: Having a sense of security is a key aspiration for many residents, and this is often discussed in terms of the provision of adequate lighting of public areas (Figure 2.16).

Detached housing: The reality is that houses take a variety of forms and people seem prepared to live in them, but when asked, people indicate an aspiration to live in a detached house, with a semi-detached house being their second preference (Figure 2.17).

Larger houses: Despite the form of the housing, a critical factor in resident choices is that their homes should be larger and have more storage space. In the UK this is often expressed in the number of rooms, although simply counting the rooms often hides the true area of a home—as in newer houses people have often found that the rooms can be too small to be really useful (Figure 2.18).

Gardens: A very common preference for families with children is the desire to live in a house with a reasonably sized garden. This, however, is not just restricted to back gardens. A significant proportion

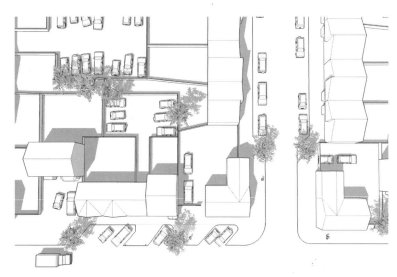

Figure 2.15   People want adequate parking

Figure 2.16   People want good street lighting

Figure 2.17   Consumers prefer detached houses

Figure 2.18   Consumers want to buy the largest house that they can afford

Figure 2.19   Adults with children often look for houses with reasonably sized gardens

of people do not want to live directly by a street and would prefer some front garden attached to their home. Communal gardens can be popular with apartment dwellers (Figure 2.19).

Appearance: The external appearance of homes often appears as a low priority for home buyers, although people might be concerned about the general appearance and upkeep of an area. Residents prefer a housing image that reflects what Cooper Marcus (1982: 10) refers to as '…local middle-class norms'. A particular concern is for 'character'. This might be genuinely historic, although in new built houses it would refer to details that stop the homes looking like bland boxes. The Popular Housing Forum (1998, p. 2) noted that people don't want features to be 'stuck on' while they like their houses to be of a common style, but different in detail to their neighbours' (Figure 2.20).

Neo-traditional or modern: Although there is a general perception that people prefer rather conservative neo-traditional forms and styles of building there is some evidence to suggest that a younger and urban population are looking for something a little more modern (Figure 2.21).

Figure 2.20   Residents involved in designing their own houses can prefer the style to conform to local middle class norms

Figure 2.21   There is a perception that consumers prefer neo-traditional styles, but there is evidence to suggest that some people are looking for something a little more modern

Landscape: In surveys the quality of the landscape has never been a particularly significant factor in shaping consumer choice, but people certainly seem to be drawn to areas which have an open character and which have views of trees and other forms of planting (Figure 2.22).

(MORI poll for, 2002; 2005; Cooper Marcus, 1982; Mulholland Research Associates, 1995; Popular Housing Forum, 1998; URBED, 1999)

In a market led economy, consumer preferences should shape the form that a product takes, but a range of other factors also shape the form and value of housing.

Figure 2.22   People like an open character and views of trees or other forms of planting

ISSUES INFLUENCING THE VALUE OF A SCHEME

Location

The location of a home has the strongest impact on its value. This influences the price of a home at a number of levels. At the highest level people demand to live within particular regions close to their work, and so compared to other regions homes will be more expensive if land is scarce. Within those regions certain locations will then be more popular, although the factors shaping the popularity will be more refined. The popularity of an area might be influenced by:

- the type of housing available in the area
- the type of population living within the area
- historic qualities which tend to give locations added character
- the mix of local facilities and businesses which might attract a particular market
- access to a significant park or other green space
- access to a significant view (Figure 2.23).

Figure 2.23   Exclusive dockland housing for sale with views out over the water is significantly more expensive than the social housing built within walking distance

Such local factors can make the value of housing vary considerably over a short distance.

The condition of the land

The value of land, and therefore of a development in general, will be greatly affected by its condition. Land that has previously been contaminated will need to be cleaned before it can be used for homes and this cost may need to be met by the returns from the development. Other brownfield sites may have previously been developed and so the costs of demolition will need to be met by the redevelopment scheme. Alternatively, remote greenfield sites will need to provide suitable infrastructure which will otherwise exist in areas that have previously been developed, such infrastructure costs might make the homes comparatively more expensive (Figure 2.24).

Figure 2.24   The cost of clearing and cleaning formerly developed land may need to be met by the development

Affordable and social housing

Effective planning systems may require a proportion of the homes that are to be built to be made affordable. This is important in areas where the costs of homes make it difficult for key worker groups to afford to live; or where, as a result of an influx of new residents, local first time buyers are priced out of the market if they want or need to buy locally. This will clearly have an impact on the value of a scheme: such homes will not maximise the return on that proportion of a site for a developer, whilst prospective buyers of the market value homes may be unwilling to pay a higher price for their home if the affordable element is not carefully integrated into the scheme (Figure 2.25).

Figure 2.25   Affordable housing is sometimes pushed to the back of a scheme

Other planning requirements

A local authority may expect a certain density of development to match that achieved on neighbouring sites, and thus maintain the character of an area. Some planning systems will also require other pieces of infrastructure, facilities or amenities to be provided as a part of larger schemes. For example, in order for a scheme to be viable it may be necessary to pay for improvements to a neighbouring road junction. Alternatively, the authority may expect the provision of open space or play areas for children (Figure 2.26). All these, and similar requirements, might impact on either the costs or potential returns from the development.

Figure 2.26   Local authorities may require developers to contribute to the provision of both open space and play facilities within or adjacent to a scheme

DESIGN AND MANAGEMENT ISSUES INFLUENCING THE VALUE OF A SCHEME

It is possible to influence the value that will be generated from a scheme by using design, and the history of housing development and layout show us how house builders have done this.

Use narrow blocks

To make efficient use of land it is common practice to configure housing in long blocks with a minimum back-to-back dimension. Deeper blocks tend to result in very large gardens for some units as an inevitable result of the block configuration (Figure 2.27). Where narrow blocks are used streets formed by the ends of the blocks need special attention to make sure that the small numbers of houses or apartments on the ends of the

Figure 2.27   Use narrow blocks

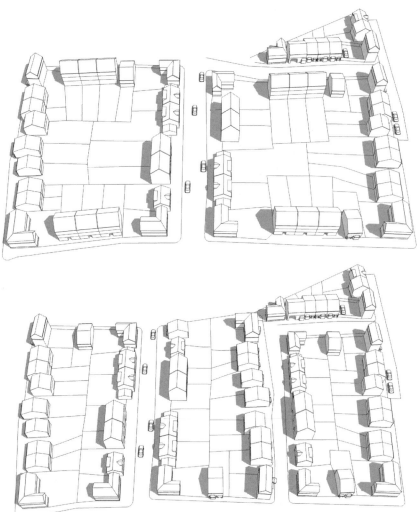

terrace face the streets. Depending on the configuration of the site, such end terraces might face the distributor road to the residential area, allowing most houses to face the quieter access roads.

Cul-de-sacs and interconnected streets

Cul-de-sacs became popular partly because developers are able to reduce the amount of road necessary to serve a particular area. They also allow difficult sites to be exploited (Figure 2.28). However, there might be a hidden contradiction here. Sometimes cul-de-sacs are connected to the wider network by larger arterial roads which have no frontage. Such roads have a

Figure 2.28   Cul-de-sacs

very expensive initial outlay and provide no return (Figure 2.29). New urbanists, however, have argued that interconnected networks may require a greater length of road but traffic is more evenly distributed across the network and so all streets can have frontage, and the roads can pay for themselves (Figure 2.30).

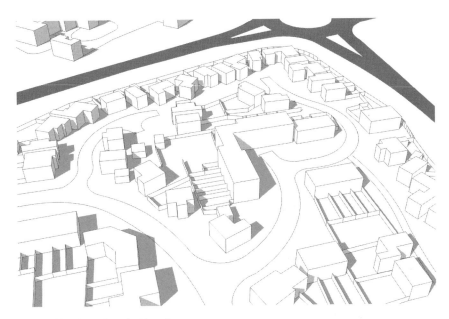

Figure 2.29   Arterial road without frontage

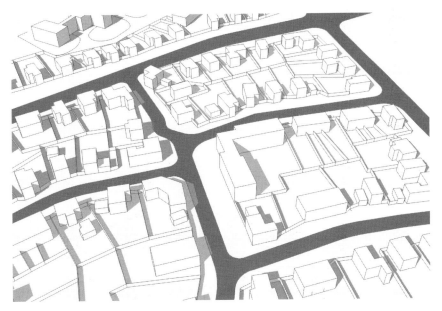

Figure 2.30   Double fronted streets

Reduce highway standards

Within some planning systems it may be possible to argue for a reduction in normal highway standards. This may result in an improvement in an otherwise road-dominated environment, but it will also mean that costs for highway infrastructure provision can also be reduced. Such an approach is common in New Urbanist developments in the USA where roads might remain in the ownership of, and be managed by, the residents (Figure 2.31).

Figure 2.31   New urbanist schemes keep costs down by developing highways to a reduced standard. The community rather than the state subsequently maintains them

Exclusivity

Cul-de-sacs, as well as gating or the use of other symbolic barriers, allow developers to enhance a sense of exclusivity within a residential area which can also add value to a scheme (Figure 2.32). Alternatively, schemes might include facilities for the exclusive use of residents such as swimming pools or a gym–facilities that are paid for as part of a service charge (Figure 2.33).

Figure 2.32   Gates allow developers to enhance the sense of exclusivity within a scheme, even if the gates are always open

Figure 2.33   Schemes can include facilities for the exclusive use of residents

Standardisation

Volume house builders will adopt standard house types within schemes (Figure 2.34). Such types may not be popular with people seeking variety and place-specific design, but they do allow house builders to control costs, quantities and standards, and they can keep the design costs down for each individual scheme. The house types can also be based on ongoing research into, and refinement of, the buildings using previous consumer feedback. More recently, some house builders have adopted types that allow them to configure the houses into more interesting layouts, whilst it is also common for house builders to adopt different facing materials or window forms to suit a particular location.

Figure 2.34   To reduce costs and control quality volume house builders use standard house types

Density

The most obvious mechanism available for increasing the value of a scheme is to build more homes on a given site. Average densities in the UK are about 25 units per hectare, although more recently, as a result of national planning policy, higher density schemes have emerged in high demand locations. Not uncommon now are schemes with a mix of houses and apartments at over 30 units per hectare, and even apartment buildings that achieve over 100 dwellings per hectare. It has been noted that this emphasis of promoting higher densities in certain locations has resulted in developers using more architects and building more bespoke schemes.

Sites adjacent to open space and with a positive outlook can be built up to a higher density, or be used for higher value properties in order to maximise the return from the more attractive position. To release this value, these open spaces can be designed into schemes such as larger parks or smaller and more incidental squares or water features. These urban design features will give adjacent properties a premium value compared to houses located in more nondescript locations (Figure 2.35).

Figure 2.35   High density schemes can also be exclusive and their design can both create and exploit attractive views

Exploit views

Views to the sea, across a land- or townscape, towards lakes, rivers, greenery or a local landmark will reinforce a sense of place and provide a popular outlook from homes, and a plan can be manipulated to make sure that as many homes as possible have access to the view (Figure 2.36). If they can't it might be possible to provide an exclusive point of access to the view for home owners. This was done at Seaside in Florida. Residents were given access to private beach pavilions, thus allowing all homes to have access to the beach even if their homes are some distance away (Figure 2.37).

Figure 2.36   Views should be exploited

Figure 2.37   Residents at Seaside, Florida have access to a beach pavilion

Exploit existing markets

Developers typically want to associate their schemes with existing popular locations so that they can exploit the higher values associated with such places. At the regional scale this will mean locating in popular towns or cities. At the local scale it will mean finding sites adjacent to popular neighbourhoods or features, like parks. At the site-specific scale it will mean trying to orientate new housing to face popular homes and features whilst, in the worst situations, turning their back on existing, unpopular communities (Figure 2.38). If left unmanaged, this local tendency can reinforce social polarisation and stereotyping.

Figure 2.38 Watercolor in Florida is located to exploit the commercial success of the Seaside community next door

USE KERB APPEAL

Kerb appeal is a term used to describe the positive, visual qualities of a home when viewed from the street (Figure 2.39). The first impression and best visual aspect is often from the street, and so developers typically invest more in the front façades of buildings to provide a suitable level of richness. Although only skin deep, the kerb appeal is one way in which similar homes will be compared and a better design might result in a quicker sale.

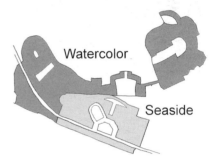

Figure 2.39   Kerb appeal involves creating the best impression of a scheme from the street

Image, style and meaning

Developers work hard to create the right stylistic impression for their homes. The dominant trend in housing for sale is homes that are neotraditional in styling. Sometimes these are relatively faithful reproductions of former styles, although, on other occasions, designers might loosely use certain motifs because they are regarded as popular. In areas where there are distinctive building traditions, such housing styles might be encouraged by the planning system and a concern to reinforce the sense of place. In other locations such a trend is thought to result from a concern for resale values as conservative buyers don't want to take a risk with the style of their home if it might affect a future sale (Figure 2.40).

Not all homes are, however, neotraditional, and within certain market sectors more contemporary forms of housing are popular, particularly in metropolitan areas. Within the UK the city centres and new or regenerating waterfront locations often contain the most contemporary apartment buildings (Figure 2.41).

Figure 2.40   Neotraditional styling

Figure 2.41   In certain market sectors more contemporary form of housing are also popular

Use a famous designer

Housing is rarely designed by anyone famous, but associating a famous architect or designer with a scheme may boost its value, raise its national profile or increase the speed of sales. A nice example from the UK is the involvement of Wayne Hemingway, the former owner of the 'Red or Dead' fashion label in the design of the Staiths South Bank scheme with George Wimpey Homes and Ian Darby Partnership (Figure 2.42). This resulted in an innovative layout that attained a high level of national media coverage for the company. Wimpey tell us, not surprisingly, that the first phase of the scheme sold in record time with buyers camping out overnight to get a home.

Figure 2.42   Staiths South Bank, Gateshead

Integrate social and affordable housing

The requirement to accommodate social and affordable housing within schemes is dealt with in a number of ways, depending on the power of the planning system or, in some cases, on the attitude of the developer. Where planning systems are weak and developers are aiming to merely maximise their profits, social housing will be grouped together in a less attractive corner of the scheme away from the market housing (Figure 2.43). This typically results in social stigmatisation. Where the social housing is dealt with in a more progressive way it will be 'pepperpotted' through the scheme so that no distinctive 'affordable' area can be recognised; whilst typically the kerb appeal of the social housing will be such that it should be indistinguishable from other homes (Figure 2.44).

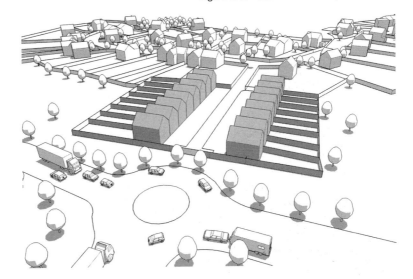

Figure 2.43   Putting social housing in a less attractive corner

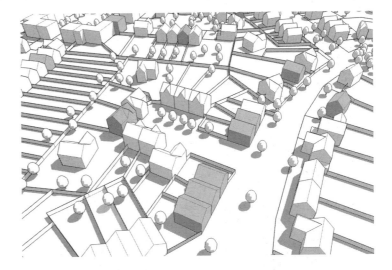

Build a 'granny flat'

Common to some New Urbanist schemes has been the introduction of living or work spaces above garages which are ancillary to the main home. If rented out, these can generate extra revenue for a home owner.

Figure 2.44   *Pepperpotting* social housing

Figure 2.45   Build a 'granny flat'

Alternatively, the space can be used by the main house occupant or a relative (Figure 2.45).

Keep away from bad neighbours

A good site analysis will highlight if there are uses or other features neighbouring a site that will detract from the value of homes. If this is the case, it may be necessary to plant a buffer of trees to hide the offending view, or if the feature is smaller it may be simply necessary to orientate the backs of new houses to it so that it is not visible from the public realm (Figure 2.46).

Figure 2.46   Keep away from bad neighbours

Management and restrictive covenants

Restrictive covenants are commonly used in some countries to control the form of housing or activities occurring within a residential area. Their purpose is to manage residential amenities and therefore maintain property values. The covenant takes the form of a legal agreement and it can stipulate, for example: the size of plot and home allowed; the need to get approval for a design from an 'architectural review committee'; what types of construction must be used; the setbacks required between the home and the boundaries; rules about the types of fencing that must be used; the lines of any easements to provide access to under or over ground utilities; any necessary fees to pay for highway or landscape maintenance; rules indicating the colours that homes can be painted; how gardens must be maintained; where residents can park; details on using homes as businesses; guidelines for tree cutting; and the keeping of pets and other animals. Such covenants are tailored to individual properties. They will vary in their depth and complexity, but they can allow one resident to enforce a significant level of influence over the lifestyle choices of others. Despite this, they can be popular because of the certainty that they create.

FURTHER READING

The Urban Land Institute has produced the excellent *Residential Development Handbook* which includes very useful chapters on the development process, project feasibility and financing (Schmitz, 2004). Further advice about costing developments can be pieced together from a number of sources including Darlow (1988), Cadman and Topping (1995) and Isaac (1996). These books tend to focus on commercial property development but residential schemes do get a look in. A useful introduction to the house development industry in the UK is Golland and Blake's (2004) *Housing Development: Theory, Process and Practice*, whilst *Delivering New Homes* by Carmona, Carmona and Gallent (2003) offers a valuable insight into the tensions that emerge between house builders and the UK planning system. These include factors affecting other planning systems such as the availability of suitable land; the effects of delay in making planning decisions; the requirement to provide affordable housing; and the concerns that planners may have about housing design. Also discussed is the impact of financial contributions required by the British planning system to help provide the necessary facilities, infrastructure or services required as a result of residential schemes. CABE's (2003) *The Value of Housing Design and Layout* tries to highlight in which situations good design is profitable, and uses cost analyses to explore the extent to which additional costs associated with designs result in greater or lesser returns from an investment.

Interesting and relatively recent publications into the types of home and environment that British people want include *Towns or Leafier Environments: A survey of family home buying choices* by Mulholland Research Associates (1995), *Kerb Appeal* produced by the Popular Housing Forum (1998), *But Would You Live There?* by URBED (1999) and CABE's (2005) *What Home Buyers Want*. Often these publications are written from the authors' perspective, although collectively they do represent an attempt to properly account for the aspirations of housing consumers. Ely's (2004) *The Home Buyer's Guide* reverses the logic of the above publications and tries to encourage a more informed approach to purchasing a house.

3 Building place and defining space

This chapter introduces the importance of designing urban form and a succession of places within residential schemes. It discusses the types of space that we create within the urban environment when we lay out homes and how these spaces should be configured. Different types of block structure are introduced and discussed. The importance of amenity standards is also considered. The chapter concludes with a brief explanation about how we shouldn't let these amenity standards dictate the form of our residential areas, and that instead we should start our designs with an aspiration towards creating different types of place within a scheme.

DESIGN PLACES

Rather than merely stringing out identikit housing along identikit roads, the main challenge for the designer of a new residential area is to create distinctive places within their scheme. The notion of a *place* is something that has complex social connotations–what one person may regard as a place or places may not match that of another–but with reference to design it can refer to a sense of individuality or difference within the environment which forms from the combination of location, landscape, building forms, urban spaces and human activity.

It is possible to be aware of, and therefore concerned about, places at a whole range of scales. Regions are environmentally, as well as socially or culturally, distinctive. This is influenced not only by environmental factors such as topography, flora and fauna or climate; but also by how societies or cultures have responded to this context when they have built buildings and put them together over time to form villages, towns or cities. If you travel between regions, therefore, you may have a sense that you are leaving and entering different places, and the characteristics of urban areas will make a contribution to that feeling.

However, within urban areas there are also distinctive places which result from how buildings, and other elements, have been combined together to create the urban environment. These places might be informed by the distinctive attributes of a region (a very simple example: all the buildings may contain a similar building material, or a distinctive type or form of building), but within the urban area the spaces created between these buildings should have a variety of both forms and functions. As you travelled through an urban area, therefore, you would experience the feeling that you are travelling between one place and the next.

Urban environments that do not have this character are called *placeless*, and often the only way to fully appreciate the contribution that place makes to our lives is to spend time in placeless environments. Relph (1976, p. 90) defines placelessness as '...a weakening of the identity of places to the point where they not only look alike but feel alike and offer the same bland possibilities of experience.'

Placeslessness in residential environments results from:

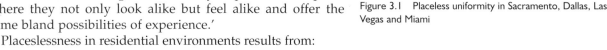

Figure 3.1   Placeless uniformity in Sacramento, Dallas, Las Vegas and Miami

- Road environments that have no direct relationship with the uses and activities along them
- Uniformity and standardisation within the built environment (Figure 3.1)
- The adoption of synthetic, nostalgic or inauthentic themes in the design of either buildings or urban spaces, which ultimately become common between different schemes.

In his thinking about how to overcome the blandness of urban development, Gordon Cullen (1961) argues simply for a recognition of both *hereness* and *thereness* in urban design. He suggests that people should have a feeling of entering or leaving a variety of places as they pass through the urban environment. As you enter a distinctive, individually designed street or square, he argues, you will have a sense of *hereness* and, by definition, the other distinctive streets and squares will have an equally considered design (Figure 3.2).

Figure 3.2   Distinctive, individual places should be the goal of residential layout

CREATE URBAN FORM

Places result from the way that individual buildings are brought together to create urban form. Streets and squares are types of urban form resulting from how individual buildings are brought together in the design, and just as we might carefully design an individual building, the form of a street or square, or the pattern of streets and squares that go together to make an entire scheme, should not be left to chance. Urban design could almost be defined, therefore, as the act of designing urban form; and the process of designing distinctive urban forms should result in physically distinctive places emerging within a scheme.

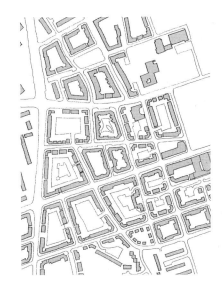

Figure 3.3   Urban form

DEFINE SPACE

In creating urban form the urban designer is helping to decide how the space of the urban environment will be used. At the most general level the urban designer is helping to decide where the solid walls of buildings will go, and in so doing choosing what will be the outside and what will be the inside environment. Figure 3.4 is a figure ground plan showing the pattern of urban form that results from this process where the distinction between the solids (buildings) and voids (outdoor spaces) is most clear. Figure ground drawings are an easy way of illustrating the pattern of urban form that is being suggested within an area.

Figure 3.4   A figure ground plan

TYPES OF URBAN SPACE

Urban space is not merely distinguishable as either *outdoor* or *indoor*. Instead, from an urban design perspective, it is better to distinguish between four types of *outdoor* space which reflect who will have access to the space and something about how it will be perceived and used.

Public space: Public space refers to urban space which is easily accessible to the general public at any time of day or night (Figure 3.5). Streets are an obvious type of public space which people can physically enter and exit. There is a degree of management or control of what you can do within street space which is influenced by laws and cultures, whilst the physical design shapes quite clearly if it lends itself to, for example, playing sports, walking, running, cycling or driving. Despite tremendous variation in what you might do in public space, however, physical access is maintained.

Semi-public space: Compared to public space, semi-public space is a type of space in which some greater degree of control is exerted over when access is allowed. These tend to be spaces which allow general public access. However, due to a far stronger management regime, they might, for example, be closed for certain hours. In addition,

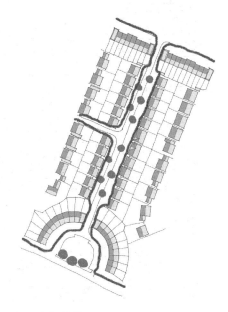

Figure 3.5   Public space

Figure 3.6   Semi-public and public spaces

Figure 3.7   Semi-private front gardens

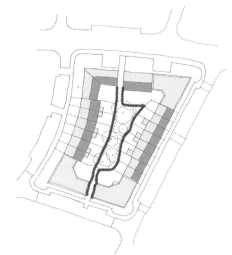

Figure 3.8   Semi-private rear courtyard

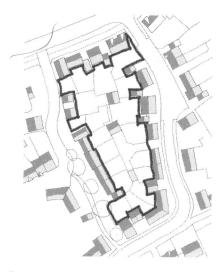

Figure 3.9   Private spaces

management may also influence who can use the space (Figure 3.6). Let's use the example of an urban square with a small park in the middle of it. If that park is always open to the public then it would be regarded as a public space. If, however, a boundary was erected, and the park was closed at night, then it would be a semi-public space. The benefit of making it a semi-public space may be that access to the public is safer, or that a slightly more sensitive environment can be protected from vandalism or other types of misuse.

Semi-private space: A semi-private space is a piece of the urban environment that tends to be private and which a member of the general public will only enter if they have a reason to. The clearest example of a semi-private space is a front garden or yard (Figure 3.7). This might be a small space that is distinguished from the paved public street by only a change of surface (a gravel path and grass lawn, for example), but still we tend to be socially conditioned to only enter that space if we are visiting the property. Another type of semi-private space might be a communal garden area for use only by specific residents. If the park, referred to in the discussion on semi-public space above, is only available to certain residents living around the square, then it would, despite its identical design, be semi-private. Sometimes, however, semi-private spaces are also included behind houses for residents living in an urban block to share (Figure 3.8).

Private space: The final space is exclusively for the use of the residents of a property. Outdoor private spaces form gardens, although sometimes roof gardens or balconies serve an identical purpose (Figure 3.9). Such spaces allow private residents complete control and a higher degree of both security and privacy, so that they can use the space for what they wish; for example, gardening, storing rubbish, sunbathing, playing or fixing the bike.

A residential area is made up of these types of space, and differently designed urban forms will result in different patterns and relationships emerging between these types of space. Public spaces tend to form a net-work which provides a pattern of access for residents (Figure 3.10). Sometimes semi-public spaces may be introduced, typically as open spaces or play areas, into the pattern of public spaces. Semi-private areas tend to be located between the public spaces and people's homes so that a *zone of control* is introduced between a public street and a private prop-erty. However, semi-private spaces can also form shared private gardens, and these may be included in a scheme between private gardens. Finally, private gardens, where they exist, tend to be accessible from the home but, as a matter of principle, they shouldn't abut a public space. Why this is will be discussed below.

INTERFACES

The boundaries between the different types of space are sometimes referred to as *interfaces* (Figure 3.11). For example, the front wall between a front garden and a public space of the street can be referred to as the

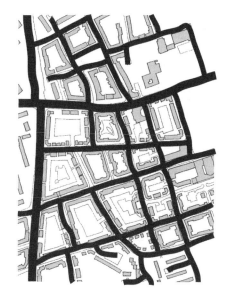

Figure 3.10   The pattern of access

Figure 3.11   Interfaces

interface between semi-private and public space, just as the front wall of the house can be described as the *interface* between the private interior of the home and the semi-private front garden. Such interfaces are impor-tant as they can be designed in a particular way to achieve a particular urban design affect. Housing schemes that have semi-private front gar-dens but no wall at the interface with the public street space may, for example, result in quite a different street character to a situation where high front walls or even hedges have been introduced.

FRONTS AND BACKS

A common concept in residential urban design is that homes have both a *front* and a *back* interface; that the public front of the homes should face the street and the private backs of the homes should face the private spaces (Figure 3.12). Why this is so can be argued from the perspectives of either achieving outdoor privacy and security around the back, or creating a focus for public life within the public realm around the front.

AROUND THE BACK: ACHIEVING OUTDOOR PRIVACY AND SECURITY

The idea that homes should have a back space stems from the observation that privacy is a very important feature of the domestic realm, and that people can enjoy privacy both inside and outside the home. The private garden is a direct result of this, although the balcony or the semi-private shared gardens are good surrogates (Figure 3.13). If private gardens are to be built into a scheme then it makes sense to group them together. This is so that the privacy between the homes is shared, and the gardens are secure.

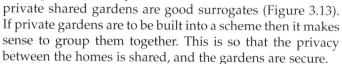

Figure 3.12   Fronts and backs

Figure 3.13   Around the back

AROUND THE FRONT A FOCUS FOR PUBLIC LIFE WITHIN THE PUBLIC REALM

The *public realm* of a residential area refers to the space that forms between the buildings which, although containing semi-public or semi-private spaces, will tend to be dominated by the comings and goings of the public street network (Figure 3.14). Despite the subtle variations in

Figure 3.14   Around the front

experience and expectation that such semi-public or semi-private spaces might allow, there is an expectation that public life will ensue. Within certain quieter parts of a residential area this may be dominated by the chance meeting of neighbours, children playing or pedestrians and vehicles passing through. In other areas the public environment will be busier, possibly with a few shops or community uses supplementing the busier comings and goings of residents. Despite this variation in the intensity of activity, the qualities of this public environment need to be carefully looked after if it is to feel safe and be convenient. One of the ways this sense of safety and convenience can be achieved is by ensuring that the front doors and windows of homes overlook the street. This allows public activity to focus onto the public realm, as people come and go from their homes through front doors that face the streets, whilst the windows allow overlooking or *surveillance* of the public realm.

PROVIDE SURVEILLANCE

Surveillance refers to the opportunity to observe activity within a street. The opportunity to observe some degree of human activity within the public spaces of a residential area is regarded as a positive feature in most residential settings (Figure 3.15). A particular benefit is the sense of security that comes from feeling that you are not alone in your neighbourhood.

Figure 3.15   Human activity within a street provides surveillance

Direct contact between people in a street going about their daily business is a form of surveillance, but the opportunity for people to see into the street from neighbouring homes also creates a sense of security, whilst those people in the street also informally observe that all is well within the homes.

DON'T CREATE DEAD SPACE

Sometimes the principle of public fronts facing the public realm and private backs facing each other is not followed, and where private gardens abut the public realm *dead space* may be the result (Figure 3.16). This is because the demand for privacy and security around the back of homes inevitably means that some sort of barrier, such as high fences, may be introduced.

Figure 3.16   Don't create dead space

For the public realm, the consequence of this is severe, as the activity associated with the front doors and the surveillance of the street environment through windows are both lost. In addition, no back fence could be as interesting as the façade of a home. This approach, therefore, results in less human activity, a poorer sense of security and safety, and an environment that is dull and uninteresting.

The consequence of this for the private gardens is equally poor. The gardens now abut trafficked streets which are noisier, whilst it is thought to be relatively easy for a thief to hop over a back fence and break into the back of a house from the public realm which is less populated and has poor surveillance.

LESS DEMAND FOR PRIVACY

Not all residential areas achieve the same level of outdoor privacy. Apartments in particular may rely on balconies above ground level to provide outdoor space, whilst in other residential schemes (including either houses or apartments) private gardens or shared communal (semi-private) courtyards can tend to be quite open. In all of these cases the compromising of privacy allows some surveillance of neighbouring spaces, whilst the visible gardens and balconies provide visual interest to residents and visitors (Figure 3.17).

Figure 3.17   Less demand for privacy

RESIDENTIAL BLOCK STRUCTURES

Residential block structures result from the way designers compose the buildings and urban spaces to create urban form. By creating residential blocks the designers are defining the location of, and relationships between, the types of urban space and the pattern of access that will be allowed in general through the area; whilst they are also starting to consider the character of the layout and whether a sense of place will be achieved.

The history of housing layout covers a great variety of residential block structures, and their enduring success shows that people can happily live in a wide range of residential settings–so long as the homes are well-constructed, the community is stable and the housing environment is well managed.

Some common residential block structures

Although a range of residential block structures have been adopted, some specific forms tend to be more common than others.

Periphery blocks

The periphery block was probably the most common form of block structure until the 1930s when other block structures were experimented with. More recently, however, periphery blocks are suggested for a wide range of contexts as a result of the influence of the publication *Responsive Environments* (Bentley *et al*. 1985). The basic principle reflects the advice given above–that the fronts of buildings should face the public realm and the private backs of buildings should face each other. The blocks are then arranged in a deformed grid of streets (Figure 3.18). Where housing is proposed the periphery block allows privacy and security for gardens, and allows the public street environment to become the focus for access, public life and social activity. Periphery blocks are not only used, however, where houses with private gardens are being considered.

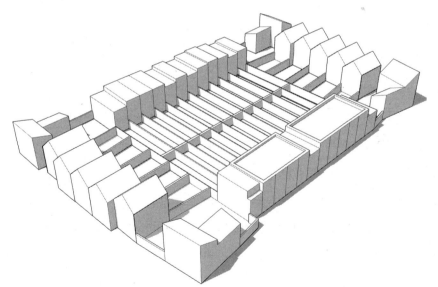

Figure 3.18   A periphery block

Apartments in periphery blocks with shared open space: Often, if apartments are developed, semi-private courtyards are introduced into the centre of the blocks where, for example, planting is introduced, residents can relax, children can play or washing can be dried. Such a space allows apartment residents access to outdoor space which is managed for the block as a whole, and which for children and some residents might be preferable to a small private garden. Sometimes it is possible for non-residents to enter the courtyards, but in other designs courtyards are only available to residents (Figures 3.19 and 3.20).

Housing in periphery blocks with private gardens and shared open space: Periphery blocks may also have housing with private gardens, but behind the private gardens a communal space for play or parking has then been introduced (Figure 3.21). This is actually a configuration that has a long lineage–during

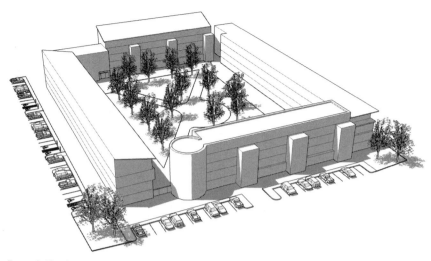

Figure 3.19   Apartments in a periphery block with shared open space

Figure 3.20   Apartments with a shared courtyard

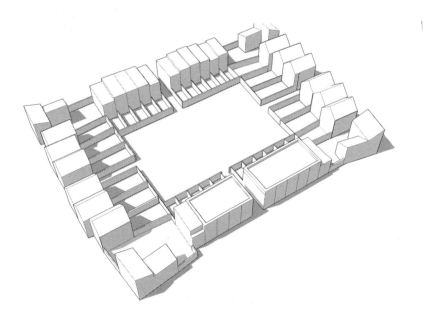

Figure 3.21   Periphery block housing with a communal central space

the seventeenth century housing was often arranged in blocks with service access in the middle of the block accommodating, for example, stables and carriages. This configuration evolved to a form of back alley access in the nineteenth century, whilst today former coach houses are sometimes converted to mews court housing.

Apartments in periphery blocks with private gardens and shared open space: Alternatively, ground level apartments in periphery blocks can have private gardens to their rear, and then residents who live on other floors have access to a communal space (Figure 3.22).

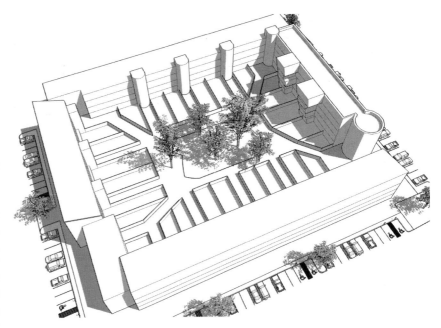

Figure 3.22   Apartments in a periphery block with private and semi-private spaces

All of the above examples demonstrate variation in how private space is considered in a periphery block, but they also allow physical definition of the public realm, as the fronts of these homes face and give a physical form to the street environment.

Free standing blocks

Since the early twentieth century, apartments in particular have been developed in free standing or *point* blocks (Figure 3.23). The rationale for this is provided by architects from the time who wished to:

- provide a form of residential environment that provided air and light to homes
- free people from what were regarded as the constraints of the depressing street environments of the nineteenth century
- provide new, and unconstrained open spaces around the homes
- accommodate the newly popular car (something that the older streets struggled to do)
- use new building techniques, technologies and materials
- provide more communal ways of living.

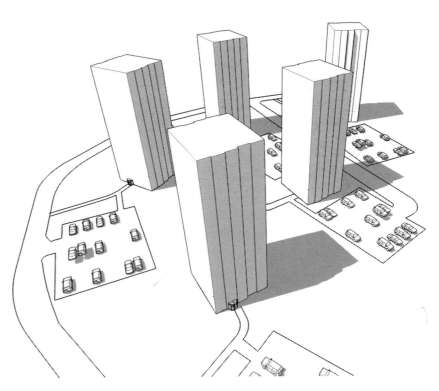

Figure 3.23   Point blocks

Today this rationale still remains relevant in certain contexts; in particular where people tend to live in apartments, and a demand for outdoor private garden space is less prevalent. In addition, on certain sites apartments in free-standing blocks provide the most effective mechanism for achieving the desired density of development. Where management processes are poor such blocks can result in vague and poorly used open spaces between the blocks which can suffer from poor surveillance and under use. However, there is no reason why a high free-standing block cannot be combined with other street level housing which is used to define a street or other public space. Blocks like this can be very high, although within European cities free-standing blocks of about five storeys are also common, allowing residents a more immediate relationship with neighbouring spaces (Figures 3.24 and 3.25).

Figure 3.24   Free standing 5 storey apartment blocks

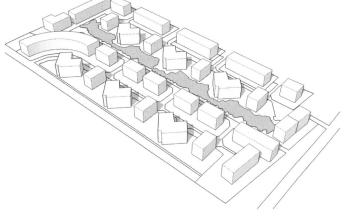

Figure 3.25   Free standing blocks can be used to define attractive public and private spaces

Linear block arrangements

Evolving during the early twentieth century, linear block arrangements are also still popular. This is a configuration of housing or apartments particularly common in parts of continental Europe, and reflects the fact that orientation of living space to the sun is given a high priority. In such a configuration the backs of houses can face the fronts of others, or the houses can face each other across a traditional street or pedestrian route (Figure 3.26).

Figure 3.26   Linear blocks

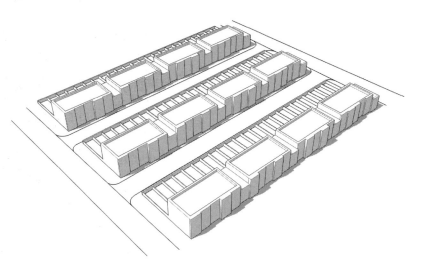

Sometimes housing or apartments arranged in a linear block can still be arranged to front and therefore provide surveillance of a neighbouring street or open space, but this does not always happen (Figure 3.27). If this is not the case, it might reflect the fact that the designers may be taking a more relaxed view of the 'public fronts must face every public street' principle–accepting instead that there may need to be areas without a public frontage, and that for small areas of public realm this will not be a major problem, especially if there is a fair degree of pedestrian activity within the street.

Super blocks

Designers often configured blocks of housing, typically in the form of apartments, to form super blocks which encircle or 'protect' other types of housing or open spaces. This is a form sometimes used where sites for development abut a difficult context such as larger urban roads or frequently used railways (Figures 3.28 and 3.29). In such a situation they allow a quieter and safer domestic environment to be realised within the

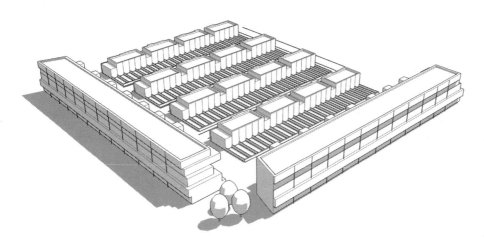

Figure 3.28   Super block

Figure 3.29   The apartment building on the left is protecting the housing on the right from the impact of a busy inner city road

scheme. The apartments in the protecting block sometimes face and animate the street, although this is not always the case. Alternatively, such a form might be considered where the site is bounded by a great view, in which case the larger apartment block allows more people access to that view (and therefore also higher profits for developers).

Cul-de-sacs

Housing arranged into cul-de-sacs do not really result in a block structure, but during the 1980s in the UK it was the most common configuration for new housing. This form creates quiet domestic arrangements, stopping any form of through traffic, and dissuading non-resident access. It is less common today as it discriminates against pedestrians and often offers areas of very poor surveillance of the public realm. Certain sites, however, can only really be developed with cul-de-sac access arrangements.

Courtyards

Rather than an organising principle for a residential urban form, courtyard housing might be added to an existing block structure. Normally the housing is grouped around a shared space which might be used for parking, otherwise it will probably be landscaped for collective use by residents (Figures 3.31 and 3.32).

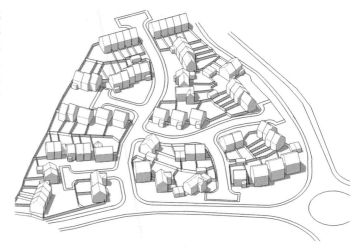

Figure 3.30   Cul-de-sac

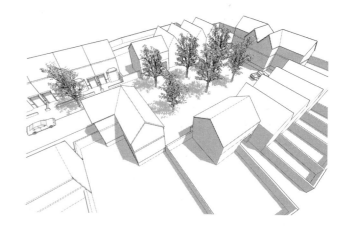

Figure 3.31   Courtyard housing

Figure 3.32   An example of courtyard houses

THE BLOCK STRUCTURE AND PATTERNS OF ACCESS

With the exception of the cul-de-sac arrangement, adopting a particular type of block structure does not have a significant impact on the pattern of pedestrian or vehicular access that might be adopted within the public realm of the scheme, as many block structures can adapt to a variety of patterns (Figure 3.33). The pattern of access should therefore be carefully considered separately and relevant issues of concern are discussed in Chapter 5.

Figure 3.33   The same block structure can accommodate different patterns of access

THE SCALE OF STREETS: INTRODUCE HIERARCHY AND SPATIAL VARIETY

Creating distinctive places within residential areas involves designing a variety of scales into the block structure that is adopted. This can be achieved in a number of ways, but when considering the block structure the most relevant thing to consider is the need to introduce some kind of spatial hierarchy into the pattern of streets and spaces to be created.

In relation to streets it is likely that some streets will have a greater degree of pedestrian and vehicular activity associated with them, and it may be desirable to make these streets more urban in scale. Other streets, by contrast, will be very quiet and used only by immediate residents. Such environments can therefore be designed to be on a more intimate scale (Figure 3.34).

The same principles can also apply, however, to open spaces. The larger streets can focus on a larger scale urban open space such as a park serving the wider neighbourhood, or a larger civic square serving, for example, a public transport interchange, civic buildings or a more central retail area. Within the residential areas the smaller and more local roads can lead to community spaces or play areas designed to be on a more intimate scale (Figure 3.35).

LIMIT THE USE OF BUFFERS

A particular characteristic of contemporary residential development is the prevalence of *buffers* or border zones around the residential communities. These are areas of open space or landscaping that isolate the new residential areas from their immediate context, but without having any obvious open space function. Sometimes they are introduced along busier roads so that no residents have to be affected by the traffic; at other times they are introduced between new and existing communities.

The impact of buffers is that they result in a very fragmented urban form with large areas of poorly used and poorly maintained open space. Often pedestrians using the busy routes

Figure 3.34   Vary the scale of streets to reflect the role of the street within the layout

Figure 3.35   Larger streets should focus on larger open spaces whilst smaller streets should lead to neighbourhood spaces

that border buffer areas feel uncomfortable in an alien environment dominated by motor traffic and without any other forms of surveillance. Buffers therefore disadvantage the pedestrian, and typically achieve little environmental benefit for residents (Figure 3.36). Buffers have a particularly negative impact on the main radial and busier routes serving an urban environment where, along stretches of the route, housing faces away from the roads. The road environment merely becomes a route dominated by traffic.

Land uses located next to such routes can, however, take advantage of the passing trade opportunities that these busier environments offer. There are also ways of managing the built form and scale of any resulting street that creates positive frontage, safe access, and a residential environment which is a positive experience for the people living on or using it. Designing the vehicular access to such environments will be discussed in Chapter 5, but the urban form and the scale of the environment still needs careful consideration.

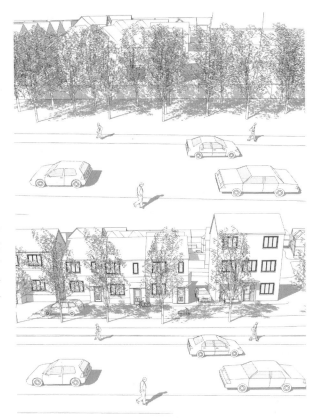

Figure 3.36   Limit the use of buffers

ENSURE A BASIC LEVEL OF AMENITIES IN RESIDENTIAL LAYOUTS

People living in residential areas expect a certain level of light to internal rooms, privacy, and possibly outdoor space. These features contribute to the residents' comfort and are referred to as *amenities*. They are also factors that are affected by the chosen layout of the scheme as much as by the architecture that might be adopted within individual homes.

Different societies have different expectations when it comes to which amenities are important to them, but there are also different ways in which the relevant amenities might be realised within the design of schemes. In particular, however, ensuring that basic levels of amenities are secured will have an impact on both the dimensions of the residential blocks used and the forms that are adopted.

FIND LIGHT

There are two types of light that concern people: daylight and sunlight. Daylight is ambient light received in rooms from all directions, whilst sunlight refers to direct rays of light from the sun. Having daylight within rooms is an essential feature of all homes, especially where sunny days are less common or winter days are shorter, whilst it also reduces dependency on electric lighting. Access to direct sunlight is also an important amenity, particularly in living rooms and well-used outdoor spaces, but its levels are influenced by both building orientation and degrees of overshadowing. When designing a housing area or block structure, it is necessary to ensure that the main rooms in all homes receive adequate daylight, whilst it will also be desirable to create a design where sunlight reaches both gardens and rooms for part of the day.

Daylight

There are two main ways of quickly assessing that the main rooms of a home are receiving adequate daylight.

Facing buildings

When planning your block, how close should the houses be built when facing each other before electric lights become necessary for the lighting of a room? A rough standard would be to take a line 25° from the horizontal from a point 2 m (the normal height of windows) above the floor level containing the necessary windows (including basements) and ensure that no building breaks that line (Littlefair 1991). If applied to normal two-storey housing on a flat site this would result in spacing of 10 m between homes. If the windows are to be on the first floor (maybe there is parking on the ground floor) then measure the 2 m and subsequent 25° angle from the base of the storey containing the windows (Figure 3.37).

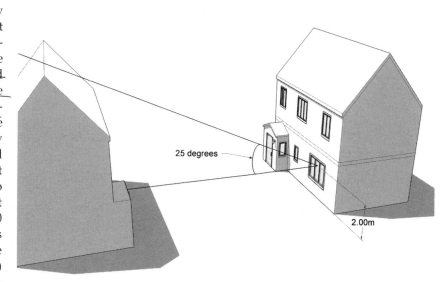

Figure 3.37   Light and facing buildings

Corner windows and extensions

Providing light to living spaces can be difficult either in the corner of urban blocks, or in areas where extensions have been built out from a façade. If a planned living space is wholly dependent on a window, you should ensure that no part of a neighbouring building cuts through an imaginary line radiating at 45° from the centre of the window (in both plan and rear elevation). If a solid building structure cuts through the line then the room may be too dark (Figure 3.38).

On difficult corner sites light can be provided by locating all living spaces on the outside of the housing block, keeping bathrooms and kitchens on the inside. Alternatively, it might be better to use a wide

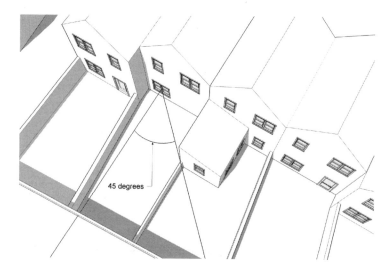

Figure 3.38   Light to corner windows and extensions

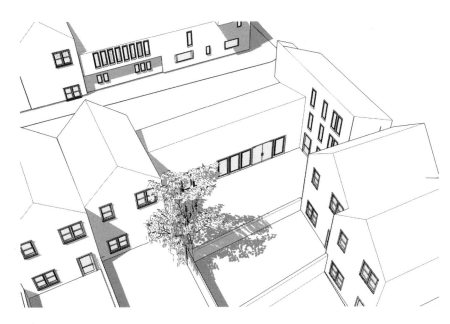

Figure 3.39   A wide fronted building may sit more comfortably on a corner

fronted building (with a wide plot but a narrow depth) which may fit more comfortably onto a tight corner plot (Figure 3.39).

Exceptions

A designer may also wish to apply any such daylight measures with some degree of flexibility, as for layout reasons it may be desirable to have less spacing between homes. Fortunately, there are a number of additional ways in which adequate light can be provided to living spaces. The window head heights could be raised, larger windows used, shallower room plans implemented or more than one light source provided to a relevant room (Figure 3.40). For example, a single room with a shallow plan could obtain light from both the front and the rear. Alternatively some form of light well or skylight could be used (Figure 3.41).

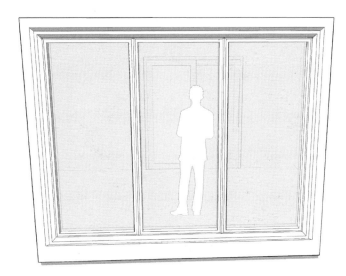

Figure 3.40   Two light sources

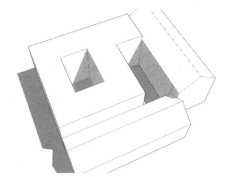

Figure 3.41   Light well

ORIENTATE FOR DIRECT SUNLIGHT

Providing direct sunlight within all homes is not always practical, although where it is possible it will be popular, so long as the amount of sunlight (and resulting warmth) can be controlled. In contrast, within a garden or courtyard access to direct sunlight should be encouraged, except in extremely hot climates, where shady courtyards will help cool buildings. In terms of planning a block structure, access to sunlight is influenced by orientation and overshadowing. The orientation of homes for sunlight is clearly affected by which hemisphere you are designing in (Figure 3.42).

In the northern hemisphere rooms and outdoor spaces that have a southerly aspect will tend to receive sunlight, whilst east and west facing rooms and spaces will receive sunlight in either the morning or evening. Homes should be designed to have living spaces orientated in these directions, and it may be most desirable to design the main living spaces so that they face in a southerly or westerly direction. When grouping buildings to form urban blocks, this may tend to result in the blocks being orientated east to west. In the Southern hemisphere the main living rooms and outdoor spaces should face to the north and west if sunlight is important.

If the scheme includes taller buildings then these should tend to be located away from the sun so that they don't overshadow neighbouring properties or outdoor spaces (Figure 3.43). Balconies, gardens or communal courtyards should be orientated to have outdoor seating, clothes drying and play spaces within the sun, and both building heights and the outdoor space designs should be adjusted to allow this, particularly for the winter months (Figure 3.44). Car parking areas, garages and busier streets can be located in areas more prone to overshadowing, where the possibility that people might stop to enjoy the sunlight will be less.

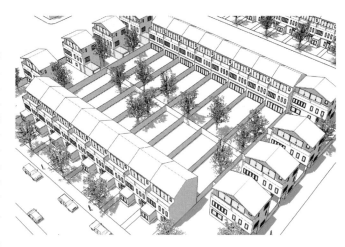

Figure 3.42   Orientation to the sun

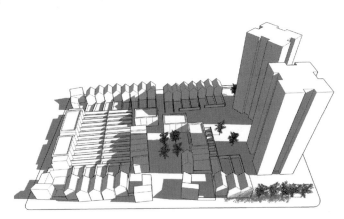

Figure 3.43   Ensure that overshadowing does not occur

PROTECT PRIVACY

Privacy is a vital requirement for rooms within a home, but complete privacy within gardens is more difficult to achieve and may be less necessary.

Internal privacy between facing homes

A common approach to achieving internal privacy is by locating facing windows at a suitable distance from each other. The distance will be

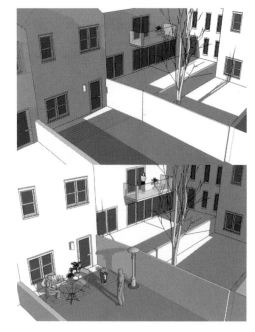

Figure 3.44   Balconies, gardens or communal courtyards should be orientated to have outdoor seating, clothes drying and play spaces within the sun

culturally determined, but a common distance is about 20 to 25 m (in the UK many planning authorities refer to a distance of 21 m) (Figure 3.45). Despite the distances, residents may choose to use net curtains to create internal privacy if they feel that it is necessary. An obvious alternative is to design homes so that they do not have facing windows and, if the detailed design of homes can be controlled so that this is achieved, the homes might be brought closer together.

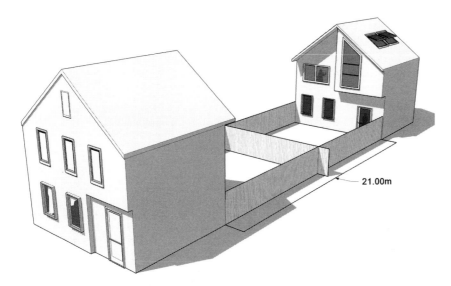

21.00m

Figure 3.45   Privacy created by remoteness

Internal privacy between homes at an angle to each other

If, within a block, homes are located at an angle to each other of greater than 30° it is unlikely that people will be able to see into neighbours' rooms. Distances between homes could therefore be reduced, although, as a consequence, overlooking of gardens will be more intense (Figure 3.46).

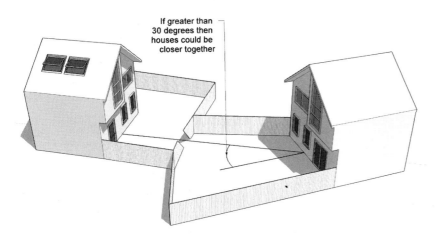

If greater than 30 degrees then houses could be closer together

Figure 3.46   Housing at an angle greater than 30 degrees can be closer together

Internal privacy from the neighbouring public realm

Homes are often located quite close to their neighbouring public realm. Privacy within a home from neighbouring public spaces can be achieved by raising the home above the eye level of people passing within a neighbouring street. Screening could be used, but this limits the surveillance of the street from the homes and can make the street feel less safe for residents and visitors (Figure 3.47).

Setting the building back from the street frontage typically increases the viewing time–or field of vision–that a passer-by might have for looking into a home, and so houses built closer onto a pavement or sidewalk will be less overlooked, despite the physical vicinity (Figure 3.48).

Figure 3.47   Privacy can be achieved by raising the house slightly above eye level

Figure 3.48   Comparing fields of vision

External privacy

Some degree of external privacy is typically a concern for private gardens, although the privacy is normally only achieved from neighbouring public spaces, rather than neighbouring homes where some degree of overlooking is common. There are a number of ways that privacy can be achieved:

Screening: Such privacy is typically achieved by locating the gardens away from the public spaces, and by using above eye level (2 m high) screening like walls, fences or hedges (Figure 3.49).

Using levels: Changes of levels resulting from topography or design features of a scheme can provide greater privacy for people who are on higher levels, and therefore cannot be overlooked (Figure 3.50).

By design: It is possible to orientate buildings and locate windows so that private spaces are not overlooked. This is a common way of controlling privacy in higher density schemes (Figure 3.51).

Figure 3.49   Screening

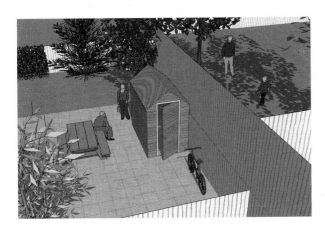

Figure 3.50   Using levels helps to maintain privacy

Figure 3.51   Privacy by design

Privacy to gardens is a particular concern in the UK where, in many contexts, there is an expectation that gardens will not be completely overlooked, but this concern for outdoor privacy might be less evident in other cultures.

PROVIDE OUTDOOR SPACE

Private or shared outdoor space is a common feature of housing layouts, and it is thought to make an important contribution to residential amenity. In some areas planning authorities require a certain amount of private outdoor space to be provided for residents, and although this is commonly in the form of gardens in lower density schemes, in others it might take the form of roof gardens, shared courtyards, balconies or even access to a nearby public square or park (Figure 3.52).

Figure 3.52   Gardens and balconies

DESIGN THE PLACE FIRST

In combining the above amenity issues together it might be tempting to think that the design of a residential layout is a technical exercise in making sure that certain standards have been met, but it is important to remember that urban design is about the creation of places within an urban form. When faced with a development site, a common first response is to design the pattern of highways and footpaths first, followed by the form of the housing which is then laid out to precisely meet the amenity standard dimensions (Figure 3.53). Don't. If you do this it is likely that the character of the environment will be dominated by the roads and the housing environment will be standardised and placeless, just like the housing illustrated in Figures 1.5, 1.6 and 1.7.

Instead, in the design of a residential environment you should consider the form and character of the spaces between the buildings before anything else. This should account for the public realm as well as any private realm that you wish to include. Only after the form of the public realm has been decided should you then include arrangements for vehicular

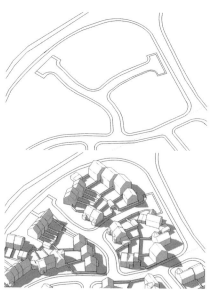

Figure 3.53   Designing the road and thinking about the amenity standards before laying out the housing results in placelessness

and pedestrian access through the public realm and provide a design in which issues of amenity are considered (Figure 3.54).

Some types of residential environment could be suggested, each with their own distinct form and character, although there is always scope for new forms. Some established types are illustrated in Figure 3.55.

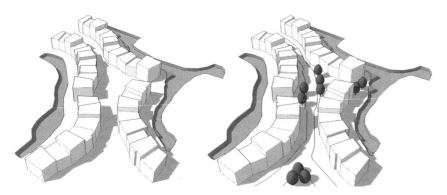

Figure 3.54   Design the urban form before thinking about the pattern of access and amenity standards

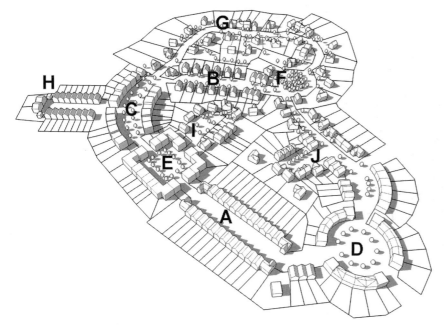

Figure 3.55   Types of place within a residential scheme A, Formal or informal street; B, Avenue or boulevard; C, Crescent; D, Circus; E, Square; F, Green; G, Lane; H, Mews; I, Close; J, Courtyard

FURTHER READING

Most introductory urban design books say something about urban form and place. Carmona *et al.* (2003–Chapter 4) provide a useful introduction to the concepts, whilst both Trancik (1986) and Panerai *et al.* (2004) bemoan the modern destruction of urban forms and blocks. A recent history of housing forms can be found in the *Design of Suburbia* (Edwards, 1981), *Housing Design: An international perspective* (Colquhoun, 1991) and the *RIBA Book of 20th Century British Housing* (Colquhoun, 1999) whilst historic housing forms and block structures also figure extensively in the book *The New Civic Art* Duany *et al.* (2003). The spectrum of private to public space types, their form, meaning and use are discussed by Madanipour (2003), whilst *Responsive Environments* (Bentley *et al.*, 1985) provides the arguments for why a concern should be given for creating public fronts and private backs in developments. Relph (1976) helps us identify 'placelessness' in our developments, whilst I have used Cullen (1961) to help define a notion of place that is useful for urban designers. Finally, there is little conclusive literature about the origin and use of standards, as all cultures adopt their own and many seem to be passed down through practice without much questioning. Littlefair (1991) does provide a useful guide to standards for daylight and sunlight within residential schemes which have informed UK practice, whilst *The Essex Design Guide* (Essex Planning Officers' Association 2005) also offers a comprehensive and very well explained set of standards that have been tried and tested in Essex over the past few decades.

4 Environmentally benign development and design

It is possible to create developments that respect natural processes, have a lower impact on the environment and generate physical conditions for a low energy lifestyle. People who live there would then be able to make a greater contribution to environmental sustainability.

Initially, this chapter will discuss the main environmental problems that could be confronted through the design of residential schemes. There are four main themes: reducing pollution and limiting the production of gases that are fuelling climate change; waste reduction and recycling; conserving water; and promoting biodiversity. There will then be a brief discussion about the features of a more environmentally benign lifestyle and the relationship between this and the design of residential areas. Approaches to design and layout will then be introduced and explained. This will start with a discussion about the role of existing and new green spaces and the need to promote biodiversity. The role of density is then considered, and in particular how higher densities might reduce the need to travel, create more energy efficient residential forms and create large enough catchments to support public transport, local shops and other facilities. Approaches to layout which support more environmentally benign forms of transport will be discussed, as well as the role that existing buildings can make to conserving energy. The design of a sustainable urban drainage scheme will be introduced, as well as the features of energy efficient residential forms. Finally, the need to consider the provision of facilities for recycling and local food production is introduced.

ENVIRONMENTAL PROBLEMS AND THE DESIGN OF RESIDENTIAL AREAS

Pollution and climate change

Urban areas are often regarded as some of the most polluted environments on the planet. Historically, the main forms of pollution affecting urban areas have been caused by the burning of fossil fuels like coal, resulting in high levels of sulphur dioxide being released into the atmosphere. Where cleaner forms of fuel are now being used for generating power, most of the pollution comes from traffic emissions. While the resulting pollutants are less visible, the forms of pollution have negative health effects on individuals, particularly with the increasing numbers of people suffering from asthma, heart or lung diseases. Climate change, on the other hand, is having a less direct impact on individuals but, instead, is affecting the equilibrium of the biosphere. This is a result of our over-dependence on fossil fuels like coal and oil, and this has produced what have become known as greenhouse gases. As fossil fuels are major, traditional energy sources for building, heating, cooking and travelling, current design is concerned with making developments more energy efficient, encouraging the use of renewable energy sources and reducing the need to travel.

Waste reduction

Waste is a big problem and countries are keen to encourage and support attempts made by local authorities to reduce waste production at source and, in particular, encourage recycling and composting. A country like the UK has an improving record. In 2001 it recycled 13% of its waste, preferring to put 81% into landfill. In 2004/5 the figure had changed to 23.9% being recycled or composted, whilst 72% went into the land (Department of Environment, Food and Rural Affairs, 2006a). The USA has a better record as it recycles 28% of its waste, a rate that has almost doubled during the past 15 years (www.EPA.gov). These countries are far behind others, however; for example, in the Netherlands and Austria about 60% of municipal waste is composted or recycled, whilst in Belgium and Germany the statistic is 50% (Department of Environment, Food and Rural Affairs, 2006b).

Given that the amounts of waste produced are increasing, the main goal in design terms is to support attempts at recycling. In particular, residential schemes can accommodate space for waste to be sorted or composted, particularly if recycling is supported by a municipal domestic collection service.

Water conservation

In a country like the UK, famous for its rain, you would assume that there are no water problems, but this is far from the truth. The average rainfall is 897 mm/year, while in the less populated mountains of Wales rainfall can be over 4000 mm/year, but and in parts of the East and South East of England the rainfall can be under 550 mm/year. The UK has a very well developed system of water distribution. However, because of the density of population in the East and South East, serving the population with adequate water is problematic (the Government's Environment Agency produces maps that highlight how unsustainable abstraction regimes are used which are causing damage to the wider environment; a situation compounded by unpredictable patterns of weather including frequent summer droughts). New housing in this region only compounds the situation, fuelling serious concern about water conservation (Environment Agency, 2001).

At the other extreme, there are also concerns. Climate change seems to be increasing the incidence of flooding and the UK's Office of the Deputy

Prime Minister indicates that: 'the latest climate change scenarios suggest that annual rainfall is expected to increase by 0–10% by the 2050s with the largest increases in the north-west. A shift in the seasonal pattern of rainfall is also expected, with winters and autumns becoming wetter over the whole of the UK, by as much as 20% under some scenarios' (ODPM, 2001a, Appendix 2, Para A7). As a result, development on flood plains in particular is not considered sensible. Increasing the areas of developed land, however, increases the likelihood of flooding as new residential developments can increase the amount and speed of water runoff across new impermeable roads and roofs. This water enters drainage systems quickly and, during periods of high rainfall, can increase the incidence of flooding downstream.

In design terms a concern for water should result in water conservation and management systems being introduced into residential areas. These would include designing sustainable drainage systems and surface water storage that retain water for longer within the scheme. Measures can also be introduced that reduce demand for water by introducing systems for storage and reuse.

Loss of biodiversity

Development can maintain, develop or destroy habitats and ecosystems that provide the environmental conditions needed to support distinctive communities of flora and fauna. Built environments can sometimes, however, be regarded as environments where little remains of a biodiversity that once prevailed, although there are approaches to planning and design which can also provide more opportunity for nature and natural processes to flourish.

The need to protect and enhance biodiversity within urban areas has been argued for from a number of directions:

Insurance: It is impossible to predict in what ways future generations may benefit from plants or animals. Nature has provided materials to create shelter and sources of fuel, food, clothing and medicine and new discoveries are always being made on how nature might assist us in our lives. Biodiversity also provides greater resilience for ecosystems to cope with ecological changes–such as changes to the climate. Glibly destroying nature does not, therefore, seem sensible.

Support for natural functions: Plants and animals play a role in maintaining the equilibrium within environmental systems. Plant life maintains and binds soils and these collectively retain water within the landscape, reducing the frequency of flooding. Trees absorb carbon dioxide, a significant greenhouse gas, and they can remove sulphur dioxide from the atmosphere. Trees and hedges, on the other hand, provide shelter from wind while plants have cooling effects in hot climates. If an ecosystem is altered to the point that these forms of life no longer survive then these protective qualities are lost (see Town and Country Planning Association, 2004, p. 7).

Health and welfare: Natural environments offer us a source of inspiration and beauty. They allow us to observe, learn about, appreciate and respect both wildlife and seasonal cycles. They supply fresh air and space in which to rest, relax and recharge. They provide us with space for food production. They also offer space for recreation, exercise, play and discovery.

Moral grounds: The UK's Action Plan presents the moral case for biodiversity (UK Government, 1994, p. 13): 'We believe that a culture which encourages respect for wildlife and landscapes is preferable to one that does not. Human beings exercise a determinative power over other creatures. Whether hundreds of thousands of species survive depends on the decisions of humans. With this dominion comes responsibility.'

For economic reasons: Natural features within an urban environment always have a positive impact on property values. People want trees in their streets, they want to overlook water, or they want to live near a park.

In design terms maintaining or enhancing biodiversity means conserving existing natural features as well as finding ways in which new natural features and processes can be introduced sympathetically into a scheme.

THE PRECAUTIONARY PRINCIPLE

Some would argue that there is still insufficient scientific evidence relating to human impacts on the environment. As a result they would argue that we don't need to concern ourselves with environmental degradation, particularly in urban development. In response to this, however, the 'precautionary principle' has emerged.

The principle appears in the Rio Declaration in 1992 and states: 'In order to protect the environment, the precautionary approach shall be widely applied by States according to their capabilities. Where there are threats of serious or irreversible damage, lack of full scientific certainty shall not be used as a reason for postponing cost-effective measures to prevent environmental degradation' (Principle 15) (United Nations Conference on the Environment and Development, 1992).

What this suggests, therefore, is that because so much degradation to the environment is irreversible, it is deemed reasonable to err on the side of caution and ensure that schemes do not result in either one-off significant or small-scale and piecemeal changes, leading to environmental damage. The result of such thinking is design that places concern for the environment at the centre of the ethic, and where accommodating particular design features might be pursued even if the short-term economic costs are higher.

ENVIRONMENTAL SUSTAINABILITY BY DESIGN?

Although it is possible to create the physical conditions for an environmentally sustainable lifestyle within a scheme it does not mean that residents will live in the desired way. It is important, therefore, not to be environmentally deterministic in your approach and assume that your design will result in an environmentally sustainable lifestyle. A common assumption, for example, is that if you provide local shops, people will use them in preference to shops that are further away. Alternatively, you might assume that if you build your housing next to an area of employment, it will be occupied by people that work there. Neither of these things can be guaranteed. Good paths and cycle routes may not dissuade people from driving, just as the provision of recycling facilities will not mean that residents will see the value of recycling their waste. Design can only create the conditions in which a more environmentally sustainable lifestyle becomes possible, although through its form it might also promote the opportunity to live in a more environmentally sustainable way. The lifestyles remain, however, the choice of the residents.

FEATURES OF AN ENVIRONMENTALLY BENIGN LIFESTYLE

People who try to live more environmentally sustainable lives typically do so for ethical reasons, and not because of the way their environment is designed. More likely, they will choose to live in an environment that allows them to pursue their desired lifestyle, or they will adapt their environment as far as possible to allow them to live a particular way.

According to research by Bedford *et al.* (2004) people living a more sustainable way would:

1   walk and cycle as often as possible, or otherwise seek to use public transport as a main form of transport within their locality. Alternatively they would prefer to car share
2   accept living at a higher density in a home that had reduced the need to use formerly undeveloped land
3   want to live in an environment where children can roam, play and socialise freely, rather than being hemmed in by traffic and highways
4   want to grow their own food or buy locally produced food
5   seek to recycle or compost their domestic waste
6   seek to conserve, collect and reuse water
7   seek to generate their own sources of energy or use renewable sources
8   try to reduce their need for energy to a minimum by living in highly insulated homes which are warmed and cooled naturally, and
9   want to see more greenery around, in and on their homes, but also accept and tolerate a less manicured landscape that supports a greater degree of biodiversity.

Sometimes residential environments might address one of two of these issues in their designs, but a scheme can only really claim to be making a significant contribution to environmental sustainability when residents have a chance to successfully achieve most of these things. Approaches to residential layout which could make a specific contribution are introduced below.

DESIGN GOOD GREEN SPACES AND FOR BIODIVERSITY

Analyse and understand the greenspace hierarchy

Urban areas typically contain a hierarchy of green spaces that allow nature and natural processes to penetrate them, while providing residents with access to a variety of green amenity spaces. In well-planned areas it may be that a network of such green spaces has been established and is being developed and so a development scheme would need to conform to these aspirations (Figure 4.1).

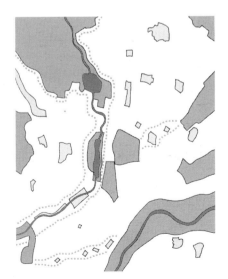

Figure 4.1   Urban areas often contain an established network of green spaces

English Nature (2003: 15) suggests that (i) large green spaces and country parks of about 60 hectares should be accessible to people within a metropolitan area; (ii) that within 1 km of people's homes they should have access to a large park of about 20 hectares; and (iii) that no person should live more than 300 m from their nearest area of natural green space in the form of a small neighbourhood park. The Town and Country Planning Association (2004) goes further to suggest that new residential areas should accommodate other types of 'green infrastructures' in the form of linear greenways along waterways and other landscape routes, as well as almost continuous tree coverage within streets. Such features would be in addition to shared and private gardens and courtyards at the most local level (Figure 4.2).

Figure 4.2   Hierarchy of green spaces

Consciously planning such spaces and opportunities into a scheme will help provide an overall structure to a residential scheme. Safe pedestrian and cyclist routes should be provided from the houses to the open spaces so that children and the elderly, in particular, can gain safe access (Figure 4.3). In addition, it might be desirable to exploit views to green spaces by ensuring developments that front the environmental assets are

Figure 4.3   Safe routes into open spaces

of a higher density and have clear views of open spaces from living rooms (Figure 4.4).

Consider different types of urban green space

In 2002, the UK Government (Figure 4.5) produced its own hierarchy of urban green space to help planners recognise the scope for introducing green space into urban areas. Residential areas may be bounded by the larger of these spaces, although some of them may be formed by the layout that is adopted, including green corridors, allotments, community gardens, amenity green spaces such as courtyards and gardens and sports pitches. The contribution that each of these types of urban green space can make to biodiversity varies, with areas like sports pitches making the least. Despite this it is worth noting the contribution that such a space can make in its location and design, and considering to what extent biodiversity can be introduced and maintained at a higher level than has often previously been achieved.

Critically consider the value of any new green space

During the early and mid-twentieth century there was a common assumption that providing green spaces in the urban environment was good, and that the more green spaces there were, the better the urban environment would be. Such a view was essentially reactionary–a reaction to nineteenth-century forms of urbanism where, unless you were lucky, there was very little open space close to your home; and due to urban poverty, long working hours and lack of transport, any green spaces were probably difficult to reach. Rudlin and Falk (1999) argue that as a result, planners started to develop generous open space standards within new developments. Today, however, it is recognised that these open spaces reduce the density of development which, in turn, reduces the viability of local shops, services and public transport. For example, people have to walk longer distances to go to the shop or doctor. In addition, these spaces cost a lot to maintain and at night, in particular, people using them can feel isolated and intimidated. Such spaces are typically also only grass, and so they make little contribution to biodiversity (Figure 4.6).

Figure 4.4   Higher densities facing open spaces

Type of Greenspace	Examples
Natural and semi-natural spaces	Woodlands, grasslands, heaths/moors, wetlands, wastelands, bare rock habitats
Green corridors	River and canal banks, road and rail corridors, cycle routes and pedestrian paths
Parks and Gardens	Urban parks embedded in the urban environment, country parks linked into the metropolitan area and formal gardens
Cemeteries and churchyards	
Allotments, Community gardens and urban farms	
Amenity Greenspaces	Informal recreation spaces, domestic gardens and courtyards, village greens and other incidental spaces
Sports Facilities	Bowling greens, tennis courts, sports pitches, school playing fields, golf courses, athletics tracks

Figure 4.5   Hierarchy of urban green spaces identified by the UK government (DTLR, 2002: 43)

Figure 4.6   Generous public space standards do not necessarily lead to attractive, well used or bio diverse public spaces

Green spaces are important in urban areas, but they should be located so that these problems do not result. Typically within neighbourhoods a number of smaller open spaces with higher quality planting, good management and a clearer use will be more valued by residents, who may then also feel some greater sense of ownership and responsibility for them.

Protect habitats

Residential schemes should be designed to protect established habitats. This has implications for context and site analysis. Identifying any features of the environment that have an environmental designation, such as nature reserves, which may contain protected species, will be necessary. Such areas should be protected from development.

Sites may also contain existing natural features which will be worth maintaining and an initial site survey should highlight these. Water features such as rivers, streams, ponds or ditches are a key source of biodiversity if kept naturalised and can be retained to form part of a sustainable drainage system (see below) (Figure 4.7). In addition existing individual and groups of trees or hedges can be integrated into a scheme. Trees and hedges add maturity to a new scheme, whilst also being important habitats. They should be carefully surveyed, located and also therefore protected during construction. Trees, in particular, might be integrated into a new public space, and will be of most value if they are visible within the public realm (Figure 4.8).

Figure 4.7   Protect existing habitats

Figure 4.8   Existing trees can be important habitats and, where retained, will add maturity to a scheme

Promote biodiversity

Many urban open spaces and green areas have traditionally been heavily manicured to look maintained, but sterile manicured lawns and exotic plants do not make a significant contribution to biodiversity. Laurie (1979: xvi–xvii) and Hough (1984) argue that ornamental parkland and manicured landscapes, designed primarily for their aesthetic appeal, can provide little habitat diversity. Instead, if biodiversity is to be encouraged, it is necessary to support or plant a greater diversity of indigenous plants and have an approach to management which seeks to enhance natural processes (Figure 4.9).

It is thought that native species usually benefit local wildlife that has evolved with them, although some exotic plants can be a good food source. A full growing cycle for plants is also encouraged, as this allows plants to form a habitat for insects as well as to seed naturally.

Figure 4.9   To promote biodiversity open spaces will need to be more naturalistic and allow plants a full growing cycle

Concern for biodiversity may result in designs that are more structured in order to create areas that are more naturalistic, in addition to areas that receive a more traditional, manicured treatment. As well as a space for nature to flourish, such naturalistic residential settings can offer greater scope for informal types of play and exploration. Hough (1984: 134) refers to high density housing in Delft:

> In the high density apartment developments at Delft, courtyards have been planted as urban woodlands in addition to providing open space... In these woodland landscapes the sheer vigour of early plant associations and their density provide a tough and highly varied environment. They withstand the pressures of play and other activities... The complexity and ruggedness of the woodland landscape can accommodate pressures that would soon reduce conventional design to ruins.

It is likely that such an approach to planting and management will require special types of knowledge and skills. Appropriate landscape architects should, therefore, be employed at an early stage in the process to help plan the form of any such spaces and then plan for their ongoing management, including management techniques that would engage with the energy, commitment and knowledge of local people.

Put trees in the urban environment

Trees are now an established part of the urban environment although Pitt *et al.* (1979) point out that trees only started to appear in plans for the urban environment during the 1800s–including Haussmann's plans for Paris, and the city squares planned in the west end of London. In the USA tree-lined boulevards became a normal element of the urban beautification movement in many cities during the nineteenth century.

Environmentally trees offer the following benefits to an urban environment:

- Trees condition air by trapping particulates and absorb pollutants such as nitrogen dioxide, sulphur dioxide and carbon dioxide

Figure 4.10   Open spaces like play areas are a good location for tree planting within residential schemes

- Trees reduce extremes in urban microclimates. Deciduous trees, in particular, provide shade in the summer and allow sunlight to reach the ground during winter. In hard urban landscapes trees reduce glare from surfaces and windows. Trees generally can reduce humidity and the effects of wind, and capture rain before it hits the ground, providing human comfort as well as reducing the likelihood of erosion of softer surfaces.
- Trees can help maintain soils allowing them to retain water in the ground reducing the likelihood of localised flooding.
- Trees also provide food and protection for many forms of wildlife.

Trees don't, however, only offer environmental benefits. The National Urban Forestry Unit (1999: 4) argue that well treed neighbourhoods typically have higher house prices as trees soften the urban scene, reinforce local character and bring nature and natural processes closer to residents.

Research by Land Use Consultants (1993) found that in the UK most urban trees were found along transport corridors, in churchyards, formal and informal open spaces, around hospitals and in areas of lower density housing. They point out that 80% of urban trees are found on private property, but that typically it is the other 20% that have the greatest visual impact.

Within a scheme, trees can be planted in areas traditionally noted for their cover such as along transport corridors like roads, railways or canals, in churchyards and in parks. However, newly designated footpaths, areas of water and green wedges should also become a focus for areas of planting. Within residential areas small open spaces used for some other purpose, such as play, can also be planted with trees (Figure 4.10).

Street trees make a significant contribution to the residents' quality of life. Where front gardens are introduced, suitable planting in the private realm will encourage a softening of the street and trees will be the responsibility of residents. Such trees may be removed and, over time, species might change, influencing the character of a street (Figure 4.11). Where houses are planned to the back of pavements, then trees should be considered for introduction into the street space with maintenance overseen by the local authority. Such trees will require a specific management regime, although street trees are not

Figure 4.11   The character of streets can be altered when trees in front gardens are removed by residents

Figure 4.12   Where houses back the pavement any trees should be introduced into the street space

difficult to maintain once they are established, and the character of a street is less likely to be changed by the whim of individual residents (Figure 4.12).

Planting can be formal and create the character of a boulevard, or it can be informal, grouped and more naturalistic. Whatever the approach it may be desirable to consider the visual as well as the environmental impact of any planting and this is discussed further in Chapter Eight.

DESIGN WITH DENSITY IN MIND

Plan the net densities

Higher net densities of residential development are often associated with areas where there is a high demand for housing, although more recently it has been argued that higher net densities of development may also allow people to live more sustainably.

The theory is straightforward: the more people that live within the vicinity of a given shop, service or facility, the more likely that its use will be sustained. The desirable distance for people wishing to walk to either their shops or a local public transport stop is typically 400 m, and so it is argued that people who live within the vicinity of such services, will choose to walk to them rather than drive. Such views are very simplistic, as often services don't just serve a local population, and people may choose to travel across town to shop, go to school or use a service (see also Chapter 6). Still, if residents are influenced by an ethical desire to reduce their travelling then local facilities should be valued and used.

Density is measured in a number of ways:

> **Gross density** a measure of the density which includes all aspects of a neighbourhood, including the housing, roads, open spaces, schools and their grounds and other uses.

> **Net density** a measure which includes everything that is developed for housing, including the housing footprints and garden areas, the pavements and access roads, car parking areas, incidental landscaping and local children's play spaces. Net density would exclude

major roads, schools and their grounds, commercial and community buildings, urban parks or other significant open spaces.

Plot ratios refer to the amount of development that there might be on a site. It is measured using the total floor area of the buildings multiplied by the number of storeys and then presented as a ratio of the total area of the site.

Dwellings per hectare/acre refers to the number of homes on a site, but ignores their size.

Bed spaces per hectare/acre refers to the size of properties and suggests approximately how many people might live within a scheme.

Figure 4.13 illustrates how the different measures give different results.

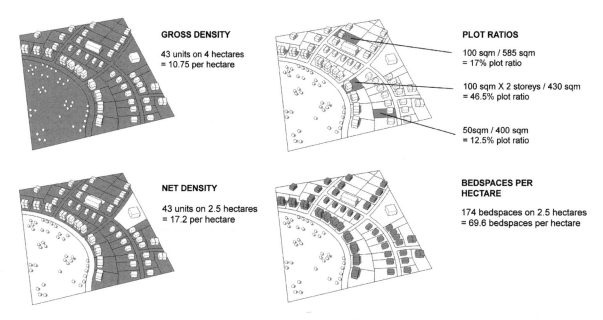

GROSS DENSITY

43 units on 4 hectares
= 10.75 per hectare

PLOT RATIOS

100 sqm / 585 sqm
= 17% plot ratio

100 sqm X 2 storeys / 430 sqm
= 46.5% plot ratio

50sqm / 400 sqm
= 12.5% plot ratio

NET DENSITY

43 units on 2.5 hectares
= 17.2 per hectare

BEDSPACES PER HECTARE

174 bedspaces on 2.5 hectares
= 69.6 bedspaces per hectare

Figure 4.13   Comparing density measures

The Urban Task Force (1999: 61) indicates that a population of roughly 7500 residents should be enough to support a range of local services. However, the area that such a population might inhabit depends on the net density of a scheme, and different countries have developed different expectations with regards to residential densities. In Australia, net residential densities of between 8–10 dwellings per hectare are common, and policies to achieve a more sustainable form of development encourage developers to increase that to 15 units/hectare in Melbourne (State Government of Victoria, 2005) and between 15–25 units/hectare in Perth (State of Western Australia, 2000). In the United States the Environmental Protection Agency indicates that Phoenix has an average net density of 5 and Minneapolis 12 dwellings per hectare (www.EPA.gov); other data suggests that net densities in medium sized cities in the USA range from an average of 7 (Charlotte in North Carolina) to 16 (Las Vegas) dwellings per hectare (North West Environment Watch, 2004). New Urbanists in the USA encourage general neighbourhood development at net densities of between 15 and 50 units per hectare (Figure 4.14). In the UK standard forms of suburban development have been at 25 dwellings per hectare for some time (Figure 4.15), whilst the UK Government hopes to raise that to 30 units per hectare through its planning guidance (Urban Task Force 1999: 187; Office of the Deputy Prime Minister, 2000). Barton *et al.* (1995: 80) and the Urban Task Force (1999: 61) suggest that the minimum net density for a bus service to be economical is about 100 people per hectare or roughly 40–50 dwellings. In Germany so called sustainable urban extensions have higher net densities: Französisches Viertel in Tübingen supports a range of services and a frequent bus service and has 60 units per hectare (Figure 4.16), while Rieselfeld in Freiburg has a range

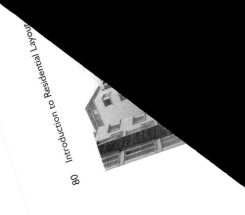

Figure 4.14 [...] schemes in the USA try and attain net densities of between 15 and 50 units per hectare, although densities will vary across a scheme

Figure 4.15 Average densities in the UK have remained about 25 units per hectare making it difficult to support a range of services

Figure 4.16 Französisches Viertel in Tübingen supports a range of local services and a frequent bus service and has on average 60 units per hectare

Figure 4.17 Rieselfeld is on average 78 units per hectare and supports a tram service to the city centre, as well as a full range of community uses and facilities

of local services, supports a tram system and has 78 units per hectare (Figure 4.17). The shift from housing to apartments occurs at between 25 and 30 units per hectare.

Consider how the same density can be achieved using different urban forms

Discussions about higher densities of development often create visions of high-rise buildings and prompts people to talk about 'overcrowding' or the loss of open space within an urban area. There is, however, no clear relationship between the net density that might be realised, the urban form that might result, or the amount of open space that might be available, unless of course the densities being considered are very high.

The desire to vary densities and increase them in certain situations has led to a re-evaluation of higher density forms of housing and how they might be configured within a scheme. The *Further reading* section for this chapter lists a number of books that provide more detailed advice about these types of urban housing. In general, however, it is worth noting that higher net densities

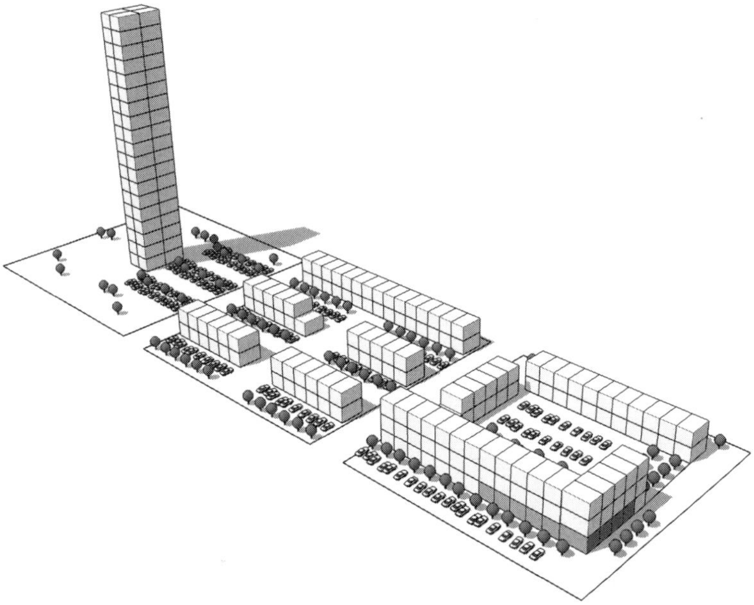

Figure 4.18 Different development forms at 75 units per hectare based on the work of Andrew Wright Associates for the Urban Task Force (1999, pp.62)

can be achieved using a number of general block configurations. This is illustrated by Andrew Wright Associates' work for the Urban Task Force (1999) (Figure 4.18) which shows how 75 units might be accommodated on a hectare:

- A point block provides large amounts of open space, but there is no private outdoor space and no direct control of the open areas by individual residents (for a discussion of defensible space see Chapter Seven). Large areas are dominated by surface parking and the public realm has no obvious form.
- The same density might be in the form of low rise apartments arranged into streets with each building providing access for residents to a smaller shared garden. Parking can be on-street.

- The final example shows the same density of development accommodated in medium rise apartments mixed with other commercial or community uses fronting a commercial street. Such a form can be used to define positive streets and public spaces. Parking can be on-street, underground or behind the block. If parking is underground, residents can have access to a semi-private courtyard, although ground floor residents might also get some private space.

It is worth considering the range of forms that higher density might take in relation to wider urban design and development objectives. Higher net densities involve some compromises over the amount of private outdoor space that residents might have or the vicinity of parking to their home, but despite these points there is no reason at all why higher net density schemes shouldn't offer the prospect of an excellent quality of life in similarly sized homes, whilst also providing benefits that lower density schemes tend not to, such as more attention to play spaces in shared courtyards for children or a greater vicinity to other uses.

Discussions about net density shouldn't ignore the provision of larger urban green spaces within an urban area and between higher density neighbourhoods. Berlin, for example, has an average of 127 people per hectare within its inner areas, although it is also one of the greenest cities in Europe, with the Tiergarten forming a large open green space in the centre (Figure 4.19). Central London has a population density of about 77 people per hectare within its inner areas, whilst the overall density of the city is 47 dwellings per hectare (Urban Task Force, 1999: 187) but residents towards the centre also benefit from relatively close access to a number of large parks (Figure 4.20). From a sustainability point of view, density measures tend to focus on net densities within neighbourhoods where the people live and the services are provided, and there is no reason why such communities should be regarded as being overcrowded or lacking access to green open space.

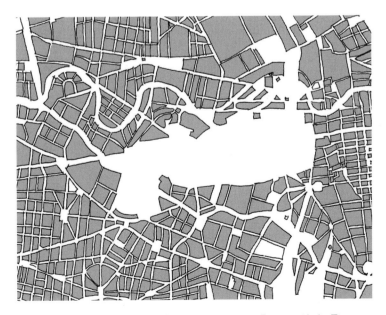

Figure 4.19   Berlin is thought to be one of the greenest cities in Europe with the Tiergarten at its core whilst it also has an average of 127 people per hectare

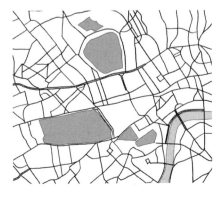

Figure 4.20   Central London has 77 people per hectare, but benefits from vicinity to a number of great urban parks

Varying the density profile: working with a transect

It is possible to vary the density and scale of a development so that within a scheme different types of residential character areas result. This means that densities overall might be increased; whilst not precluding the fact that people will be attracted to live in a variety of forms of housing within one neighbourhood. To explain this approach, new urbanists have developed the concept of the transect (Figure 4.21).

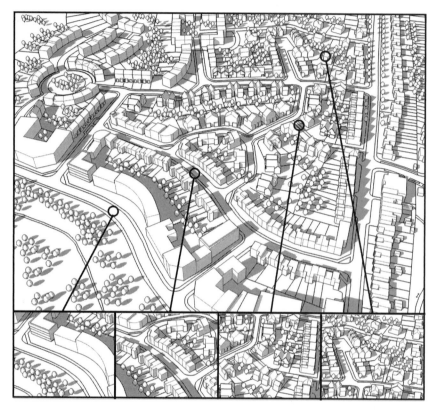

Figure 4.21   New urbanists encourage us to think about the transect as a way of creating a diversity of residential characters and densities within a scheme

Studying the form of older towns it is possible to suggest that densities of development tend to be higher towards the centre, along the main streets and within walking distances of commercial activities and public transport stops. Towards the periphery, in contrast, they might tend to fall off. The higher densities at the centre have traditionally reflected the demand to live close to local shops and services that existed prior to the automobile, whilst lower densities reflect the impact of cars on the urban environment and the fact that people could finally live at lower densities without affecting their accessibility to other uses. Noting that some old centres and higher density areas still remain very popular because of their distinctive urban character and convenience, the transect seeks to recreate various forms–and therefore densities of development–by using different housing typologies and street tissues in a positive way, so that an increase in density is created but residents don't have to compromise on their amenity.

The transect describes the types of environments you might experience as you pass from the centre of a neighbourhood to its edges. New urbanists identify core areas as the most urban and mixed use in character; the general neighbourhood as medium density and mainly housing (although the odd corner bar or shop might creep in); and the edge as the most suburban, with housing located in a dominant landscape. Two sides of a street should share a character so that they appear unified–so the form and character of development should be split within a block. The plan for a neighbourhood could reflect this potential change in character with higher density and more formal developments fronting the major commercial roads, urban spaces or attractive views; while lower density and more arcadian forms of development merge with neighbouring lower density development or the wider landscape.

EXPLORING TISSUES

The transect idea encourages us to look back at the forms of popular development that have gone before to understand how their forms and mixture of uses have been designed. We can learn a lot from how the public and private spaces of existing areas are composed from an analysis of their tissues. Often existing environments have many of the qualities that we might like to encourage in new schemes and their analysis is worthwhile so that we can determine how the forms are composed and managed (Figure 4.22). In analysing an existing tissue you might like to consider the following questions which consider not only aspects of the physical form, but also how a scheme is lived in, used and managed:

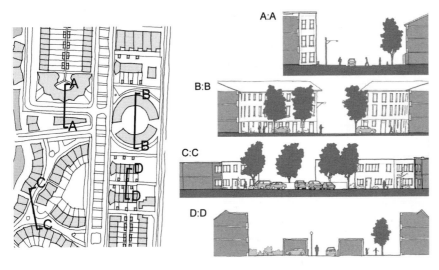

Figure 4.22 A piece of housing tissue illustrating different typological configurations

- What are the height to width ratios of spaces created within the scheme?
- How is the plan and section of the scheme composed in terms of:
  - its overall form
  - the nature of plot widths and any building lines
  - relative dimensions of highway, pavement, other hard or soft open spaces or service areas
  - the location and form of boundaries such as front or rear walls

- ○ the rhythm of building entrances and windows
- ○ the nature of the interfaces between public areas and private interiors, including porches or verandas
- ○ the location, form and type of trees or other landscaping
- ○ the use of street furniture and hard landscaping to support the desired pattern of use
- ○ The location and extent of provision of other facilities such as play equipment
- ○ the nature of both planned and incidental use of the streets and spaces by people?

- How is use of the public areas managed by, for example access or parking controls, limits to delivery times or frequency of street cleaning?

FAVOUR ENVIRONMENTALLY BENIGN TRAVEL

Compared to a more traditional residential area, a scheme that allows for an environmentally benign lifestyle will place greater emphasis on forms of travel that have less impact on the environment. Such a residential scheme will connect directly by footpath, cycleway and public transport to nearby existing centres, creating the shortest possible distances for both pedestrians and cyclists between their homes and other uses or areas of the scheme. The higher densities should also make it possible to economically sustain a public transport service, although willingness to use public transport appears to be heavily influenced by culture, access to a car, and issues around how traffic is managed, such as the availability and cost of parking at a destination.

As residential densities increase there is evidence that people generally travel shorter distances to shops and services and tend to use cars less and other modes more (Balcombe *et al.* 2004: 123–124). There is also some consensus that having higher densities of development, and therefore more people within a given area, helps to support public transport systems, providing a higher level of service at greater frequency and for longer periods of the day (Addenbrooke *et al.* 1981; Del Mistro 1998; White 2002). As a rough guide new urbanists suggest, for example, that an average net density of about 24 units/hectare will provide a critical mass for a viable bus service, but higher average net densities such as 45 units per hectare are necessary for light rail or a more frequent bus service (Calthorpe 1993: 58). As stated previously, in the UK the Urban Task Force (1999: 61) quote a slightly higher figure for a viable bus service of about 100 people/hectare.

For public transport to be successful, a high proportion of residents should live within about 400 m or a 5 minute walk from stops linking directly to key destinations. This suggests that development should focus along and link directly to public transport corridors and that higher density development could be focused around stops. This would result in what is conceptually known as a *beading effect* (Addenbrooke *et al.* 1981: 31) (Figure 4.23).

With new housing schemes it is important to carefully plan the walking routes to public transport for residents. Routes should be well lit and overlooked from neighbouring homes. Distances should be measured as if walked and not 'as the crow flies', as distances can be increased

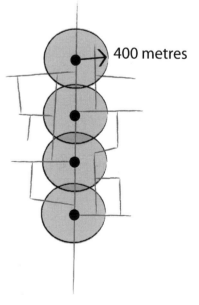

400 metres

Figure 4.23   Beading effect

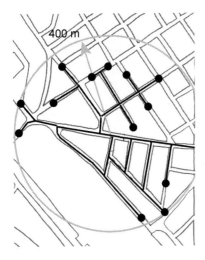

Figure 4.24   Don't measure walking distances 'as the crow flies'

Figure 4.25   Ensure that public transport stops are integrated rather than ignored by a scheme

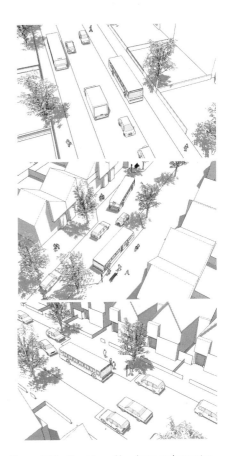

significantly by impermeable blocks (Figure 4.24). Public transport stops should also be well integrated into schemes, well lit, overlooked from neighbouring homes; and in certain situations, might be a location for the local shop, services or other facilities (like public telephones or post boxes) (Figure 4.25). Unfortunately this is not always considered, and people may find themselves waiting for a bus in a bleak and unsafe area, away from other signs of life (Figure 4.26).

Strategic public transport routes could be planned to have a designated space in the carriageway so that it is not hindered by other traffic. On access roads going through schemes, bus stops could be in a lay-by, thus allowing the free flow of other vehicles–although on some routes the presence of public transport might contribute to traffic calming as it will slow down through traffic as it stops to let off or pick up people (Figure 4.27).

Figure 4.26   Ensure that public transport stops are integrated rather than ignored by a scheme

Figure 4.27   Provision of bus lanes and stopping bays should vary according to the status of the route

REUSE OLD BUILDINGS AND LAND

Within any site designated for residential development, it is desirable to consider the scope and viability of reusing previously developed old

Figure 4.28   Within any scheme it is always desirable to consider the scope and viability of reusing existing buildings so that resources are recycled

buildings and land (Figure 4.28). Environmentally, reusing older buildings is encouraged as a conversion should require less raw materials and energy than buildings that are built from scratch. Sometimes such buildings are a valued part of the environment and have historic significance. They often provide unusual forms of living space, and these spaces can be more generous than those achieved in new buildings. Buildings like this can also be well located relative to existing services which their reuse may subsequently help to support (this is discussed further in Chapter 6).

Another environmental reason for reusing land is that it protects non-developed land from development. Despite this, land that is to be reused may require reclamation, especially if the land has formerly been used for an industrial process. Such reclamation will require specialist advice and will dramatically influence the costing of a scheme, unless the polluter has been required to pay.

WATERCOURSES AND SUSTAINABLE URBAN DRAINAGE

Previously it has been suggested that greater concern should be shown for the conservation and management of water in residential areas. Architecturally it is possible to introduce, for example, water efficient household appliances or grey water recycling into the design of individual buildings. Such matters are beyond the scope of this book (see Howarth 2000 or Kennedy 1997). In terms of site layout and urban design, however, it should be possible to maintain existing watercourses in a naturalised state, as well as introduce a sustainable urban drainage system (SUDS).

Maintain naturalised watercourses

Studying and understanding how water drains off an existing site should be an important element of any site analysis, and the role that existing watercourses make should be particularly explored. In a natural state, rivers and streams can offer an approach to drainage that is in equilibrium with

Figure 4.29   Maintain naturalised watercourses through a scheme

broader environmental conditions and that requires little management. The natural state of the watercourse also offers a great source of biodiversity and is a good resource of both educational and amenity value (Figure 4.29).

Develop a sustainable urban drainage system (SUDS)

In traditionally drained residential areas drainage has been designed with dedicated pipe systems to remove rainwater from the environment as quickly and efficiently as possible. In extreme conditions this might result in flooding elsewhere in the catchment once this water is returned into the river system, whilst the runoff from urban areas can carry pollutants into groundwater which is then far harder to clean. In particular, the environmental and amenity value of retaining water and water features within the environment is overlooked.

Martin *et al.* (2000:2) and Kennedy (1997:65) argue that SUDS can protect and enhance water quality by encouraging a more natural rate of groundwater recharging and help replenish groundwater supplies. They can also provide habitats for wildlife within urban areas, and improve the local microclimate during hot weather. They do this by dealing with runoff closer to where rain occurs. Because the runoff is retained in the locality for longer, the flow of water into the wider catchment is far slower.

As a technical area it is important to gain comprehensive advice about how to plan SUDS (see, for example, Martin *et al.* 2000), but the principles and basic approach are relatively easy to understand.

Use green roofs

Where traditional pitched roofs are replaced with roofs containing grass sod or other relevant plants, water is retained in the earth on the roof. In such roofs runoff can be minimal (Kennedy, 1997: 61). Such roofs also have other advantages. They can: help insulate a building from both heat and noise; reduce extremes of heat in hot weather; provide a habitat for wildlife; as well as look attractive as a result of the natural planting (Figure 4.30).

Figure 4.30   An example of a green roof which would reduce runoff

Figure 4.31   Minimise impermeable surfaces

Minimise paved areas

Traditionally, drained residential areas are often dominated by impermeable surfaces that take water from roofs or off surfaces to a piped drainage system. SUDS encourage the use of permeable surfaces which allow water to drain straight into the ground. A simple example would be the use of gravel instead of tarmac in domestic driveways (Figure 4.31).

Drain into a permeable area

Rather than draining water off roofs, paths or lightly trafficked roads into a complex system of pipes, SUDS would mean that water drains as soon as possible into one of a number of permeable features that would allow a more natural rate of groundwater recharging:

Figure 4.32   A soakaway

> **Soakaway:** A soakaway is a specific area that has a permeable surface and which, following rain, is able to temporarily store water prior to its infiltration into the ground. A grassed or semi-paved area could, for example, be put over a coarser gravel area which is able to accommodate a larger volume of water in the void between the gravel–water isn't usually retained on the surface (Figure 4.32).

> **Swale:** A swale is a long, shallow and vegetated channel. The vegetation slows down the water flow trapping organic matter and sediments. A swale retains water within the locality of a scheme following rain and can temporarily store larger amounts of water at the surface prior to its infiltration into the ground (Figure 4.33).

> **Retention ponds:** To accommodate more significant volumes of runoff, swales might be connected to a retention pond where water can be retained prior to the natural process of infiltration into the

Figure 4.33   A swale

Figure 4.34   A retention pond

ground. Such ponds offer significant scope for interesting planting and will become a home for a more diverse wildlife (Figure 4.34).

Typically, water drains away from roofs and surfaces by either pipe or surface drain into these features. These can then be connected to the local stream or river system or might ultimately connect to a traditional piped drainage system within the vicinity of a scheme, although the demands made upon the traditional system should be far less.

SUDS features can be designed to promote a positive resident amenity as well as biodiversity. The drainage areas and water environment should form part of the public open space within the scheme, and might be used for play, recreation and education. With regard to wildlife, the SUDS offer scope for the development of distinctive habitats for both flora and fauna, and the advice of landscape architects should be sought to ensure that selected plants can deal with the specific conditions created by a scheme.

Concrete	11 – 17
Plaster	31 – 200
Bricks	76
Cement	106 – 174
Indigenous Softwood	158
Plasterboard	167 – 220
Imported Softwood	195 – 306
Bitumen	278
Mineral Fibres	389 – 528
Steel	473 – 834
Glass	528
Paint	667
Plastics (pvc)	1629 – 2224

Note: figures show variation of results from 3 research projects, and give only a general indication of embodied energy levels

Figure 4.35   The embodied energy in building materials (kWh/tonnes) Based on Newton and Westaway (1999:6)

ENERGY EFFICIENT RESIDENTIAL FORMS

There are now many architectural solutions which help provide more energy efficient homes, thus relying less on fossil fuels. Homes and landscapes can be designed for construction using a combination of recycled materials and materials which contain low levels of 'embodied' energy used in their manufacture and delivery (Figure 4.35) (see Edwards, 2000; Newton and Westaway, 1999; Harris and Borer, 2005).

South facing surfaces can be fitted with photovoltaic cells (Figure 4.36) or solar water heating systems, or they might benefit from geothermal energy, the use of biofuels, wind or water power. In addition, there are now approaches to building that allow homes to be more highly insulated against extremes of temperature, as well as more naturally ventilated (see, for example, Roaf et al. 2001). Arguments are also made for developments to make more use of combined heat and power systems (see, for example, Barton et al. 2003; Rudlin and Falk, 1999).

Figure 4.36   The sun can passively and efficiently create electricity using photovoltaic cells or heat water using passive solar water heating systems which should be located on south facing surfaces

In terms of site layout, however, there are also approaches to the configuration of homes that allow them to be more energy efficient.

Energy efficiency and housing forms

Homes with less exposed external surfaces are more energy efficient, as heat is always lost through roofs, walls and floors. As a result, apartments and terraced houses are more energy efficient than semi-detached or detached homes. Denser buildings may also be more sheltered from cooling winds by surrounding buildings (Figure 4.37).

Figure 4.37   Apartments and terraces are more energy efficient whilst denser configurations provide more shelter from winds in exposed locations

Orientate homes to manage access to heat and light from the sun

In hotter climates natural lighting is desirable, but the excesses of heating need to be managed. In such a context deep balconies or overhangs on sun lit elevations will provide natural shading; wall and roof insulation will keep heat out of living spaces; while natural forms of ventilation off shaded surfaces or areas will help air flow through a home and allow natural cooling (Figure 4.38).

Figure 4.38   Balconies and overhangs on sunlit elevations will create naturally cooling shade

In cooler and more temperate climates the sun can still passively heat interiors through windows, reducing the need for other forms of heating. This is a process that is helped particularly if interiors contain materials, or thermal mass, that retain and radiate heat (concrete, stone or brick). Such a process is also helped if, in the northern hemisphere, the main windows of a home face within 30° of due south and where the window-to-wall area ratio is 25–35 per cent. Some houses that seek to make the most of passive solar heating might, for example, include a sun space (Roaf *et al.* 2001) or conservatory on the façade towards the sun (Figure 4.39). Such spaces convert solar radiation into heat, and heating effects can be managed using the building mass, natural forms of ventilation, or shading. They might form stairwells in apartments, or form or abut living spaces where appropriate. Where this logic is followed it might also be desirable to ensure that on northern façades the amount of window area is kept to a minimum–just enough to light relevant rooms, so that heat is not then lost through glass, which is also a less insulating material.

Such architectural features need to be accommodated within the layout of homes, and so it is important to coordinate the architectural design and the choice of house types within a residential scheme with the features of the layout itself. A tighter urban form–courtyards, water features and vegetation, etc.–can be used in hot climates to provide shadow and a cooler microclimate, just as natural breezes might be exploited to the same effect (Figure 4.40). In cooler climates housing should be located within the landscape and in a configuration so that sunlight reaches relevant façades all year. This requires modelling, but would probably preclude large amounts of development heated in this way on northern slopes of valleys as they will be in shade for long periods of a year (Figure 4.41). With reference to the more detailed arrangement of the urban form, ensuring that such glazed areas face south doesn't mean that houses must have their front door facing south, or that other matters, such as orientating homes to front a street, need to be overlooked. At the same time, it is important to make sure that, despite the use of more glazed façades on some elevations, people within homes feel that they can manage their privacy.

Consider the impact of wind

The qualities of wind affecting a site can be found by researching wind roses which indicate the typical direction, strength and cooling affect of winds impacting on a site at different times of the year.

Some winds may be positively used to cool the urban environment in hotter climates, and so homes need to be

Figure 4.39 Sun spaces on southerly facing façades help to warm a home, particularly when combined with thermal mass within the building structure

Figure 4.40 Use site layout features like courtyards, water and landscaping to help natural cooling in hot climates

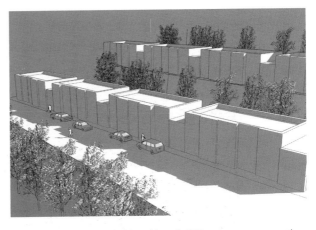

Figure 4.41 It may not be desirable to build housing on steep northern slopes where the housing will be in shadow for long periods of the year

spaced and orientated so that breezes can penetrate the urban form. Orientating streets in the direction of the wind will achieve this (Figure 4.42).

In other areas wind may unnecessarily cool homes and so schemes may seek to be more sheltered. Finbow (1988: 45) points out that shelter from wind can reduce energy needs by between 3% and 5%. Shelter can be achieved by:

- locating development suitably in the landscape (Figure 4.43)
- using denser patterns of development (Figure 4.44)
- orientating streets away from the direction of wind (Figure 4.45)

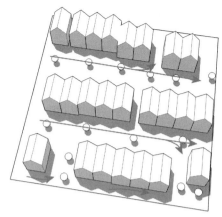

Figure 4.42   In hot climates in might be desirable to orientate streets towards the direction of a cooling wind

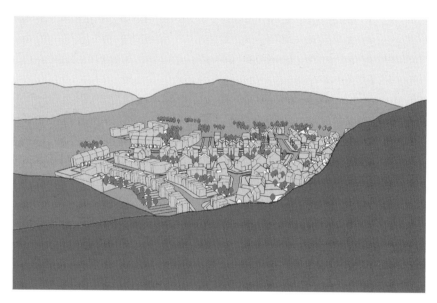

Figure 4.43   Locate developments carefully in the landscape rather than in very exposed locations

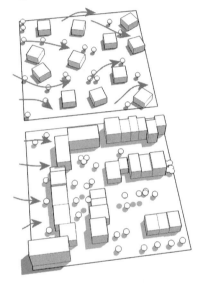

Figure 4.44   Use denser patterns of development

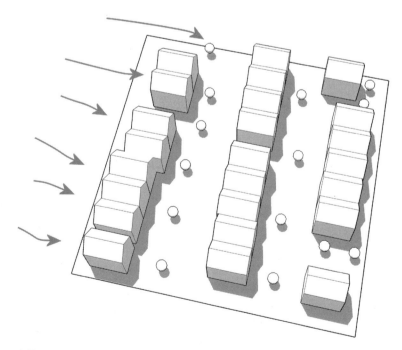

Figure 4.45   In more temperate and exposed locations orientate streets away from the wind direction

- maintaining a smooth building profile, roof line and a dispersed landscape canopy within an urban environment. This is so that turbulent wind eddying doesn't impact on homes and outdoor spaces (Edwards 2001) (Figure 4.46)
- planting shelter belts (Figure 4.47).

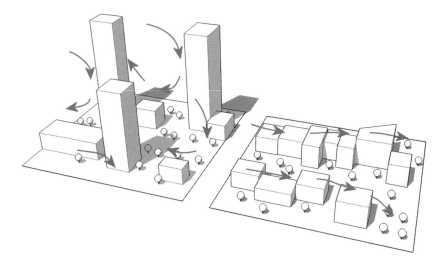

Figure 4.46   Maintain a smooth building profile

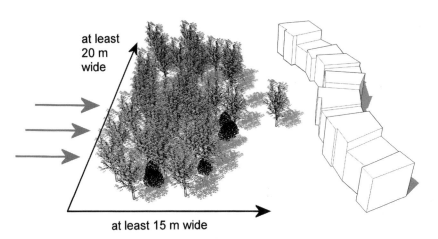

Figure 4.47   A shelter belt

A shelter belt is created by planting on the windward side of a development where it protects the development from the full force of a wind. Shelter belts should be planted perpendicular to the direction of dominant cooling winds, but they can remain effective when planted up to an angle of 45°. They are also effective if they are both tall and have a wind porosity through the vegetation of about 50 per cent. This can be achieved by planting a mix of deciduous and evergreen trees and lower bushes. To be most effective, a shelter belt should be at least 15 m deep and at least 20 m long. A shelter belt of this porosity and dimension should reduce wind speeds to a maximum degree (approximately 65%) at a distance of about four times the height of the belt. If the belt is therefore 20 m high, it will be most effective at 80 m from the belt. The wind speed should, however, still be halved at a distance of eight times the height, or 160 m away from the planting (Finbow, 1988: 40–45).

PROVIDE FACILITIES THAT ALLOW RESIDENTS TO RECYCLE THEIR WASTE

Localities have very different approaches to the management of waste, and it is important that schemes should dovetail with local collection schemes. Within a layout, however, the design implications of supporting recycling need not be complicated. For example, within some schemes it might be possible to have collection points for sorted waste within walking distances from people's homes; in other areas, where doorstep collections occur, it might be desirable to provide more space for the separation and temporary storage of waste within and around the home (Figure 4.48).

Figure 4.48   Provide opportunities for residents to sort and recycle their waste

CREATE OPPORTUNITIES FOR LOCAL FOOD PRODUCTION

Gardens and allotments have traditionally been important spaces for people who wish to grow their own food, and increasing awareness of the distances that supermarket food travels nowadays (Roseland 1998; AEA Technology Environment, 2005) has encouraged environmentally aware people to revisit the extent to which they might use the principles of permaculture to grow food within the vicinity of their home. From a design point of view this means providing room for useful gardens or allotments (Figure 4.49). From a management point of view it means ensuring that bylaws, codes and covenants do not restrict the use of open space to manicured lawns–as occurs, for example, in Springwood Estates, Indiana:

> Landscaping: ...All front yards and side yards must be planted with grass, which shall occur within thirty (30) days of occupancy, weather permitting.
> Springwood Estates Subdivision, Indiana, Covenants and Restrictions

Figure 4.49   Provide opportunities for residents to grow their own food and compost their own vegetable and plant waste

FURTHER READING

There is a lot of relatively recent literature about environmentally sustainable forms of urban development and so this list is merely indicative of what is available. For a straightforward introduction to the issues, see Rudlin and Falk (1999) and The Urban Task Force (1999), or pick up the *Rough Guide to Sustainability* by Edwards (2001). Excellent general guides about how to lay out housing and other services and facilities include those by Barton *et al.* (1995 and 2003) and Girling and Kellett (2005), while the State of Western Australia (2000) has produced *Liveable Neighbourhoods* to show the policy and guidance implications of trying to secure sustainable forms of development. Recently, there have been a number of books and reports looking more specifically at how to design higher density forms of housing such as those by PRP (2002), Lewis

(2005), Zhou (2005) and Towers (2005). For an introduction to ecological housing, where energy efficiency is of paramount concern, have a look at *The Whole House Book* by Harris and Borer (2005), *Ecohouse: A design guide* by Roaf, Fuentes and Thomas (2001) or *Sustainable Housing: Principles and practice* edited by Edwards and Turrent (2000). For discussions about public transport provision have a look at White's *(2002) Public Transport: Its planning, management and operation* or *The Demand for Public Transport: A practical guide* edited by Balcombe (2004). The Town and Country Planning Association (2004) discuss the role of design in promoting biodiversity, whilst Hough (1984) discusses how to respect natural processes in both urban and landscape design in *City Form and Natural Process*. The provision and management of urban green spaces gets more specific attention in *Green Spaces, Better Places* by the UK's Department of Transport, Local Government and the Regions (2002) and English Nature's (2003) *Accessible Natural Green Space Standards in Towns and Cities: A review and toolkit for their implementation*. The value of trees in the urban environment is considered by Pitt *et al.* (1979), Arnold (1980) and the National Urban Forestry Unit (1999). Reasons for trying to conserve water in the provision of housing are discussed by the UK's Environment Agency (2001) in *Water Resources for the Future* and by Howarth (2000) in *Water Conservation and Housing*. More detailed design guidance on sustainable urban drainage systems is provided by Kennedy (1997) in *Water: Use and value* and Martin *et al.* (2000) in *Sustainable Urban Drainage Systems–Design Manual for England and Wales*. The thinking behind transects is further explained in a comprehensive guide to new urbanist practices published by New Urban News (2001–2002).

Finally, advice on shelter belts and how to design them can be found in Finbow (1988) *Energy Saving Through Landscape Design*.

5 Access and movement

The built environment must accommodate the modes of transport that residents will use to get around. Modes of travel vary but the dominant methods that need to be accommodated for include walking, cycling, using public transport and driving. A designer should consider the different environmental requirements for each mode of travel, as good routes for walking or cycling are not necessarily the same as good routes for driving, although some can obviously share space within a street.

This chapter introduces the issues surrounding the design of access for these different modes. It starts by considering the extent to which design can influence the travel choices that people make. It then moves on to consider the concept of permeability and how this might be achieved within a scheme and between a scheme and neighbouring areas. This discussion starts by considering the concept in general, but then the link between patterns of physical accessibility and social and economic exclusivity, or inclusivity, is introduced. Following this, we consider how permeability can be achieved when applied to overlapping networks supporting different modes of travel. A distinction between physical and perceived access is then discussed. Different types of networks are then introduced, including a discussion about how these different networks have historically emerged to accommodate different relationships between travel modes. Specific advice about how to design for public transport, busier routes and cyclists is then introduced. This is followed by a discussion about the different types of highway you might provide within a scheme, the provision of traffic calming and also the different ways that parking can be accommodated.

TRAVEL CHOICE OR PRESCRIPTION

It is quite common amongst planning and transport professionals to think of ways to encourage people to, for example, cycle or use public transport more, and designs of the urban environment can support people's preferences, prescribe a range of travel choices or, more commonly, create the conditions in which a particular travel mode can be supported.

Design of the physical environment could be used to determine how people travel or, more particularly, modes of travel that couldn't be used. There are housing schemes that are car free (usually with car parking at the periphery of the project) and people choose to live in such schemes, benefiting from the car-free spaces around their homes. The Vauban in Freiburg is such a place (Figure 5.1). A large residential area, people can drive to homes to deliver things, but private cars are parked in the car parks at the edge of the scheme. The remaining street and other spaces accommodate foot and cycle paths, planting, sitting out, and play areas. A new idea is the 'car-free city', in which the design would make it physically impossible (and presumably undesirable) to drive through (Figure 5.2). Such initiatives remain rare, although they can offer good living conditions, and they are generally only introduced where there is a market and/or the political will to encourage that form of innovation.

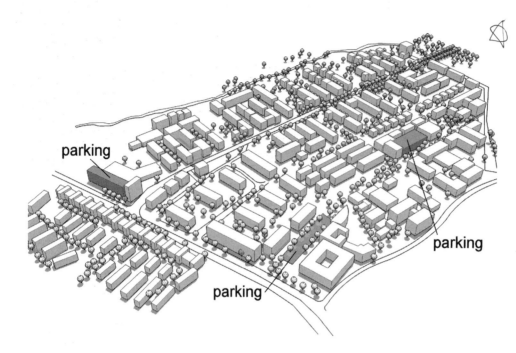

Figure 5.1   The Vauban in Freiburg is a car-free residential area

Figure 5.2   Car-free cities

Such places might otherwise be rejected by residents who may decide to move elsewhere.

More common are attempts to shape the decisions that people might take about how they travel. A good example of this is the plan for Houten in the Netherlands, a town for which the plan encourages cycle use by offering short and direct routes for cyclists, whilst drivers of cars or other vehicles must take a more circuitous route (Figure 5.3). The combination of the Dutch cycling culture and this plan means that cycling is particularly popular in the town, although people still have the opportunity to drive if they wish.

Design, therefore, can play a role in making it easy or difficult to use a particular mode of transport. Urban designers should be very explicit about the forms of movement that they wish to allow and encourage whilst, in principle, they should ensure that the most environmentally benign forms of travel are particularly encouraged.

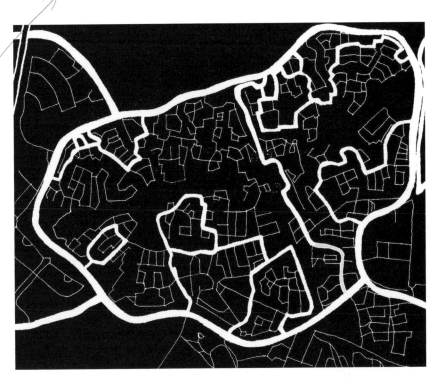

Figure 5.3   The route pattern in Houten provides direct access on smaller routes for cyclists

THINK ABOUT THE LEVEL OF PERMEABILITY

The term *permeability* (used by Bentley *et al.* 1985), refers to the amount of access that is possible within the adopted residential block structure, and it is an important quality to consider, particularly for pedestrians and cyclists. Places can be more or less permeable. A more permeable environment offers people a wider number of more direct routes between various possible destinations. This results from a smaller block structure. For a pedestrian and cyclist this would mean that routes will be short and more direct (Figure 5.4).

An area that is less permeable will have, for instance, an urban form of larger blocks or a cul-de-sac layout. As a result people have a far more limited number of routes between possible destinations, whilst the distances that they must travel will be longer. Such layouts tend to discriminate against both pedestrians and cyclists.

Figure 5.4   Levels of permeability

AREA ACCESSIBILITY AND SCHEME PERMEABILITY

Thinking about permeability does not mean only thinking about the permeability within the scheme. The location of a scheme within an urban area has a big impact on the extent to which people will get access to other parts of an urban area–where they, for example, work, shop or go to school. Schemes that are in existing permeable areas should make use of the direct links and maintain the level of permeability that has already been established. Schemes located in areas with existing poor levels of permeability will need to maximise connectivity into the existing network, and, in particular, provide good pedestrian or cyclist routes to services like local shops or schools (Figure 5.5).

An analysis of the site and consultation with existing residents in an area will determine if they require or expect access through the future scheme. It will also determine if those people are happy for future routes to be connected directly to their own neighbourhoods.

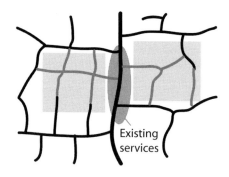

Figure 5.5   Schemes should seek to enhance the permeability within an area especially for pedestrians and cyclists

EXCLUSIVITY OR INCLUSIVITY

Economic and social issues often directly influence the patterns of access that might be introduced into a scheme. Developers may request that the number of routes through a new scheme is limited to use by only the new residents in order to increase the desired level of exclusivity. However, exclusive schemes often turn away from their context and limit the routes through an area, thus reducing the permeability of the area **generally**.

It is also common for residents neighbouring a new scheme to complain if the new housing has either pedestrian or vehicular access through their own streets. This is often not only because they are concerned about additional traffic and noise, but also because they would wish to retain the level of social exclusivity that they have previously enjoyed.

If an urban designer wishes to create a permeable layout that would benefit pedestrians and cyclists, it may be necessary to negotiate on behalf of the idea–and use design skills to convince both developers and existing residents that such a layout is desirable and would not result in negative consequences. For example, where any commercial or community uses are being considered, it makes sense to provide direct and safe access to them through neighbouring areas, although often there is genuine controversy if new schemes impact too heavily on the existing tranquillity of established residential areas (Figure 5.6).

Figure 5.6   Direct linkages between existing and new residential areas may need to be carefully negotiated

OVERLAPPING NETWORKS

It is possible to create a permeable layout for pedestrians and cyclists whilst limiting the through routes available for vehicles. This would require a designer to plan the patterns of access for the different modes separately within a pattern of urban form.

The periphery block structure discussed in Chapter 3 creates a clear pattern of streets and other public spaces that can provide good, direct routes for pedestrians. A separate network of routes can be added for vehicles which rationalises a little more which routes they might take. In general, this allows the designer to create quieter areas within a scheme with less through traffic, although sometimes the decision might also be taken to make car access less convenient in the hope that people might consider walking or cycling instead (Figure 5.7).

DON'T COMPROMISE PRIVACY OR SURVEILLANCE

The need to create a good level of pedestrian and cyclist permeability should not be at the cost of ensuring homes have privacy and pedestrian routes have adequate surveillance. Sometimes, in order to be able to say that a scheme is more permeable, a designer might be tempted to put a public route through a private courtyard or between gardens. Such routes, if not carefully planned, may compromise the privacy of residents or create a route that lacks surveillance, thereby impairing the security of a scheme (Figure 5.8).

Pedestrian and cyclist network

Vehicular network

Figure 5.7   It is possible to create a coarser network for vehicles compared to pedestrians and cyclists

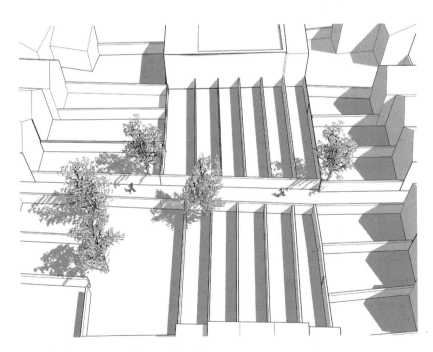

Figure 5.8   Compromising privacy and security

PHYSICAL AND PERCEIVED ACCESS

This chapter is concerned with providing physical access to residential areas, but providing access does not just mean providing the physical opportunity to move through an area. It is also necessary to create the clear impression that a route will take you where you want to go and that the route will be safe. There are many routes through the built environment–especially for the pedestrian–but some are not used as their destination is unclear or, because of a lack of surveillance or lighting, people feel that the routes may be unsafe. In order to encourage permeability, creating perceived access is therefore as important as creating physical access. In contrast, designers sometimes have to deliberately manipulate the form of a street so as to limit the perceived access, especially if the scheme is to appear as exclusive–this would discourage non-residents from entering the scheme as they would assume that it did not connect to anywhere else (Figure 5.9). How you might design a residential area to create or limit perceived access is discussed more fully in Chapter 8.

DETERMINING THE PATTERN OF ACCESS WITHIN THE SCHEME

The adopted urban form will influence the rough pattern of access through the site, and there are five principle forms: the *grid*, the *tree*, the *closed loop*, *Radburn* and the *Poundbury*.

The grid

The grid has a long tradition of use in all forms of urban planning and design, and it comes in a range of types. Rectilinear grids are very common in the United States, whilst deformed grids are more evident in the UK and older settlements in other parts of Europe (Figure 5.10).

Grids can provide an even pattern of access between urban blocks, although the profile of streets and spaces can vary, and traffic management measures can also limit access for vehicles in certain directions. Small grids do particularly benefit pedestrians and cyclists as they offer direct routes and a choice of directions.

Grids, despite their apparent uniformity in plan form, can accommodate a very wide range of environments and levels of vitality, whilst the land uses, densities, levels of economic viability and social mix can also vary and evolve.

Grids tend to accommodate commercial uses at busier junctions and along busier routes, and a range of suitable sites is typically available, although from a large-scale commercial point of view, the grid may water down passing trade as people can move through the environment in different directions (Figure 5.11).

If **perimeter blocks** are adopted, the resulting streets will be defined and have surveillance, whilst private spaces can be secure within the block. Where **free-standing blocks** are planned they might be imposed on a grid, although free-standing blocks tend to produce a poorly defined public realm, unless other housing around the towers creates this form. Where *linear blocks* are proposed, these can be orientated to the main street frontages which will then have a form and surveillance, although lateral streets will have less form or surveillance unless the end buildings

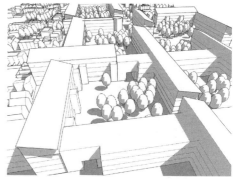
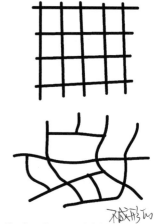

Figure 5.9   Routes can be indirect so that although access is possible people may not perceive it to be so, alternatively routes can be direct and obvious

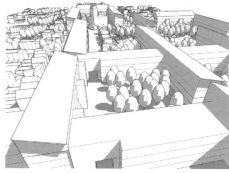

Figure 5.10   Rectilinear and deformed grids

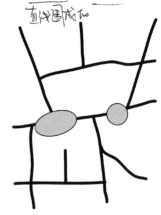

Figure 5.11   Commercial locations on a grid

Figure 5.12   New urbanist schemes in the USA often have rear parking alleys as part of a grid

relate to these routes more closely. New urbanist schemes often contain rectilinear or deformed grids that also include rear parking alleys as another variation on the grid form (Figure 5.12).

The tree

Building a pattern of access in the form of a tree allows a designer to create a series of quiet cul-de-sacs that become the focus for domestic life. This pattern of access rigorously manages the route choices available to people, and environments are designed with close regard to the amount of vehicular activity that is expected. At the ends of the cul-de-sacs, the environments can be intimate and quiet. When they leave their homes, however, people are then necessarily funnelled onto main routes, which tend to be dominated by faster-moving traffic, whilst some of the junctions need to be large and free flowing to accommodate the projected traffic levels. Because the main routes are inevitably busy, they often don't have any form of frontage, which makes them feel less safe, whilst any pedestrian environment that results is poor. With the tree design, pedestrians also have far fewer choices and walking distances tend to be longer, whilst shortcuts between cul-de-sacs can also result in poor quality environments (Figure 5.13).

Locations for commercial uses tend to be more limited, but well selected sites can be found, where a significant number of people can pass–although typically these people have to drive, as the commercial areas tend to be situated away from where people live (Figure 5.14).

The closed loop

The closed loop is a form of access that allows a residential area to connect to its context at a more limited number of locations, although circulation within the scheme might be as efficient and direct as a grid. A closed loop could be used in a scheme that is bounded by a super block where the context only allows access at a small number of points.

Figure 5.13   Tree network

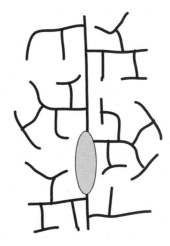

Figure 5.14   Commercial locations within a tree network

Where closed loops are created, commercial activities can be located at the entrances where passing trade can also be exploited (Figure 5.15).

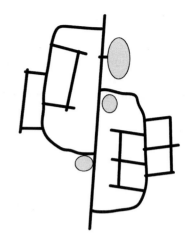

Figure 5.15   Closed loops

Radburn

The name Radburn refers to the community in Fair Lawn, New Jersey. Here, Clarence Stein and Henry Wright created a neighbourhood where the patterns of access for pedestrians and vehicles are completely separate. A radburn layout involves creating a form of block where one side of a home faces the vehicle access and parking, whilst the other side faces pedestrian routes and community spaces (Figure 5.16).

In this scheme, locating private gardens becomes difficult as the pattern of access to both sides of a home means that there are no private backs to these homes. As a result, a private garden has a negative impact on either the pedestrian route or vehicular route because any high fences reduce surveillance.

The duplication of access can also result in more land than is necessary being given over to circulation. This might be expensive, especially as good quality public landscaping, drainage and lighting infrastructure need to be provided over a wider area.

A final issue resulting from a Radburn layout is the extent to which pedestrian activity isn't focused onto particular routes. This means that the public realm around the housing is extensive, and that pedestrians are forced to use environments that might feel more isolated than elsewhere. An observation of some Radburn layouts show that pedestrians generally choose to use the roads for access as they feel safer having contact with people in cars, rather than feeling alone and less secure in the pedestrian areas.

The Radburn layout is common in some apartment developments where no private outdoor spaces are provided. One side of an apartment block will have the car parking court, and the other side will provide pedestrian circulation and sitting areas or play spaces (Figure 5.17).

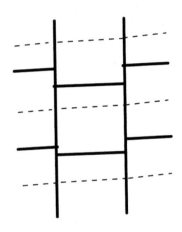

Figure 5.16   Radburn

Figure 5.17   Vehicular access and pedestrian routes on either side of an apartment block

The Poundbury block

The Poundbury block is a relatively recent innovation initially used in Britain at Poundbury in Dorchester, and has subsequently been used elsewhere. The areas are very similar to residential blocks containing mews courts common in some older parts of Britain.

The Poundbury block includes a relatively normal periphery block of housing that provides frontage and form to a distinctive street environment–parking for residents tends to be to the rear in parking courts. This reduces the number of parked cars on the street frontage. These parking courts also provide a supplementary pedestrian network, and a number of houses or living spaces above the garages provide surveillance to the areas. These routes can be connected together to provide routes through a site in addition to the streets (Figure 5.18).

The courts need to be well designed and attractive to be successful–houses overlooking the parking courts are an important feature so that people will not feel too isolated if they choose to walk away from the normal streets. However, schemes need to be well-designed to make sure that privacy is not compromised for residents in surrounding houses and gardens, and that pedestrians are not required to walk long distances along poorly lit, quiet alleys. In general, it is not clear if it is really necessary to provide supplementary pedestrian routes through areas that already have relatively small perimeter blocks.

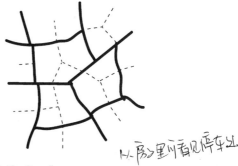

Figure 5.18   Poundbury

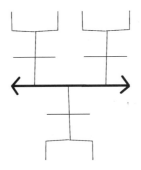

Figure 5.19   Tributary networks

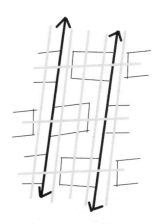

Figure 5.20   Pedestrian and vehicle separation

Figure 5.21   Walkways create 'streets in the sky'

DESIGNING FOR MODES

The history of housing design during the twentieth century is full of experiments on how to design a scheme that enhances a good relationship between pedestrians and vehicles, and five principal forms of access have emerged. The following options have been tried:

Using tributary networks: The tree and closed loop networks, discussed previously, partly resulted from the suggestion that roads should be combined together in a tree form, taking account of the role of the roads within the route hierarchy. Busier roads should be designated and designed for free vehicular movement at higher speeds, linking residential area to the wider route network, and having a higher capacity. Smaller roads to provide access to residential areas, encourage vehicles to slow down, and provide improved facilities for pedestrians should be designed. Still smaller routes should then provide access to groups of houses primarily used by pedestrians (Figure 5.19).

Pedestrian and vehicular separation: More radical housing areas have seen pedestrian and vehicular networks completely or partly segregated, based on the reasoning that pedestrians slow vehicles down, whilst vehicles can be dangerous and should be as remote from pedestrians as is practically possible (Figure 5.20). Sometimes, as with Radburn, this separation has been horizontal, but schemes where the separation is vertical, with pedestrians using walkways or 'streets in the sky', have also been introduced (Figure 5.21).

Traffic calming: More recently, progressive design practices have seen attempts made to civilise vehicles in residential areas by introducing traffic calming onto residential streets. This means that drivers have to drive at a restricted speed and in a style that matches the needs of pedestrians and cyclists. Traffic calming means that segregation is not necessary. It can also be used to reduce vehicular access through an otherwise permeable layout. Grids, including the Poundbury block structure, have this character and rationale (Figure 5.22).

Figure 5.22   A combination of traffic calming techniques produces an environment where vehicular access is possible but only at a very slow speed

CONNECTING TO PUBLIC TRANSPORT

In some development cultures, public transport is regarded as so important that any new residential area is planned around the train, tram or bus stop. A good residential plan would provide access to enough residents to serve the system and the pattern of access would provide clear, short and safe routes to stops, with the stops themselves being overlooked, having shelter and being well lit at night.

Stops of this nature can be on segregated routes; or for buses and trams, they can be integrated into the main vehicular routes through the scheme. For trams, the tendency is to integrate the stops fully into busy points of the scheme, whilst segregating the routes so that vehicles can still move freely. Some schemes have segregated bus routes, although as land is expensive, within quieter areas of a scheme this will be unnecessary.

The plan for the new community of Rieselfeld in Freiburg has a segregated tram route running

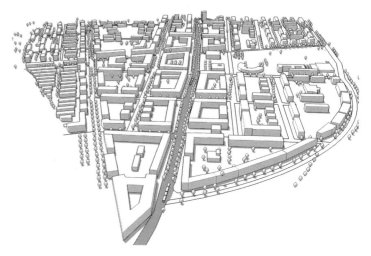

Figure 5.23   The public transport core through Rieselfeld in Freiburg

through the centre of the scheme, and along the main business street. The route has a number of stops on it with direct routes into residential areas. The route connects residents directly with the city centre and other parts of the city's integrated public transport system (Figure 5.23).

SPECIAL CONCERN FOR BUSIER ROUTES

Where road hierarchies are adopted, the busier routes tend to pose a particular design and environmental problem. Because of the traffic, people may not want to live on such environments. In addition, it is very common for highway engineers to want to limit the number of access points to residential areas from arterial roads, as this would slow down the traffic passing through.

As a result, developers often build housing facing away from these roads. This is a problem as these roads are often the routes that connect together neighbouring residential areas, and the fast traffic, the lack of surveillance, and the lack of urban form mean that the environment feels more dangerous and will be unpopular with pedestrians who might wish to visit neighbouring areas. Housing that backs onto a busy road are no more remote from housing that fronts onto it; however, housing that backs onto it has compromised privacy and amenity as gardens will be adjacent to the traffic and passing pedestrians (Figure 5.24). The challenge for designers of new residential areas is to ensure that housing also fronts directly onto what would then become the most important streets (Figure 5.25). These busier routes used to be the business streets of our urban areas as they were the locations for public transport stops, and the routes that were most busy with pedestrians. As a result, shops and other

Figure 5.24   Housing often faces away from busier routes resulting in a poor quality environment

Figure 5.25   Busier routes should still have frontage onto them

businesses would locate on these routes; shops that still thrive in many urban areas that have retained their form (Figure 5.26). We can learn a lot from these older business streets for patterns of new development.

DESIGNING FOR THE CYCLIST

Cyclists require specific attention when designing a scheme, as they may need specific routes and types of infrastructure to be planned for them. There is lots of good advice available on how to design a cycle-friendly infrastructure (see *Further reading*) and this should also be read, so the discussion here aims only to cover some of the most basic points.

Cyclists should be able to follow most routes provided for pedestrians, and their network should typically be finer and more direct than for motorised vehicles. This should encourage people to consider cycling instead of driving as routes will be shorter and more convenient (Figure 5.27).

Planning the network of cycling routes should be considered as a distinct task and the network of routes from housing to destinations should fully accommodate adequate infrastructure. On very busy (40 mph/60 kph) roads cyclists may require segregated lanes. These will typically follow the line of the roads and still have priority over traffic joining the routes from side roads (Figure 5.28). On 30 mph (50 kph) roads, distributing traffic within a neighbourhood, cyclists may require designated

Figure 5.26 Busier routes used to be the business streets where local shops and services would locate

Vehicular Network   Cyclists' Network

Figure 5.27 The cyclist network can be finer and more direct than that provided for other vehicles

Figure 5.28 Cyclist provision on busier routes with a 40 mph speed limit serving the wider urban area

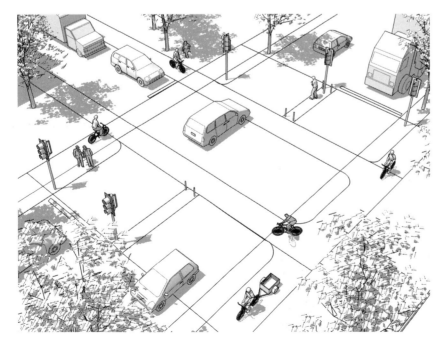

lanes within the carriageway and forward stop lines at signalled junctions. Cycles can safely share bus/taxi lanes but, again, this must be clearly sign-posted (Figure 5.29). On roads providing exclusive access to a smaller number of homes, cycles can share the road space (Figure 5.30). In addition, it is rarely necessary to plan one-way streets to include cyclists, as these should be planned to accommodate contraflow cycling (Figure 5.31).

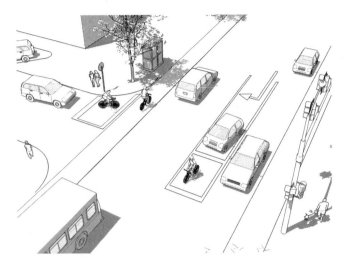

Figure 5.29   Cyclist provision on the main access routes serving a residential area

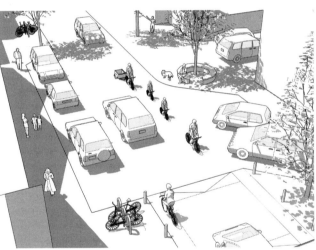

Figure 5.30   Cyclist provision on very local and quiet streets

Figure 5.31   One way streets can be planned to allow contraflow cycling

Ensure that the widths of cycle lanes are adequate for cyclists and the level of use that is anticipated. A minimum width of 100 cm should be achieved wherever possible, although ideally 150 cm should be the standard. Busier routes could be wider. Where cyclists share a route with other users, it may be helpful and safer to highlight the cycle lanes with a change of surface material or colour (Figure 5.32).

If cyclists turn off a route without crossing oncoming traffic it may be possible to preclude them from having to stop for traffic lights. If cyclists turn across oncoming traffic on busier routes a designated waiting lane should be provided for safety (Figure 5.33).

Within residential areas it is important to consider where bikes will be parked if cycling is to be encouraged. Adequate cycle parking should be provided in any areas that might form likely destinations for cyclists, including at home, near shops and other business areas, parks and open spaces, leisure centres or at public transport stops (especially tram stops or railway stations). Racks or stands should allow bike frames and wheels to be securely chained, whilst parking areas should be adequately lit and well signed. Some form of shelter is also desirable, especially if it is likely that bikes will be parked for long periods. It is important to note that cyclists will always park their bikes near the entrances of the buildings that they are visiting and in areas that are heavily populated and well lit (Figure 5.34). Many people will prefer to park their own bikes

Figure 5.32   Cycle lanes might be highlighted with a change of material or colour

Figure 5.33   Cyclists may not need to stop if they don't cross oncoming traffic. If they do then a waiting lane should be considered

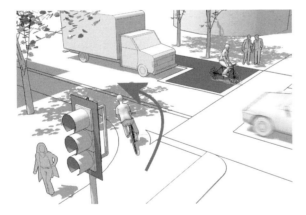

Figure 5.34   Examples of cycle parking

within their homes and gardens, although in apartments basement and ground floor rooms may be desirable (Figure 5.35).

Unlike other vehicle users, cyclists are sometimes expected to transfer between 'on road' and 'off road' routes during a journey. It is important to make sure that transitions between these routes are as smooth as possible and that cyclists do not need to dismount continually in order to go up kerbs or between bollards. Such transitions are particularly important for people with trailers carrying children or bulky items (Figure 5.36). The surface quality of cyclist routes is also particularly important as rough surfaces and uneven drainage gulleys can make cycling considerably harder (Figure 5.37).

Figure 5.35   A ground floor room dedicated to cycle parking

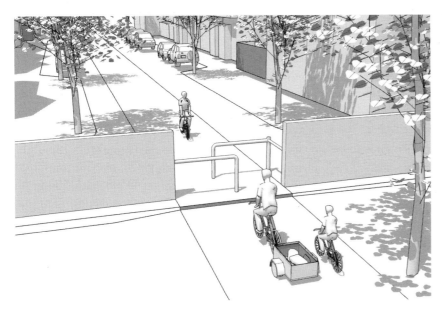

Figure 5.36   Keep transitions between routes as smooth as possible

Figure 5.37   Rough surfaces and uneven drainage gulleys make cycling considerably harder

HIGHWAY TYPES AND DIMENSIONS

In Chapter 3 under the heading '*Design the place first*' it was suggested that when designing a residential area the block structure and forms of the places within the block structure should be designed before the specific highways that people will use to gain access to the different parts of the scheme. After these features have been designed, it is necessary to consider further the form of vehicular access and, in particular, ensure that routes and junctions are sensibly designed in detail in order to accommodate the types and levels of traffic that are anticipated.

The pattern of access selected will determine how many vehicles will be using the different highways at different times of the day and, as such, the highways should be designed to a standard. This standard should be met to ensure that routes can accommodate the appropriate types and levels of traffic. It indicates the minimum dimensions needed; but in areas where it is desirable to control both the numbers of vehicles and how they travel, it may also come to represent a maximum standard.

Highway standards vary considerably and standards that have been applied locally should always be checked. As a general guide, a set of standards are provided here based on UK provisions to illustrate how standards work (Figure 5.38). Standards change over time, and hopefully they will continue to change as this will ensure that a variety of residential layouts can be achieved, as well as ensuring that cars are accommodated within schemes but without dominating the character of residential streets.

Highway type		Local distributor	Major access road	Minor access road	Minor access way	Home zone
Maximum number of dwellings served		No limit	400 (200 on a cul-de-sac)	200 (100 on a cul-de-sac)	50 (25 on a cul-de-sac)	No limit
Maximum traffic flow		-	-	-	-	100 vehicles per hour (peak time)
Carriageway width		7.3m (if a bus route) – 6.75m	6.75m	5.5 – 4.8m	3m with 4.8m at passing places.	3m with 4.8m at passing places.
Frontage Development		Yes	Yes	Yes	Yes	Yes
Direct access		No	Yes	Yes	Yes	Yes
Junction spacing	Adjacent	60	30	-	-	-
	Opposite	30	15	-	-	-
Forward gear access necessary		Yes	No	No	No	No
Corner radii		10.5m	6m	4m	4m	-
Junction viewing distance		X=6m, Y=90m	X=2.4, Y=60	X=2, Y=33	X=2, Y=33	X=2, Y=12
Servicing verge		2m	-	-	-	-
Maximum design speed		50kph/30mph	30kph/20mph	30kph/20mph	30kph/20mph and slower	16kph/10mph
Across traffic turning facility		Yes	-	-	-	-
On street parking		No	Yes	Yes	Yes	Yes
Footway requirement		2m on both sides	1.8m on both sides	1.5m on both sides	Delineated 1.8m margin adjacent to 3m carriageway	-
Cycling requirement		Off carriageway	On carriageway	On carriageway	On carriageway	On carriageway

Figure 5.38   A typical set of UK highway standards

Local distributor routes

These are 50 kph multipurpose routes providing access to and between parts of the urban environment (Figure 5.39). They are typically quite

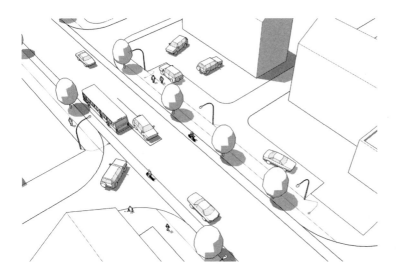

Figure 5.39   A local distributor

busy and will often accommodate bus routes. The width of the carriage-way is 7.3 m (with bus access) or 6.75 m. Buildings need to front these roads, but it shouldn't be possible to drive off the road straight into a private business or home, and parallel service roads or shared drives need to be introduced instead. All vehicles need to emerge onto this route in forward gear. Crossroads for motor vehicles will not typically be acceptable, and junctions need to be spaced at 30 m distances from each other. At the junctions the corner radii need to be 10.5 m and the viewing distance for a vehicle approaching the junction needs to be 90 m from a point 6 m from the stop line. The carriageway requires a servicing verge of 2 m on either side to accommodate underground utilities as well as 2 m wide footways. A separate cycle lane needs to be provided in both directions, and vehicles turning across traffic require their own lane for queuing. Car parking will be off street.

Major access road

Cars turning off the local distributor road will drive onto a 30 kph-route that provides access to the residential area (Figure 5.40). These roads

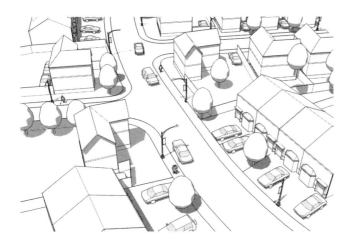

Figure 5.40   A major access road

serve up to 400 homes (or 200 homes if they form a cul-de-sac). The width of the carriageway is 6.75 m. Buildings front these roads, and it is possible to get direct access off the road into a private business or home. Vehicles can emerge from neighbouring properties onto this road in reverse gear. Crossroads for motor vehicles are not typically acceptable, and junctions are otherwise spaced at 15 m distances. At the junctions the corner radii need to be 6 m, encouraging slower driving and the viewing distance for a vehicle approaching the junction needs to be 60 m from a point 2.4 m from the stop line. Footways of 1.8 m are required on both sides of the road for pedestrians. Cyclists share the road space and car parking can be on street.

Minor access road

A minor access road serves 200 homes (or 100 homes if they form a cul-de-sac) (Figure 5.41). Buildings also front these roads, and it is possible to get direct access off the road into a private business or home. The width

Figure 5.41   A minor access road

of the carriageway for vehicles is between 5.5 to 4.8 m with 1.5 m footways provided on both sides. Vehicles can emerge from neighbouring properties onto this road in reverse gear. Crossroads for motor vehicles become acceptable, and there is no minimum distance requirement between junctions. At the junctions the corner radii need to be 4 m, encouraging very slow driving and the viewing distance for a vehicle approaching the junction needs to be 33 m from a point 2 m from the stop line. Cyclists share the road space and car parking can be on street.

Minor access way

A minor access way serves 50 homes (or 25 homes if they form a cul-de-sac) and has a design speed of 30 kpm (Figure 5.42). Buildings also front

Figure 5.42   A minor access way

these roads, and it is possible to get direct access off the road into a private business or home. The width of the carriageway for vehicles is 3 m but with passing places of 4.8 m width at approximately every 40–50 m. Between passing places a 1.8 m, shared surface footway for pedestrians should be included. Vehicles can emerge from neighbouring properties onto this road in reverse gear. Crossroads for motor vehicles are acceptable, and there is no minimum distance requirement between junctions. At the junctions the corner radii need to be 4 m encouraging very slow driving, and the viewing distance for a vehicle approaching the junction needs to be 33 m from a point 2 m from the stop line. Cyclists share the road space and car parking can be on street if space is available.

Home zone

A home zone is a residential street where the living environment clearly predominates over any provision for traffic (Figure 5.43). It is an environment where the design of the spaces between homes provides areas for motor vehicles, but where the wider needs of residents are also fully accommodated. This is achieved by adopting approaches to street design, landscaping and highway engineering that control how vehicles move without restricting the number of vehicular movements.

Figure 5.43   A home zone

In a home zone, people share what would formerly have been the carriageway and pavements. If these are designed well, vehicles can travel at a maximum speed that is only a little faster than walking pace (less than 16 kph). This means that other things can be introduced into the street; for example, areas for children to play, larger gardens or planting including street trees, cycle parking, and facilities such as seats where residents can congregate.

A home zone could be introduced where less than 100 vehicles use a carriageway during the peak hour of the day. Buildings front these roads and people must get direct access off the carriageway into their homes. The width of the carriageway would be the minimum 3 m with passing places and vehicles are able to emerge from neighbouring properties onto this road in reverse gear. Crossroads for motor vehicles are encouraged and there is no minimum distance requirement between junctions. At the junctions the corner radii could be as small as is practical to encourage very slow driving and the viewing distance for a vehicle approaching junctions would need to be only 16 m from a point 2 m from the stop line. Pedestrians and cyclists share the carriageway with vehicles. Further details for how to design home zones are discussed in Chapter Nine.

HIGHWAY TYPES AND NETWORKS

There isn't necessarily a relationship between the highway types discussed above and how they might be configured into a network. For about 30 years highway engineers have conceived of these types being configured into a tree network. This has frustrated urban designers trying to achieve permeability, whilst it has also been felt that these highway types have dictated, and standardised the built form qualities of local streets. Marshall (2005) has argued, however, that in planning a route network we should adopt less hierarchical concepts and use instead what he calls a *constitutional* approach. Instead of imagining an ideal configuration of routes forming grids or trees, we should be able to plan the use of a variety of street types into a wide number of networks where only *necessary and allowable connections* are controlled using allowable *junction types*.

Necessary and allowable connections should be guided by the need to achieve *arteriality* and the desire to enforce types of *access restraint*.

Arteriality is a quality of all movement networks and refers to the need for all strategic routes (highway, cyclist or pedestrian) within a network to connect contiguously. Smaller routes are free to form localised sub-networks that don't need to (but could if desired) connect with each other.

Access restraint refers to the extent to which particular types of street either must or may connect to other types of street of the same or a different type. Some forms of access restraint may be necessary for cars and public transport, but it will probably be unnecessary for pedestrians and cyclists (Figure 5.44).

Junction types refer to the whole range of junctions available for use where two vehicular routes meet. For example, a grade-separated junction (unlikely in a residential area), signalised junction,

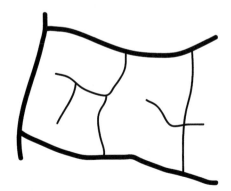

Figure 5.44 Arteriality: The larger routes must join together. The smaller routes must join to the larger routes but don't need to connect to each other

roundabout, prioritised T-junction or prioritised crossroads. Within the UK, crossroads have become uncommon in residential areas, and are only really found where less busy routes cross. More common and likely are T-junctions, which are regarded as safer. Roundabouts are common between larger roads, but for urban designers either T-junctions or signalled junctions are preferred as they are safer and more convenient for pedestrians and cyclists, whilst they also allow a more vivid built form.

Using these types of control Marshall (2005) argues that a whole range of networks might be achieved without compromising on any of the controls that engineers wish to enforce, and Figure 5.45 illustrates this by showing how different networks have been achieved using the same highway types and network rules.

Rules: Only T Junctions
          Each route type can only connect
          with its own type or the type above
          or below in the hierarchy

Figure 5.45   Engineers' rules about arteriality, access restraint and junction types shouldn't stop a whole range of networks being achieved (Marshall, 2005: 223)

TRAFFIC CALMING

Traffic calming is a practice that has become particularly common in residential areas where planners and designers hope that physical measures might encourage driving at speeds that are below the designated speed limits. Slow driving speeds improve the environmental quality for neighbouring residents and other road users, and the lower speed provisions mean that less space is required for vehicles.

Traffic calming replaces other techniques previously used to reduce the impact of traffic in residential areas, such as pedestrian and vehicular segregation; 'traditional' traffic management like using road closures and one-way traffic systems; or reliance on speed limit signage. Segregation creates environments that discriminate against the needs of pedestrians who are forced to use underpasses and areas with poor surveillance. Road closures and one-way streets increase the distances vehicles have to travel and force more traffic onto what become unpleasant distributor roads. Signage is sometimes introduced into environments where streets have been laid out with dimensions that are too generous, and therefore it is often not obeyed.

In environments that are heavily used by children, other pedestrians and cyclists, calming can be used to create designated 30 kph zones. Research has shown that the incidence of child pedestrian accidents occurring in and around residential areas has reduced by about two-thirds where calming measures have been installed. UK government research into such zones found that average driving speeds were reduced by 9 mph, annual accident frequency fell by 60%, the overall reduction in child accidents was 67%, and there was an overall reduction in accidents to cyclists of 29%. Traffic flow in the zones was also reduced by 27% (Department of the Environment, Transport and the Regions, 1999a).

Such zones usually cover a group of streets and involve the use of clear signage and possibly an entrance feature. Following this, the calming features are introduced at least every 50 m along an otherwise normal vehicular carriageway and at junctions.

Traffic calming can increase the amount of space dedicated to non-traffic activities or planting and greenery, which itself can make residential areas more attractive and environmentally diverse. Residents experience less noise and pollution as more consistent driving speed restrictions are introduced–drivers at slow speeds drive less erratically. They may also experience less through-traffic, as drivers are dissuaded from using the calmed street. Residents themselves might also be encouraged to use alternative modes of transport for short journeys.

The most radical form of traffic calming would see the introduction of home zones with design characteristics implemented so that vehicles travelled no faster than, say, walking pace. These adopt traffic calming measures, and they will be discussed further in Chapter Nine, where we consider how other types of activity in public space can be encouraged.

MEASURES TO ACHIEVE SPEED REDUCTION

Vertical measures

The most common and effective form of speed reduction measure involves a vehicle moving over an obstacle which, if hit at too high a speed, will make the driving experience uncomfortable. These vertical measures include road humps, plateaus, cushions and ramps. Flat humps and plateaus can also provide a route between adjacent pavements for pedestrians without a change of level. Cushions can provide a flat route between the measures for cyclists and larger vehicles like buses (Figure 5.46).

Figure 5.46 Vertical traffic calming measures

Horizontal measures

Horizontal measures require drivers to slow down as they have to turn and progress through narrower routes with forward views that might be deliberately constrained (Figure 5.47). These lateral shifts are created using chicanes, 'build outs' in the footways (Figure 5.48), islands in the middle of the carriageway, mini roundabouts, or the realignment of on-street parking. Sometimes the constrictions can require traffic to give way to each other forcing vehicles to stop and negotiate progress. A most common form of horizontal measure is the use of small corner radii at junctions that require vehicles to slow down considerably in order to turn

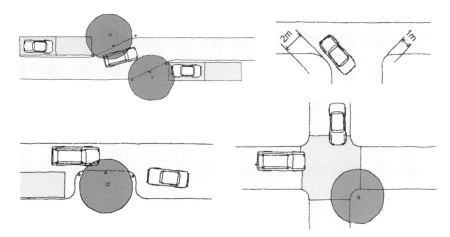

Figure 5.47   Horizontal traffic calming measures

Figure 5.48   Horizontal traffic calming measures include build outs to narrow the route

(Figure 5.49). Such tight corner radii also benefit pedestrians who can progress without deviation, particularly if a ramp across the junction maintains their path. Radii like this can make manoeuvrability for very large vehicles difficult and so they are introduced on routes that people driving larger vehicles tend not to use.

Junction priority measures

Changing what might be the intuitive priorities at junctions can also assist in slowing down traffic. This might involve giving priority to traffic using smaller streets crossing a larger route or even traffic turning into a road. Alternatively, it might mean either removing any indication of junction priority or requiring all drivers to give way. Either way, the approach forces drivers to have greater awareness of other road users and to negotiate their own progress carefully (Figure 5.50).

Figure 5.49   Tight corners slow down vehicles, but so does putting a building directly onto a corner to reduce the opportunity for a driver to see passing traffic until the point that the junction is reached

Narrowing the optical width

Moving beyond the design of the carriageway, this measure involves the use of both buildings and landscape to limit views down a street. A 'wider' street provides no visible reason to slow down, but a 'narrower' one encourages slower driving. This width can be created in the space between building frontages or, if buildings are to be set back, through the use of walls, hedges or street tree planting (Figure 5.51).

Figure 5.50   Changing intuitive arrangements at junctions might slow cars down

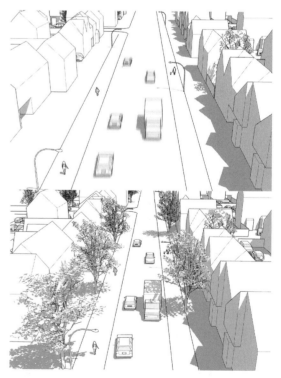

Figure 5.51   Narrow optical widths will slow down drivers

Setting buildings forward at corners can play a particular role in encouraging drivers to slow down as they approach junctions and this is a key measure for limiting the junction viewing distances that have been outlined in Figure 5.38. Figure 5.49 also illustrates this quality.

Narrow carriageways with occasional strips

Minimising carriageway dimensions helps to reduce the optical width of a road forcing vehicles to progress slowly. Occasional strips can be used adjacent to the main carriageway surface, or to divide the carriageway. These allow the odd larger vehicle to use the carriageway when necessary, but at a slow speed (Figure 5.52).

Figure 5.52   Occasional strips provide surfaces suitable for larger vehicles on narrower routes

Surface changes

Different surface materials can be used to emphasise a change in the status of a carriageway, or to highlight pedestrian or cyclist features. Concrete, brick or stone paviours, for example, are a common surface used when enforcing slower speed limits along certain streets, crossing areas or occasional strips (Figure 5.53).

Planting and street furniture

Trees, planters and street furniture such as light standards, post boxes or bollards can, if carefully used, act to reduce the optical width of a street, create physical barriers to protect areas for pedestrians, and also reduce forward visibility. Such features are typically used to

Figure 5.53   Surface materials can help give an impression of a suitable driving speed and help to define areas designated for types of activity

Figure 5.54   Planting and street furniture can be used with other traffic calming measures to slow traffic and add other features to a streetscape

support and control other traffic calming features previously discussed (Figure 5.54).

Entrances and gateways

At the entrance and exit to a traffic calmed area, it is sometimes desirable to introduce a feature that indicates to drivers that they are entering or leaving an area where the highway has a different status. This encourages them to adjust their expectations and driving style. Such features might result, for example, from the configuration of buildings creating a narrowing or gateway effect; the use of either planters or trees; the use of a ramp; a change of surface; or a realignment of the carriageway. Such features usually supplement necessary signage, indicating the legal status of the highway (Figure 5.55).

Figure 5.55   This access road to a new residential area has many of the features that would slow down entering traffic

PARKING

How you accommodate cars into a residential area will have a big impact on its character and appearance. A common complaint about residential areas is that the streets are car dominated–meaning that when you look down the street all you see is parked cars (Figure 5.56). This is despite the fact that a variety of measures exist to accommodate the car conveniently within the vicinity of people's homes. What follows is a discussion about how cars might be accommodated.

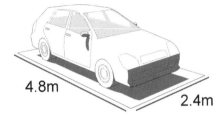

Figure 5.57   Parking dimensions

Figure 5.56   Too often the street environment is dominated by parking

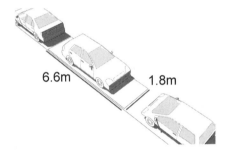

Figure 5.58   Parking dimensions for cars parked parallel to a pavement

Standards and dimensions

Parking spaces vary in size and local authorities often have detailed standards that they want all new developments to adhere to. In the UK, the simplest common dimension for a free-standing parking space is 4.8 m long and 2.4 m wide (Figure 5.57). Larger vehicles, like sports utility vehicles, create new demands for more space to be designated for parking.

Cars parked parallel to a pavement will require longer spaces (6.6 m) so that they can manoeuvre in and out, although the width of these spaces could be slightly narrower (1.8–2 m) as car doors can open over pavements (Figure 5.58).

Parking perpendicular to a route or rows of parking spaces facing each other should have a turning distance of at least 6–7 m to allow manoeuvring in and out of spaces. Where parking is arranged at an angle of, for example, 60 or 45°, the manoeuvring distance between the facing spaces can be reduced to 4.5 m or 4 m, respectively (Figure 5.59).

Cars parked up to wide walkways could also allow their fronts to overhang the walkway, thus reducing the depth of the dedicated space to about 4.5 m. The profile of the surface, however, needs to stop parking on the pedestrian area (Figure 5.60).

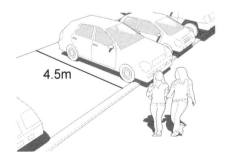

Figure 5.59   Cars need about 6–7m manoeuvring space if they are parked perpendicular to a route

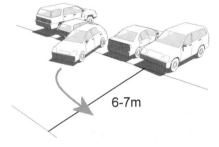

Figure 5.60   Cars can park overhanging a wide pavement

Parking for people who are physically disabled

In comparison to a regular parking space, a parking space for a person who is physically disabled should be more generous. Countries and states may have standards for the provision of such facilities and these should be reviewed. As a general rule, a parking space should be about 3.6 m wide to allow the manoeuvring of a wheelchair around the vehicle. Such parking spaces should also be level and have no kerb to any walkway. Spaces should also be clearly marked and located directly adjacent to relevant homes and other destinations (Figure 5.61).

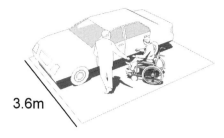

Figure 5.61   Parking space for a person who is physically disabled

On-plot

On-plot parking is very common and popular as parking is controlled by the resident, whilst the car is regarded as more secure. Neither does a parked car interfere with other traffic movement. On-plot parking can be in front of the home, to the side, or to the rear. Parking in front means that the car is highly visible in the street. This aids surveillance of the car but is also less attractive. Parking at the side hides the car but increases the overall plot width, which may have implications for the density of a scheme. Parking at the rear hides the car, but can reduce the dedicated garden area whilst increasing the area of land that is sealed (Figure 5.62).

Garages are a common feature of on-plot parking and, if carefully integrated, can limit the impact of cars within a scheme, particularly if combined with wide-fronted houses. Used extensively, however, they can come to dominate the character of a street, creating extensive areas of blank frontage. Some houses in the USA have been criticised because they have no front door, as designers assume that people will gain access to their homes from their cars–thus turning the garage into the main entrance. In the UK small houses with a lack of storage space often means that garages are used for storage, thus increasing the amount of visible car parking.

Figure 5.62   On plot parking

Ground floor parking

Parking is sometimes accommodated on the ground floor of residential schemes. If other rooms are located on the ground floor facing the street then the impact of the car on the character of the street can be minimised. This is often not achieved, however, and so the public environment is dominated by blank ventilation grills and shadowy views of parked cars (Figure 5.63).

Figure 5.63   Ground floor parking

Basement parking

Basement parking is very common in northern European countries like Germany where most apartments include parking underground, with access through the façade or from an adjacent space. Parking is typically either under the building or under the adjacent space (Figure 5.64). Such a parking arrangement significantly increases the cost of a scheme, but in areas of higher density it removes cars from view and provides a high degree of security. Separate routes for cars in and out are common to control access and reduce the impact of entrances onto the streets. Access to such car parks is usually electronically controlled, with drivers gaining access to homes from within the scheme.

Figure 5.64   Basement parking

On-street parking

On-street parking is common in residential areas that were designed before cars became a common feature of the urban environment. For some time, on-street parking was frowned upon by engineers who thought that it slowed down through-traffic–until it was pointed out that this was a good feature for any residential area. Since then, on-street parking has been cautiously welcomed where it is consciously introduced to assist in traffic calming.

On-street parking can be parallel to a walkway, or arranged at 45, 60 or 90° angles (Figure 5.65a–c). Parking at these angles increases the calming effect but widens the streets and can make parking highly visible if landscaping isn't also included. Parking islands can be introduced into residential areas as part of a widening in the street (Figure 5.66). Parking schemes on street can also be used to create discontinuity and chicanes in

Figure 5.65(a)   Parallel on-street parking   (b)   On-street parking at 60 degrees   (c)   On-street parking at 90 degrees

Figure 5.66   An on-street parking island at 90 degrees

the highway so that it is physically difficult to drive fast. Such an arrangement is particularly common in early Dutch home zones.

Facing garages

A common arrangement in some schemes in Europe is to locate parking garages directly opposite homes with access via a simple, shared surface route perpendicular to the busier streets. Garages such as these are easily seen from homes and can be used for storage of garden equipment, bikes and toys. This arrangement allows residents to extend their living environment over the street. The weakness with this form of development is that the streets have frontage only on one side (the other side is garages), and such a design may result in a greater length of highway per home which could be more expensive. This could be compensated for by having simpler forms of highway, or even short one-way blocks with narrower carriageways (Figure 5.67).

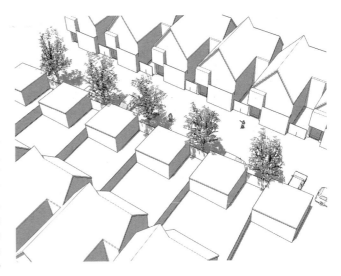

Figure 5.67   Facing garages

End parking

Another common arrangement for parking in Europe is end parking, where parking is arranged perpendicular to the residential block at the end of a terrace. Access to homes is then via narrow pedestrian-dominated routes, although generous dimensions still allow for delivery of goods. Often the parking area is also the location for waste and recycling facilities. This arrangement keeps the parking a short distance away from homes, allowing space around the homes to be used by residents and, in particular, children. The end of terrace houses or apartments can easily provide some surveillance of the space (Figure 5.68).

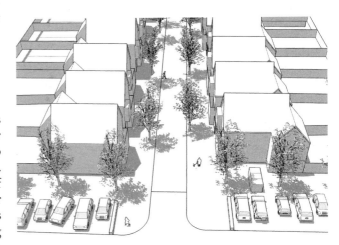

Figure 5.68   End parking

Parking courts

Parking courts arrange cars collectively into a courtyard or mews either in front or to the rear of homes (Figure 5.69). To the front, cars can be seen from the houses. To the rear the space must be planned to have surveillance–the Poundbury block discussed above shows how this can be achieved successfully, with houses or apartments included within the parking court but away from the main street. Successful parking courts, particularly to the rear, tend to have controlled access, or are designed to dissuade non-residents from entering so that a greater degree of security is achieved. Not all parking court arrangements are, however, successful. Some parking courts to the rear of homes or

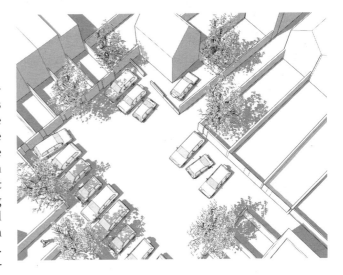

Figure 5.69   A parking court

Figure 5.70   Larger parking courts might be less attractive

apartments can be over large, creating the impression of a car park rather than a more domestic environment, and residents might feel a little remote from their own car. Larger parking courts may also have problems with security (Figure 5.70).

Parking alleys

In the USA, alleys are particularly common in New Urbanist residential schemes. This involves providing rear access to homes for cars, and removes parking and garages from the main street frontages, allowing them instead to be dominated by the character of the buildings, their entrances, and features such as porches. The alleys tend to have a minimum dimension, and the garages often have living spaces above them (Figure 5.71). In the UK, alleys like this are regarded as problematic, particularly if there is no surveillance of them from homes or if access is not easily controlled.

Figure 5.71   Rear lane parking with 'granny flats' above the parking spaces

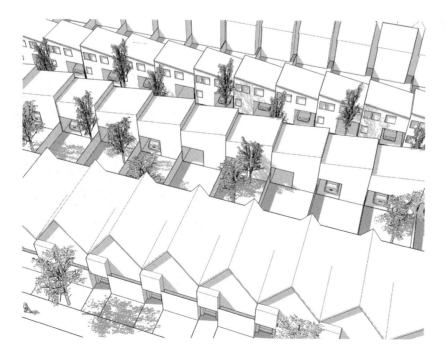

Multi-storey parking

A less common, but equally viable, form of parking is the use of private multi-storey garages within a community. Car-free communities, such as the Franszösischen Viertel in Tübingen or The Vauban in Freiburg, have community managed multi-storey car parks that allow people to own cars whilst keeping them away from the environment of their homes. If the multi-storey car parks are located carefully on the edge of a community, this can significantly reduce the impact of cars within a scheme, whilst still providing convenient access (Figure 5.72).

Mixed arrangements

Some of the best residential schemes accommodate parking in a variety of ways, rather than allowing one particular approach to dominate the character of a scheme. On-street parking is very convenient–particularly for visitors or deliveries–whilst it can also calm traffic and maintains activity within public spaces. Where all parking is on-street, however, the streets quickly become dominated by parked cars. Schemes, therefore, should be designed to accommodate a bulk of parking away from public view (Figure 5.73).

Figure 5.72   Community managed multi-storey car parks offer secure parking a short distance from people's homes

Figure 5.73   Mixed parking

Car sharing and car clubs

To reduce the need for a high level of residential parking–as well as to support residents with their desire to live more environmentally-friendly lives–some residential areas accommodate car sharing schemes or car clubs (Figure 5.74). Such schemes or clubs allow residents access to their cars when they need them and they may have dedicated parking areas within a scheme for parking vehicles when not in use.

Figure 5.74   Car sharing schemes could have designated parking areas within a scheme

Buying a space

In areas where the demand for parking spaces are high, or where a specific effort has been made to reduce parking provision, residents may even be required to purchase these separately when buying their home.

FURTHER READING

The concept of permeability is discussed as some length in Bentley *et al.* (1985). This discussion has driven a recent move away from cul-de-sac forms of development dictating the configuration of new residential areas in the UK. Transit-oriented developments, focusing on public transport, are introduced in *The Pedestrian Pocket Book* (Kelbaugh, 1989) and reviewed along with permeable configurations that support 'walkability' in the comprehensive report on new urbanism produced by New Urban News (2001–2002). Walkable suburbs are also reviewed by Southworth (1996). Marshall (2005) presents a very in-depth analysis of street configurations and their performance, offering a whole range of concepts for comparative analysis of different types of network. Southworth and Ben-Joseph (2003) provide a very useful history of the evolution of streets and their standardisation, whilst also comparing new configurations and discussing standards.

A comprehensive set of highway standards, including standards for traffic calming, can be found in the Dutch *ASVV: Recommendations for Traffic Provisions in Built-up Areas* (CROW, 1998). This might be compared to the American *Residential Roads* (Kulash, 2002). In the UK the main sources of advice are *Design Bulletin 32: Residential Roads and Footpaths* (Department of the Environment and Department of Transport, 1992) and its supplement *Places, Streets and Movement* (Department of the Environment, Transport and the Regions, 1998) which provides more recent advice about residential roads and street character. At the time of going to press, both of these documents are being revised, and the new report *Manual for Streets* is planned for publication in 2006/2007. Within the UK some county or local authorities translate the national guidance into local design guidelines for residential areas, of which the Essex (Essex County Council and Essex Planning Officers' Association, 2005) and Kent (Kent Design Initiative/Kent County Council, 2006) design guides are the most comprehensive and quoted. Radical thinking about car-free cities can be found in Crawford (2002), whilst the best advice on providing cycle friendly infrastructure can be found in the Dutch CROW (1993) publication *Sign Up For The Bike: Design manual for a cycle-friendly infrastructure* or the UK's *Cycle-friendly Infrastructure Guidelines for Planning and Design* (Department of Transport, 1996). A more recent guide *Designing for Cyclists: A guide to good practice* has also been produced by Essex County Council. Traffic calming techniques are discussed in a wide number of publications. In the UK *Traffic Calming Guidelines* has been produced by Pharoah and Devon County Council (1991), *Traffic Calming in Practice* by the County Surveyors' Society (1994), or *Traffic Calming Techniques* for the Institution of Highways and Transportation (Lovell, 2005). In the USA and Canada the Institute of Transportation Engineers has written *Traffic Calming: State of the practice* (Ewing, 1999).

6 Integrating other uses

INTRODUCTION

No residential scheme should be considered in isolation to other land usage, as most people live within the vicinity of schools, leisure, shops and other local facilities. Unfortunately, however, it remains the case that many residential areas are developed without any particular regard to their surroundings. There are a number of reasons for this. Firstly, and the main reason, is the increasing reliability on cars. These days, most people use cars to do things that, only decades ago, they would have done on foot, by bike or by using public transport. Many businesses are now located some distance from town centres, taking advantage of the larger populations who can access their services by car–inevitably, their profitability is accused of killing off local shops and services closer to homes. Secondly, house builders typically only build houses, while other developers specialise in commercial schemes, and investors like the security of investing their money in single uses–rather than in mixed developments–thus maximising their profits. Neither of these groups tends to be prepared to consider the increased complexity and risk of creating mixed-use schemes. Thirdly, although it is less relevant in some planning cultures, planners often like to zone, and therefore separate, different types of uses so that conflicts of amenity do not occur. This approach is a legacy of both the Garden City Movement and the functionalist approach to urbanism presented in earlier drafts of *The Charter of Athens*. Such thinking, developed before the 1950s, was based on a very nineteenth-century notion of what urban environments might be like (a mix of pollution-belching factories and poverty-stricken slums) and such thinking really needed updating.

This chapter is concerned with exploring ways in which other types of developments might be mixed with housing and, in particular, looks at the design and layout considerations that should be taken into account. Such thinking would appear to be contrary to development trends in some countries. However, it is an approach actively encouraged by policy makers because:

- local shops and facilities allow residents to access them without depending on a car. This may have the knock-on effect of reducing car use generally within local streets, making them feel safer and quieter
- having other uses, including schools or community facilities, near to where people live allows everyone, including children, young people

and the elderly in particular, to have a greater degree of autonomy as they can access these facilities more easily

- mixed uses create the variety and vitality which are popular features of urban areas. You see a variety of people using streets and other public spaces for longer periods of the day. Different uses also require some variation in building types which can encourage an attractive variety in the form and townscape of the built environment (see Chapter 8)
- more walking or cycling encouraged by mixed uses improves health and gives more scope for residents to socialise within their local streets, whilst reducing car dependence helps address wider policy issues such as concerns about global warming (see Chapter 4).

WHAT IS MIXED USE?

The term 'mixed use development' has become shorthand for describing any schemes that is not made up exclusively of 'one use'; but it also hides some complexity. Figure 6.1 shows that uses can be mixed **vertically** in individual buildings. Where a residential scheme is concerned, vertically mixing uses typically involves providing commercial properties on the ground floor and residential properties above them. Such patterns of development are quite normal in countries like The Netherlands and Germany where streets that have a commercial function will normally have living accommodation above them. Such mixed uses are also perfectly normal in cities like London and New York, where demand for living accommodation is very high and space is at a premium.

A **horizontal** mixing of properties would refer to uses changing within neighbouring buildings (Figure 6.2). Therefore, a street would have a horizontal mix if a bank is situated next to a community building; the community building is situated next to a school; the school is situated next to housing, and so on.

The mixing of uses might also vary in its **grain**. In some areas, uses might vary between a large number of small buildings. This is known as a 'fine grain'. In other areas, the mix might be coarser as uses are situated in larger buildings or groups of buildings and sit side-by-side, but at a greater distance from each other. A finer grain of uses tends to be preferred, although any grain is appropriate so long as they are comfortably accessible on foot (Figure 6.3).

CATCHMENTS AND USE HIERARCHIES

Most uses require a certain number of customers to become viable in the form and location where they are situated. If we look at food stores, for example, we can see that residents in a particular area might be served by a number of shops or markets, depending on their catchment thresholds:

- A local food store selling daily convenience items might be located within the community

Figure 6.1   Vertically mixed uses

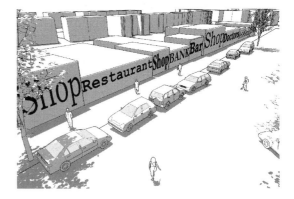

Figure 6.2   Horizontally mixed uses

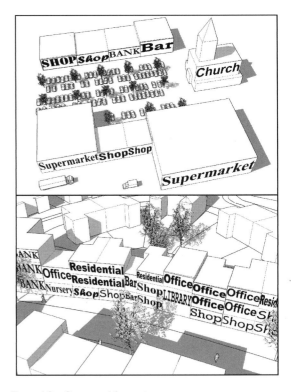

Figure 6.3   Coarse and fine grain

- A supermarket where residents can do their weekly shopping might be located between communities
- A wide range of specialist stores providing access to specialist foods might be located along a retailing corridor, or in a town or city centre and might be visited at least once every couple of weeks
- A weekly farmers' market, serving the town or city as a whole, might traditionally be in a central location.

This complexity is desirable as it provides residents with a choice of stores and, in these examples, foods (Figure 6.4).

In planning any residential area it is necessary to understand the existing distribution of uses, their necessary catchment thresholds for viability and their position in the use hierarchy. Only then will it be necessary to determine what additional uses could be considered to provide an additional level of service to the new community.

Barton *et al.* (1995) (Figure 6.5) cautiously use a number of sources to formulate a list of likely catchments for a range of uses found within the urban area.

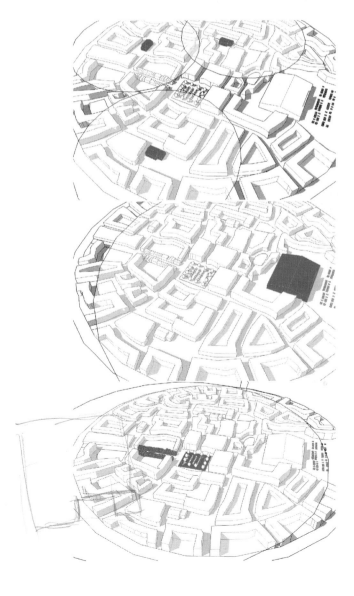

Figure 6.4   Catchments for local shops (top), a supermarket (middle) or specialised shops and a farmers' market (bottom) overlap and create a more diverse mix of retailing opportunities for residents

	Population
Corner shop	2000 – 5000
Doctor's surgery	2500 – 3000
Primary school	2500 – 4500
Bar/public house	5000 – 7000
Post office	5000 – 10,000
Local shopping centre	5000 – 10,000
Youth club	7000 – 11,000
Community centre	7000 – 15,000
Secondary school	7000 – 15,000
Church	At least 9000
Health centre	9000 – 12,000
Library	At least 12,000
Superstore	At least 25,000
Sports club	At least 25,000

Figure 6.5   Suggested catchments for a variety of uses (Source: Barton *et al.*, 1995: 113)

Newpoint	I'On	Orenco Station
130 homes	762 homes	1900 homes
2 commercial buildings	30,000 sqft	57,000 sqft
• Small general store • Ice cream café • 2 realty offices • Holistic medicine centre • Massage therapist	• Food store • Hair salon and beauty spa • Realty office • Baker, flower and coffee shop • Pub/restaurant	• Post office • Medium sized organic supermarket • Italian restaurant • Indian restaurant • Steak restaurant • Coffee shop • Flower and gift store • Insurance office • Dentist • Women's clothes store • Dry cleaners • Wine and cigar store • Sweet shop • Kitchen shop • Opticians

Figure 6.6   The range of other uses achieved in a spectrum of residential schemes gives an indication of what might be achieved elsewhere in similar schemes

Looking at actual schemes it is possible to get a sense of the types of uses that might be attracted to an area given the scale of development. Three examples are presented in Figure 6.6 for illustration only as they are all context specific, and the viability of any use will need to be judged on a case-by-case basis. Some of these areas, for example, have other commercial uses within the vicinity that would limit further development within the scheme.

GETTING A CATCHMENT

There are three ways of maintaining a catchment to support a greater variety of uses. The first is to mix primary uses within an area to support secondary uses. The second is to get more custom by having a larger number of people living within a local area. The third is to get custom by taking advantage of passing trade.

Mixing primary uses

Areas might contain one or more **primary uses**, and then a number of supporting or dependant **secondary uses** (Figure 6.7). Primary uses are the main reason why most people would be in a particular area. Therefore, in housing areas, it is the residential function (i.e. going to and coming from work/school) that means an area is populated during certain periods of the day, say the morning and evening. Secondary uses, like local shops, bars and restaurants within an area that have one primary use, only benefit from passing trade when the area is populated. If, as in residential areas, this is limited to the morning and evening, then the viability of local uses is harder to achieve. If a primary use is mixed with another, i.e. a range of offices, then the area might be populated for a longer period. Residents would frequent the secondary uses during the morning and evening, replaced by office workers during the day.

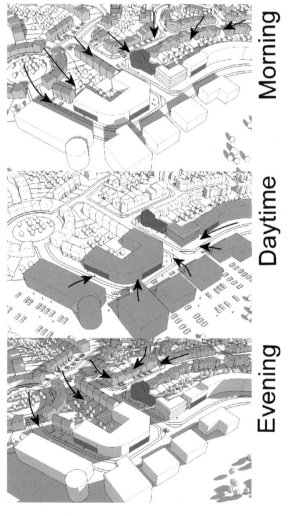

Morning

Daytime

Evening

Figure 6.7   Mixed primary uses like housing and offices can provide customers for shops and other commercial uses at different times during a day

Densities and mixed use?

Increasing densities are also thought to supply the people needed to provide a catchment for a wider number of businesses within an area. Acceptable densities for an area vary due to a number of interrelated factors, including:

Cultural expectations: People in Paris are prepared to live at a far higher density than people in Los Angeles

Demand to live within an area: Demand to live in central London is higher than demand to live in central Sheffield

The character and quality of the local built environment: The existing density of development in Berlin is relatively high, making it desirable to match that density with future developments. The same high density, however, would be unacceptable in Beaufort, South Carolina, where such development would destroy the existing character and might overburden the local infrastructure, even though demand to live there might be equally high (Figure 6.8).

Figure 6.8   The existing character of central Berlin involves good quality higher density housing, but the same density would be unacceptable in Beaufort, South Carolina

Densities, affluence and commercial viability

Chapter 4 discusses how net densities vary and points out that 30 units per hectare is argued to be necessary to create some variety of use if density is to be the main driver behind diversity. Such a statistic, however, is a little simplistic. If, for example, residents living in 30 units per hectare are quite affluent, you might expect more money in the local economy to support the local uses, whereas a more deprived community might struggle in similar circumstances. This is one reason why it is desirable to achieve a balanced mix of affluence within a population; or at least rely on a mix of primary uses or passing trade to help support a degree of diversity.

Retail 'realities' and patterns of life

Promoters of higher densities often suggest that having commercial uses within walking distance from people's homes *will* result in more people walking to those services rather than using the car. Research suggests, however, that this is not always the case and that local shops provide only the opportunity or choice for people to use them. There is evidence that:

- if people have access to a car that they will travel farther to a wider choice of places
- people from poorer backgrounds will travel to still cheaper stores rather then use the local, and possibly more expensive ones
- sometimes local stores are not of a good quality and people may ignore them and travel to better quality stores farther away from their homes
- people also use stores close to where they work, or which they pass on their journey home.

Picking up on passing trade

The third and possibly most flexible approach to supporting a mixture of uses within a scheme involves making use of passing trade. Commercial uses today, in particular, often rely on car or public transport-based custom to achieve their required catchment and make them viable–if you have plenty of passing trade, then you wouldn't need a mixture of primary uses or high densities to make your business viable.

To help support the viability of both existing or new shops and community uses designs should:

- locate commercial activities where they are clearly visible to potential passing trade. It is well known that if a business is even a few metres from a main road frontage, the amount of custom will fall off significantly and might make its business less viable
- take advantage of existing levels of activity by fronting new retail uses directly onto street frontages with an established level of footfall from pedestrians
- focus the pattern of streets within the new scheme onto existing or new commercial areas so that these locations are convenient and become the obvious focal point for future shopping
- exploit the added accessibility, and therefore commercial potential, provided by well-used corner locations where passing trade comes from more than one direction
- provide adequate short-stay parking for new commercial uses either on street or in a form that allows people to conveniently visit more than one location (Figure 6.9).

In deprived areas passing trade might help to make commercial uses more viable as they become less dependent on support from the local population only.

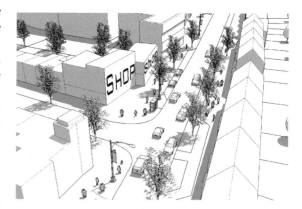

Figure 6.9 Pick up on passing trade

Passing trade and the urban grid

The value of passing trade to commercial businesses cannot be underestimated, and any designer will need to consider how best to attract passing trade when planning a layout. Hillier (1996) analyses urban grids and street networks to predict the extent to which any street in the urban environment is integrated with all others. The most integrated streets will be able to support passing trade, as they will be the routes that are, or could be, used by the most people.

We know which routes are the most frequented by observing them, but Hillier provides us with a tool for predicting the extent to which new routes added to the established urban grid might change patterns of movement and integration, and subsequently which routes might be busiest in the future. In Figure 6.10, the level of integration between each route (indicated as a line), and all other routes in a network, has been calculated. The darker routes are the most integrated, whilst the lighter routes are less so. You can expect that the darker routes will have the most passing trade, whilst the lighter routes are the quiet residential streets.

If you want commercial uses, it makes sense to create routes within a scheme which really integrate well with the established movement patterns and only locate commercial uses on these routes. In the example illustrated above, we would locate these commercial uses along the darker routes, as along the lighter routes there wouldn't be enough activity to make them commercially viable.

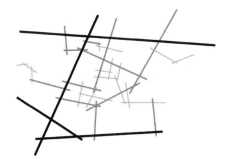

Figure 6.10   Illustration of an axial map produced as a result of space syntax analysis and based on Hillier (1996, Figure 4.7c). The darker routes are the most integrated and would be the better locations for uses requiring passing trade

THE SPATIAL DISTRIBUTION OF USES

The type of uses that might be possible within an area also depends on how they are to be developed spatially. Four arrangements would seem to give an indication of how urban areas and patterns of use might develop. People needing access to shops and other facilities within the new residential schemes will probably find them provided in one of these four forms.

1 **Centralising shops and facilities:** Some designers, having studied traditional patterns of urban development, locate a mix of uses at their centre. Such patterns of use are common in older and smaller towns and cities which still have strong centres, and where older buildings have been conserved; thus, to a certain extent, preserving the diversity of land uses. In new schemes, this is difficult to replicate. However, where such uses are at the centre, residential areas would circle the commercial and community uses, while providing direct access to them. Such areas typically require a complex relationship of mixed primary and secondary uses in order to remain commercially robust. This pattern of development is sometimes referred to as monocentric (Figure 6.11). An example is Kirchsteigfeld in Potsdam, a new urban extension (Figure 6.12) where both commercial and community uses are located at the core of the new development around a relatively large open space.

2 **Corridors:** Mixed use corridors often develop in a linear form along main streets. These corridors fall between the main residential areas and they get trade from both neighbouring residents and people using the through route

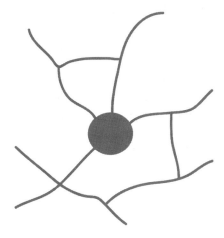

Figure 6.11   Centralising shops and facilities

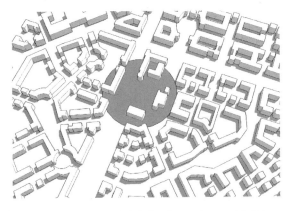

Figure 6.12   Kirchsteigfeld, Potsdam has its shops and facilities in the centre of the scheme

travelling by car or public transport (Figure 6.13). In larger towns and cities, the corridors might supplement the uses provided in the core, although corridors tend to provide more localised shops and facilities that are closer to many people's homes.

Figure 6.14 shows the centre of Neu-Karow in Berlin whose commercial properties are built along its main through-street. The street has developed to provide a diverse range of shops, restaurants and other services. It is on a good route connecting across the neighbourhood and therefore benefits from passing trade, but is also within walking distance of the large local population.

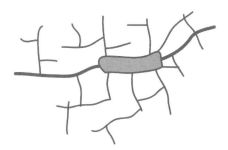

Figure 6.13   A commercial corridor

Figure 6.14   The commercial corridor through Neu-Karow in Berlin

3   **Planned neighbourhood shops and facilities:** Zoned shops and facilities in planned neighbourhoods may struggle if they serve only a single, small neighbourhood, as they don't benefit from the vicinity to other primary uses or passing trade. New urbanist planning concepts acknowledge this, and typically locate any retailing element at the entrance to a community so that all residents have easy access, whilst passing trade from the main road users is also possible (Figure 6.15). The extent of the facilities may vary depending on the size of the planned neighbourhood. The Newpoint development, near Beaufort in Southern Carolina, is a small scheme in a suburban location, but two mixed-use commercial buildings are viable due to the scheme's location on a main road (Figure 6.16). This compares with I'On in

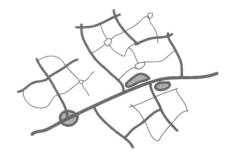

Figure 6.15   Planned neighbourhood shops and facilities

Figure 6.16   Two mixed use buildings located at the entrance of the small community of New Point in South Carolina pick up on passing trade

Figure 6.17   I'On's commercial and community uses at the entrance to the scheme

Mount Pleasant where a grouping of commercial and community uses is located within the entrance to the 243 acre development. It benefits less from passing trade, but is well used by local residents (Figure 6.17). Orenco Station is a new 'transit oriented' settlement on the outskirts of Portland, Oregan. Its shops and facilities are located to draw in as wide a population of potential users as possible. It has a town centre adjacent to a light rail station linking the town to Portland, whilst the centre is also located on Cornell Road, offering a good level of passing vehicular trade. The form of the town centre allows direct pedestrian access from within the community with car parking behind the buildings. Above the shops are commercial offices that also support the viability of the retailing when they are in use, whilst the office workers benefit from their location within an attractive and convenient town centre environment (Figure 6.18).

Figure 6.18   The mixed use commercial centre in Orenco Station near Portland is located on the main road and with direct linkages to the local light rail station which links the new community to the city centre

4   **Decentralising retailing:** Taking advantage of car-borne residents, large shops are in decentralised locations, situated at the junctions of major roads and providing extensive car parking. Although they may have bus, pedestrian or cyclist access, their viability is dependent on

car users and their ability to draw custom from a relatively wide geographic area. Typically, the schemes can turn their backs on neighbouring housing, whilst the development of large retail 'sheds' accessible from major roads and across car parks also segregates neighbouring communities. This form of development is, therefore, typically remote from specific residential areas and is a less environmentally sustainable form of development (Figure 6.19).

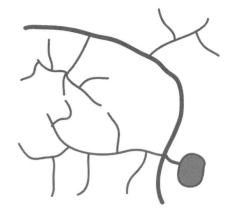

Figure 6.19   Decentralised retailing

Figure 6.20 shows new housing in Pontprennau, Cardiff and its neighbouring retailing area. The shops are located to take advantage of the major highway junction so that they are accessible for cars from across the city, but they are also the local shops for neighbouring residents. Unfortunately, however, the scheme isn't integrated within the community and walking there is unpleasant. Residents also have a far smaller choice of only large businesses within their vicinity, compared, for example, to the older shopping areas that have a wider mixture.

Figure 6.20   The retail centre in Pontprennau, Cardiff is peripheral to the community, isn't convenient and is not that easy to reach on foot

MIXED USE AMBITIONS

Compared to older residential areas, many new areas like Pontprennau in Cardiff, tend to have far fewer smaller businesses planned into their form. Developers in such situations tend to, rather lazily, just provide commercial space for national chain stores rather than create opportunities for local entrepreneurs. The plan for New Islington in Manchester is an interesting contrast. Extracts from the project's website (http://www. newislington.co.uk/) illustrate the positive ambition for promoting a diverse range of smaller uses as well:

> Living our lives is about the uses we bring into the area. At the moment there's one dimension–housing... We want it to be much, much more. We want New Islington to have:
>
> * the best fish and chip shop
> * a greengrocer, a newsagent, a bookies
> * an Indian takeaway
> * a hairdressers, a coffee shop
> * a beautiful launderette
> * a poncey wine bar, a great pub
> * a caff, a café, a greasy spoon

- a chic little Italian with red checked tablecloths
- and a restaurant with 3 Michelin stars
- a new clinic–that's state of the art
- alternative therapists, witch doctors, potions and national health
- a new primary school that tops the league tables
- a fantastic nursery and a wonderful crèche
- a footie pitch that's safe to use
- a farmers market to buy local food.

> Our ambition is to create the best place in Manchester… We propose to set up a company that will manage the area, in which the residents will be the shareholders and will receive the ground rents so that they have an income and an asset, to protect, govern and safeguard the future of the area… assuming we get it right.

It is very unusual for developers to show such positive ambition, particularly within the UK.

SCHOOLS IN RESIDENTIAL AREAS

It is common within schemes accommodating between 2500 and 4500 people for a primary school to be built as part of the scheme, whilst the quality of local schools is also a critical selling point for housing generally. Early designs put the school at the centre of the neighbourhood, as it was felt that the institution helped with community cohesion; children could safely walk the short distance from their homes, whilst the playing field and hall could be used for community events (Figure 6.21). Today some proponents of new urbanism suggest that the school should be at the edge of a neighbourhood so that its playing fields don't divide the community and the use can be shared with neighbouring areas (Figure 6.22).

Whichever approach is adopted it is desirable to ensure that children have access to safe walking and cycling routes to and from schools from within the catchment area, whilst streets adjacent to school entrances should have traffic calming systems. The school in the neighbourhood of De Aker in Amsterdam (Figure 6.23 on the right in the image) shows how the schoolyard can become part of the neighbouring streets. The shared surface is regarded as the best way to ensure safety as car drivers must

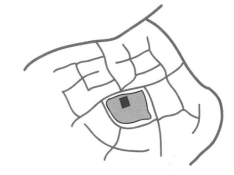

Figure 6.21   Early neighbourhood concepts put the school at the centre of the community

Figure 6.22   More recent new urbanist thinking has put the school on the edge of neighbourhoods so that they can be shared and the playing fields don't divide the communities

Figure 6.23   A school in De Aker, Amsterdam showing how the school yard can become part of the neighbouring streets

drive slowly around the area; as they clearly have no priority. This contrasts interestingly with the new school provided in the Greenwich Millennium Village in London (Figure 6.24): this also has shared surface streets neighbouring it and the school is architecturally interesting, but it is far more defensive in its form and style.

Figure 6.24   The new school in the Greenwich Millennium Village in London showing how defensive a school can be within its context

STUDYING BUILDING TYPOLOGIES

Mixed-use building typologies are common, and existing precedents can be understood and their basic forms recreated in new schemes if the conditions are felt to be right. Homes for Change in Manchester is one such innovative group of buildings (Figure 6.25). The scheme contains 75 homes, a theatre, café, artist studios, workshops and offices. It is common

Figure 6.25   Mixed use buildings like *Homes for Change* in Manchester can be studied to examine how uses are successfully mixed within the schemes

for designers to consider precedents like this. In analysing an existing typology you might like to consider the following questions:

- Where is the building located in relation to the pattern and hierarchy of streets and neighbouring uses?
- How are the uses arranged either horizontally or vertically within the building?
- What types of access arrangement and floor area are required to make the particular uses viable?
- Do the particular uses need a shop window and individual entrance for customers, and how are these highlighted in the form of the building?
- How is signage and lighting used in the promotion of non-residential uses?
- How is parking arranged and managed for the different types of uses?
- How is servicing arranged for the commercial uses?
- Are residential areas provided with outdoor amenity spaces or not, and if so how is privacy maintained?
- Are the different types of uses expressed in the form, scale or massing of the building?
- Are the buildings designed in any special way to reduce the impact of one type of use on the amenities of the other?
- Is there a management regime in place to ensure that relative amenities are protected; for example, limits to opening times or controls over delivery times?

RETAINING OLDER BUILDINGS

A diversity of use is best realised where a neighbourhood retains older buildings. This is simply because a greater number of uses will be able to afford the rents or building costs, in comparison with the commercial rents required to occupy newly developed space. Only uses that are very profitable or subsidised can afford to pay for the costs of new construction. Chain stores, chain restaurants and banks go into new buildings, whilst privately owned shops, neighbourhood bars and locally managed restaurants and takeaways might go into older spaces. Bentley *et al.* (1985) note that there is a far larger number of businesses and potential businesses that will enjoy the cheaper rents.

Residential neighbourhoods do not typically offer highly profitable commercial business opportunities. Instead, as they are 'off centre' and in deliberately peripheral locations where residents' amenities are not affected negatively by large amounts of through traffic. Because of this, it is relatively easy to predict that businesses located in these areas may need more affordable spaces as their turnover can be low. To help promote a greater diversity of neighbourhood uses, it makes a lot of sense, therefore, to retain older buildings that are on a site and consider how they might be used for some type of commercial activity or community facility (Figure 6.26).

SUBSIDISING OR PHASING-IN OTHER USES

Residential populations develop slowly, particularly in a new neighbourhood and, as a result, the necessary catchments for certain businesses might take some time to develop. Therefore, it may be necessary to subsidise the use of commercial space developed early within a scheme, to provide the

Figure 6.26 Retaining older buildings may provide space for commercial and community uses that would not be able to afford the cost of occupying a new building

Figure 6.27 It may be necessary to reserve sites for future developments which can only be realised once funding has been secured

businesses with time to become profitable as the population grows. Alternatively, it may be necessary to designate sites for future developments which can then be built as the population gets to the right level (Figure 6.27).

ANCHORS

Commercial areas will benefit from the correct location of an 'anchor' to attract people to use the businesses within a neighbourhood. Anchors are typically larger uses that might be common destinations for people. Sometimes they might be a collection of smaller businesses, like bars, that people would also regard as a destination. Other uses might then be located adjacent to, and within walking distance from, the anchors in order to take advantage of the coming and going that they generate.

We can learn how anchors support the diversity of other uses when we look at the layout of shopping centres; large stores are carefully planned at a reasonable and convenient walking distance to each other, and smaller stores are located along the routes to take advantage of the passing trade (Figure 6.28). Such principles should also be applied to the locating of anchor uses in a larger neighbourhood centre.

Figure 6.28 Anchors should be located to support additional neighbouring uses

Within the university town of Davis a new residential area was built adjacent to the town centre, but between the housing and the centre a new commercial area was built. The anchor here is a bookstore, which also attracts the university students, whilst a series of smaller units take advantage of the location next to the store (Figure 6.29).

Car parking is carefully planned as an element of the layout. People often want to drive and park near an anchor, so other uses might be located around the car park. In Davis,

Figure 6.29   The anchor book store in the new development next to the town centre of Davis, California, where secondary uses take neighbouring units

Figure 6.30   The car parking shown here in Poundbury, Dorchester is conceived of as a function of the main square

California, the car park also serves the wider area so the commercial schemes take advantage of people passing by to other locations. In Poundbury in southern England, cars park in a central urban square. The square is fronted by an anchor supermarket and surrounded by other commercial uses, but it also manages to serve as a distinctive *place* at the centre of the scheme, rather than as merely a car park (Figure 6.30).

CATCHMENTS AND PERMEABILITY

Catchments are heavily influenced by patterns of accessibility, and when assessing a catchment for a business it is necessary to measure the real distance that residents will have to travel if they want to use a given service. Businesses established in areas with a low level of permeability will need to have larger catchments than businesses established in areas where routes are more direct (Figure 6.31). The level of permeability therefore combines with the pattern of uses to make an area easier to use without relying on a car.

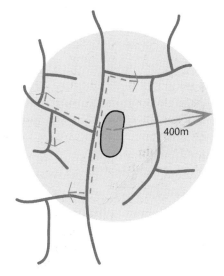

Figure 6.31   Measuring catchments as the crow flies ignores the true distances that people may need to travel and the quality of routes available to them

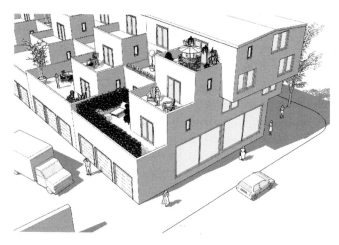

Figure 6.32 Commercial buildings can have larger footprints which can provide space for balconies or access to apartments above

Figure 6.33 Keeping the residential and commercial entrances separate will reduce conflicts between the uses

MIXED-USE BUILDING ACCESS, SERVICING AND SOUND

It is important for vertically mixed-use buildings to ensure that conflicts do not occur between the uses during the life of a scheme.

Sometimes commercial buildings have a larger footprint than residential uses and so it may be possible to use the additional area on the exposed roof for residential gardens, balconies or access (Figure 6.32).

Access for residential and commercial businesses should be kept separate so that each type of use is secure, and activities–like repeated commercial deliveries–do not come into conflict with domestic life. Residential uses above ground level will typically have separate entrances either in the façade or from a residential courtyard or parking area located at the rear (Figure 6.33).

Commercial buildings often need servicing areas for deliveries, for operational parking or for the storage of rubbish. It is important to make sure that such areas don't come into conflict with residential uses and that they aren't easily overlooked by people living above (Figure 6.34).

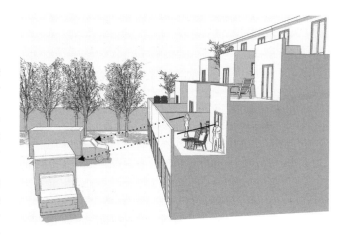

Figure 6.34 Try and find ways to reduce the impact of service areas on views from homes

OUTDOOR SPACE

Residential uses located above other types of activities can have access to outdoor space (Figure 6.35). All apartments can have balconies. Where a ground floor activity is serviced from the front, residents can have access to a rear courtyard, and where ground floor activity is serviced from the rear, then semi-private space can be

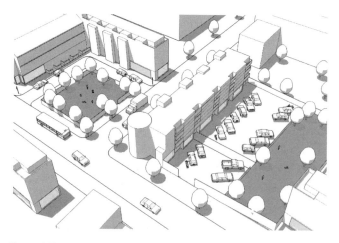

Figure 6.35 Homes above other uses can still have access to outdoor space

created beyond the service area or within a square located within the street. Within the street, outdoor space might be public or even semi-public, the latter form being common in British squares built during the 1700s and still sometimes exclusively managed and used by neighbouring residents today.

LIVE/WORK

The idea of introducing live/work units provides another opportunity for the creation of mixed uses within a scheme. The idea is not new as Europe, in particular, has a long tradition of people 'living above the shop' but it certainly appears to have been reinvented and its image transformed. The concept is relatively straightforward: that people live and work in their accommodation. The idea emerged following observation of how artists live in or next to their studio space, usually in low cost buildings. The form has subsequently emerged as a building type that is thought to be attractive to self-employed people who run small studio or office-based businesses–such as artists, craftspeople, designers or even lawyers. Live/work units could also be in the form of shops.

There is no point in suggesting live/work units unless there is a market for them–and where there is, they might take a number of forms (Figure 6.36). Some may merely include an additional workroom

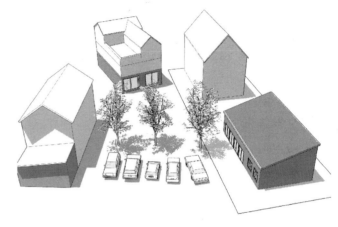

Figure 6.36   Different configurations of live and work units

within the residential space. Some may have the workspace on the ground floor and living space above. Others may involve the construction of a separate work building within the curtilage of a residential plot. Grouping such buildings might help to reinforce the distinctive character of the area and reduce any potential conflict with purely residential uses. It could also help to reduce the potential isolation that might be felt by people who don't go out to work. Planners might be reluctant to include live/work units within an exclusively residential scheme but, where a commercial area is included, it would seem reasonable to introduce live/work developments between the purely commercial or residential buildings.

OTHER BUILDING TYPES WITHIN RESIDENTIAL AREAS

Other uses common in new residential areas include community or religious buildings and kindergartens. Community and religious buildings can form a prominent traditional and meaningful focus within a layout. Where the building forms are particularly distinct, and they are located at important junctions or adjacent to significant public spaces, such buildings can make a useful orientation point within a layout (Figure 6.37) (see Chapter 7). Kindergartens often appear in European schemes where they are frequently located in separate buildings within the block structure, protected from traffic and have safe outdoor play areas (Figure 6.38).

Figure 6.37   Community or religious buildings are sometimes found at key focal points within residential areas

Figure 6.38   Kindergartens can be located within the centre of periphery blocks made up of apartments or houses. This is a protected space free of traffic.

FURTHER READING

The creation of a balanced mix of uses in neighbourhoods was addressed by Clarence Perry (1929) in his model neighbourhood unit presented in the *Regional Plan of New York*. This model remains influential today. A concise, but also influential discussion about the value of mixed uses to urban vitality and character, can be found in Jane Jacobs' (1961) *Death and Life of Great American Cities*. This thinking formed a chapter on creating variety in *Responsive Environments* (Bentley *et al.* 1985), a chapter that looks at mixed uses and considers, usefully, how their commercial viability might be tested.

During the 1990s, influenced by the emerging awareness on environmental sustainability, mixing uses became a common theme in policy and practice debates. Shankland Cox (1994), Alan Rowley (1996), Andy Coupland (1997), and the Department of Land Management of the University of Reading (1998) provide good critical reviews of the concept and its general relevance. The notion of mixing uses receives attention in the UK Government's *Planning for Sustainable Development Towards Better Practice* (Department of the Environment, Transport and the Regions, 1998b), *Towards an Urban Renaissance* (Urban Task Force, 1999), *Making Places: A guide to good practice in undertaking mixed development schemes* (English Partnerships and Urban Village Forum, 1998) and *Mixed Use Development, Practice and Potential* (Office of the Deputy Prime Minister, 2001b).

In their book exploring the concept of the sustainable urban neighbourhood, Rudlin and Falk (1999) discuss the concept of density and its relationship with promoting a greater diversity of uses. Hillier and Hanson's technique for exploring patterns of integration and segregation within the urban grid in order to predict patterns of passing trade is discussed in *The Social Logic of Space* (1984) and Hillier in *Space is the Machine* (1996).

The UK's urban village concept involved endorsing many qualities but mixing uses was one of them. The original concept is outlined in Aldous (1992) but a recent source on the concept is Neal (2003) which also reflects on how such uses might be funded. In the USA, a lot of literature exists which explains new urbanist approaches to neighbourhood planning and design, but *New Urbanism: Comprehensive report and best practices guide* offers many insights into thinking about the location and form of 'main street retail' and the use of the transect concept–written and published by New Urban News, my version is from 2001 but it has since been updated.

In a slightly more critical vein Farthing *et al.* (1996) explore the relationship between the provision of local facilities and their use, whilst Biddulph *et al.* (2003) consider, amongst other things, the viability of mixed local uses within urban villages. Biddulph (2000) and Madanipour (2001) reflect critically on contemporary neighbourhood planning concepts and the tendency to develop polycentric patterns of use.

Community buildings are an important feature of the urban landscape and might be encouraged within a scheme. Marriott (1997) provides a useful discussion of their value whilst Hudson (2000) discusses how they might be managed.

7 Safe and easy to find your way around

REAL AND PERCEIVED SAFETY

Residents should feel safe within their urban environment. They should feel comfortable within the streets and public spaces around their home, and on routes leading to neighbouring homes, shops, work or places of recreation. Feeling safe is tied up with both knowing where you are and where you are going, as well as feeling confident that, as a resident or someone passing through an area, you will not become a victim of crime.

Kevin Lynch (1961) argued that you can design the built environment so that people will be able to fully identify with their surroundings, orientate themselves and then find their way around. He wrote '{a} good environmental image gives its possessor an important sense of emotional security. He can establish a harmonious relationship between himself and the outside world. This is the obverse of the fear that comes with disorientation' (p. 5). This chapter will explore the qualities of a *good environmental image* and consider how they might be accommodated in the design of a residential area.

In addition, we will look more closely at design and safety. Statistics from different urban areas around the world show us that crime rates vary considerably. In the UK, crime rates vary between areas, although they tend to be slightly higher within urban areas (as a result of the higher number of households and people otherwise using the area) and more deprived areas, whilst certain crimes affect certain groups more; for example, violent assaults affect young males in particular. Discussion about crime is always a heavily emotive issue, but these statistics show that concern about crime shouldn't affect us equally. Despite this, a British Crime Survey points out that despite the low percentage of people who become the victims of crime, between 51% and 41% are worried about becoming a victim, whilst 13% are very worried (Dodd *et al.* 2004). Such a fear has a significant impact on people's quality of life and planners have looked to design in an effort to deal with some of these fears. In this chapter we will, therefore, consider how a concern for safety might infuence a residential layout.

KEY CONCEPTS FOR THE DESIGN OF A GOOD ENVIRONMENTAL IMAGE

A clear pattern of main streets

If you ask people to draw a map of their neighbourhood it is likely that they will start by drawing the pattern of main streets and they will try, in particular, to show how these streets connect together. Onto this pattern of main streets they will then put the minor streets and other qualities of the locality. This illustrates how important the clarity of the main streets is to a sense of orientation within a locality. A clear pattern of main streets, with direct and obvious connections to other streets, will help people make connections between one part of an environment and another, and therefore help them find their way around (Figure 7.1).

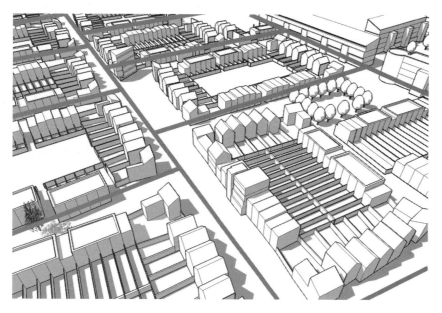

Figure 7.1   A clear pattern of main streets

It has been suggested that creating continuously clear routes may result in the loss of some of the mystery that is often enjoyed by visitors to new urban areas, and in his work Kevin Lynch (1961) recognises this. He feels, however, that despite areas of complexity, those areas should form part of a clear and coherent overall plan. As he puts it: 'The surprise must occur in an over-all framework; the confusions must be small regions in a visible whole' (Lynch 1961:6).

Nodes or focal points

Where main streets meet there is the opportunity to change the environment slightly to make it more distinctive or memorable. Within residential areas, in particular, this would allow an otherwise indistinctive place to stand out a little more. People will then be able to re-orientate and locate themselves before having to make a decision about how they should continue. Lynch (1961: 47) called these points 'nodes'–this now common jargon for part of an urban design where an important junction has received some kind of emphasis in its form in order to make it distinctive. Alternatively, such points might be referred to as 'focal points'. Within residential areas, the entrance to an area or other key junction might be emphasised by distinctive building forms or elements of landscape to make them more memorable (Figure 7.2).

Figure 7.2   A distinctive node at a road junction where the buildings and space create a special emphasis

A clear edge to a neighbourhood

It has long been recognised that people are territorial and have some sense of 'their patch' and often, although not always, physical elements define the boundaries that exist between these territories. Such territories result from economic, social, cultural or racial differences between people. Studies of housing markets, for example, highlight how one side of a street, railway or river might be highly desirable, whilst on the other, despite the close proximity, houses might be cheaper and harder to rent or sell. A study of development and change in Garston, Liverpool generated a map showing both strong and weak boundaries within the community as residents distinguished between it and neighbouring communities located on the other side of a major road and railway line, and between particular groups within the community who lived in different house types developed at different times (Figure 7.3).

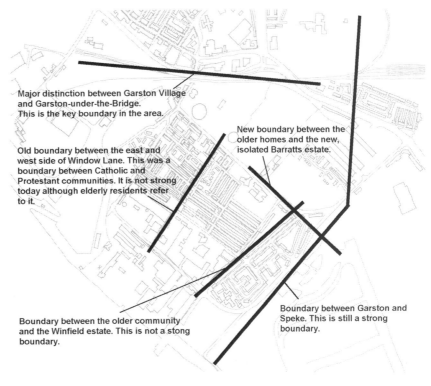

Major distinction between Garston Village and Garston-under-the-Bridge. This is the key boundary in the area.

New boundary between the older homes and the new, isolated Barratts estate.

Old boundary between the east and west side of Window Lane. This was a boundary between Catholic and Protestant communities. It is not strong today although elderly residents refer to it.

Boundary between the older community and the Winfield estate. This is not a stong boundary.

Boundary between Garston and Speke. This is still a strong boundary.

Figure 7.3   Neighbourhood boundaries in Garston, Liverpool

Whether such territories are desirable is debatable, although they would appear to be almost inevitable. However, more significant here would be to ask 'to what extent should design be used to reinforce such territories?' On the positive side, it has often been argued that these types of territories provide people with a sense of identity and belonging to their particular group or area; while on the negative side, they might inhibit interaction, maintain stereotypes and promote intolerance.

Lynch argues that roads, rivers, railway lines or open areas–like parks–can form edges which help define one area from another so that people can organise their mental image of the extent of that area. This, he states, would help people find their way around as they would know when they were entering or leaving a particular area as they came across the edge. It could be argued that all new residential neighbourhoods should have strong edges and therefore be relatively self-contained. This would allow residents to develop a sense of 'group identity'. When applied to affluent areas, this sense of identity is often exclusive–restricting access to non-residents. When applied to more deprived areas it merely allows the area to become cut-off, isolated and the subject of negative stereotyping by 'outsiders'. Edges to a neighbourhood, like major roads, might also create significant and undesirable barriers between neighbouring communities, or between communities and neighbouring facilities or amenities (Figure 7.4).

Edges therefore need to be treated carefully. There will inevitably be boundaries between areas of the built environment and, as stated above, these can be used to help people orientate themselves while providing a sense of belonging, but we should also be critical of how such edges are created to ensure that their contribution is positive.

Figure 7.4 A major road creating a significant and undesirable barrier between a neighbourhood and neighbouring facilities

Districts

Urban areas often contain districts that people recognise. Such districts may contain a particular population or, in design terms, might contain buildings from a particular period, or even of a distinctive style. Often where the character of an area is regarded as particularly positive, new developments might be designed to reinforce that character and therefore help to maintain the distinctive identity. However, where areas are homogeneous and monotonous, a design opportunity for new development might be to use a scheme to create something new and memorable that people will then proudly recognise as a distinctive new district (Figure 7.5).

Figure 7.5 New apartment buildings in the Pearl District of downtown Portland reinforce the scale and massing of existing traditional buildings within the area

Landmarks

Creating something that stands out within its context will result in a point reference within a scheme which people will find memorable, and which they will be able to use to orientate themselves. A distinctive building,

Figure 7.6   This piece of public art located within its own space helps to create a memorable point within the scheme in which it is located

structure (like a bridge), or a well-located piece of public art would form such a landmark (Figure 7.6). Such landmarks can be combined with other qualities to make them memorable; for example, a square containing a piece of public art will certainly be more distinctive. People will recognise the landmarks and use them to get a sense of position and progress, whilst hopefully the landmarks might also become popular and be used to give a positive meaning to an area.

KEY CONCEPTS FOR DESIGNING SAFE RESIDENTIAL LAYOUTS

When thinking about creating a sense of security a number of concepts help in understanding why certain design approaches might be considered.

Possibilism not Determinism

Every crime has a perpetrator and a victim, and it is important to remember that crimes occur for social and economic reasons. In other words, it is incorrect to say that the built environment causes crime, whilst it is also not correct to say that design characteristics might reinforce criminal behaviour. In other words, the relationship between the design of the built environment and criminal behaviour is not deterministic. During the last few decades, however, it has come to be recognised that the way that the urban environment is designed, and then subsequently managed, can have an impact on whether it is possible or easy for people to commit crime, or as importantly, whether people feel that they are safe within an area. There is, however, less consensus about how safe environments might be designed, whilst some also point out that too much emphasis on merely creating safe environments undermines the extent to which other urban design qualities might be achieved. A good urban designer should be aware of the issues and approaches, while being able to design in a balanced way to ensure that a range of qualities is achieved.

Territoriality and defensible space

A design of the built environment can create, in residents, a sense of responsibility and control for a defined area if particular qualities are achieved. Oscar Newman (1972) called this 'defensible space'. In his research, he explored the extent to which residents felt they had control over the spaces within and around 14-storey apartment buildings in deprived housing projects in New York. Using the categories of space that were defined in Chapter 3, he found that between the public streets and the private apartments were extensive areas of semi-public space that individual residents didn't feel that they had any control over (Figure 7.7). In practical terms, because of a lack of control this meant that anyone could wander off the street, into the buildings, into a lift and along a corridor without anyone knowing who they were or why they might be there. Such a situation can be compared to that of a traditional house on the street (Figure 7.8). Many houses typically have clear boundaries, and it is easy for residents to have a sense of control over who might be visiting. Some apartments located on streets have entrance-controlling devices or staff who monitor who enters the building. In both of the latter examples, due to the clear distinction between public and (semi) private space, and the adoption of special management measures, residents feel a sense of control or responsibility over the comings and goings within spaces immediately beyond their home, and would know when to call for help should something unacceptable be observed.

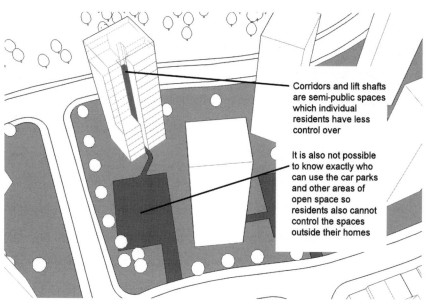

Corridors and lift shafts are semi-public spaces which individual residents have less control over

It is also not possible to know exactly who can use the car parks and other areas of open space so residents also cannot control the spaces outside their homes

Figure 7.7   The shaded areas highlight the lift areas and outdoor spaces that residents don't feel that they have much control over

Figure 7.8   The shaded area highlights the area of semi-private defensible space in front of the traditional house on the street that residents find easy to control

Opportunities for surveillance

Surveillance is the opportunity for people to observe the activities occurring within a place. While in their homes, residents can observe the activities going on in the street immediately outside–just as people coming and going within the street can passively observe the homes and their front gardens (Figure 7.9). Jane Jacobs (1961: 45) referred to this as the quality of 'eyes on the street'. In terms of security these 'eyes' help to reinforce the social norms of what might be acceptable behaviour within a street–you wouldn't break into a house or a car knowing that people were watching you.

Signs of life

Desolate or little-used streets feel less friendly and safe than populated streets where people are going about their daily lives. Residents generate signs of life within their own homes. However, as important, if not more important, are the passing strangers using routes as part of their daily life. To ensure a reasonable degree of coming and going, it is important to ensure that key routes through a scheme link important destinations, and that most streets and open spaces within a scheme are only a few turns away from these key streets. Activity within streets is also generated by having entrances to buildings, whilst windows provide an opportunity for surveillance from within homes. Surveillance is inhibited, however, by blank walls or garages, ground floor parking, extensive dense landscaping, changes of level that take pedestrians away from ground level, high-rise buildings where residents can't see the street clearly and/or the general distance between homes and the street (Figure 7.10).

Target hardening

This refers to the activity of stopping access to particular parts of a development with the use of physical measures such as strong doors, locks, bars, security phones and gates. It could also refer to the adoption of special management techniques,

Figure 7.9   Surveillance is when people in their homes can observe the coming and going in the street and the people in the street can observe the homes and front gardens

Figure 7.10   Opportunities for surveillance are reduced by (a) blank walls or garages (b) ground floor parking (c) extensive and dense landscaping (d) changes in level (e) high rise schemes where residents are remote from neighbouring streets (f) distance between homes and neighbouring public spaces

such as the employment of security guards or the use of cctv cameras. Target hardening is typically beyond the scope of urban design, although the configuration of housing might encourage a particular approach to target hardening being adopted.

Conflicting approaches

Writers on safety and design have adopted varied approaches to how design might be considered, reflecting very different attitudes that the writers have to the public and the private realm within schemes. During the 1980s, authors tended to focus heavily on the need to ensure the safety of residents in their own home, whilst showing less concern for the safety of people–especially pedestrians–coming and going in neighbourhood streets. Some authors also tended to argue that the purpose of design should be to exclude non-residents from schemes in order to make the areas more secure and exclusive whilst reducing what the police refer to as 'potential escape routes'. More recently, theorists have begun to view this same group of people as being the 'eyes on the street', creating vitality and a greater perceived sense of safety. The purpose of design is therefore to ensure that residential areas are fully integrated with neighbouring areas so that they aren't cut off, but instead have an appropriate degree of coming and going along residential streets.

The former approach resulted in a limiting of through routes and promoted the use of cul-de-sacs and enclaves within residential areas. In addition, the advice suggested that all access roads, open spaces and commercial areas should not be fronted by housing, as their 'publicness' might result in antisocial behaviour. The continuation of this thinking has also resulted in the proliferation of gated residential areas in more recent years (Figure 7.11). The alternative approach now recognises the wider urban

Figure 7.11   Gated communities are becoming a common feature of the urban townscape. They create security by excluding non-residents

design agenda by encouraging permeable through routes that the public can use, whilst all open spaces and commercial areas should be fully integrated into schemes, and fronted by residential developments. In this way,

Figure 7.12   Permeable street patterns use the presence of the public in clearly defined streets to create a sense of security for residents and other users of the space

the public spaces are populated, feel safer and there is mutual surveillance between building and space users (Figure 7.12).

APPROACHES TO LAYOUT DESIGN TO ENHANCE THE ENVIRONMENTAL IMAGE

Create views to somewhere

Long winding streets are a common feature of housing in many layouts. In some earlier designs, it was thought that, by not allowing people to see a destination straight in front of them, non-residents might be put off entering an area. However, such designs often result in visitors arriving in an area unsure of where they should be going, and the constantly changing route makes it difficult for them to work out which direction they might be facing (Figure 7.13).

In addition, such housing configurations can be overly complex and result in a labyrinthine quality. People will generally know how to find their way around if their destination is just a few turns away from a main route through a town or city. However, if housing schemes result in too many turns down different

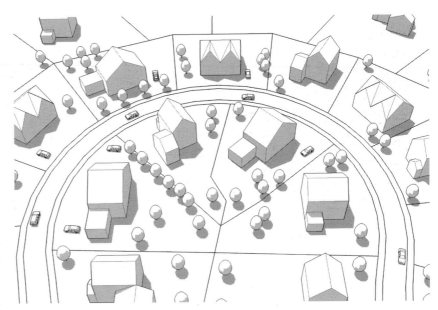

Figure 7.13   Winding routes can be disorientating

roads towards the required destination, then it will be harder to find–and the streets located deep within the scheme will be less well-used by people coming and going. As the streets will feel under-populated, they will feel less safe, and residents may possibly feel it necessary to worry about why non-residents might be in the area (Figure 7.14).

Rather than using winding routes, therefore–and to help people find their way around–it is important to compose the built form of a residential area so that visitors get a sense of where they are going, and what potential connections might be possible via particular routes. For the larger routes linking through a neighbourhood, it is important that views are directional and create a feeling of linkage so that people can have a sense of the routes that connect the areas of the neighbourhood together (Figure 7.15).

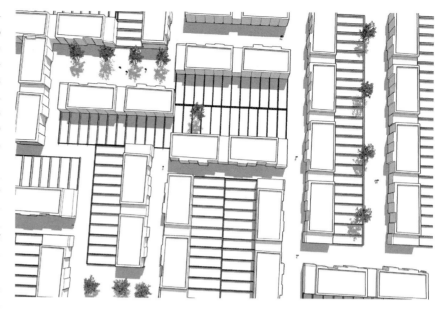

Figure 7.14   Some housing layouts can be overly complicated and so they will be less well used by people coming and going

Figure 7.15   Housing schemes should be composed so that routes appear to connect to somewhere

Design 'shallow' schemes

Building on the above theme it is equally important to make sure that all parts of the housing scheme are a short distance away from a main route so that the labyrinthine design is avoided; people wishing to find a particular residence, can use these main routes for guidance. They will remember the one, two or possibly three turns they made from such a street once they leave it, but four or five turns–especially if the housing area is featureless–might be more difficult to retread, whilst with every turn the street will probably feel less populated and more isolated (Figure 7.16). 'Shallow' schemes will still be quiet enough for residential purposes, as traffic will drop off very quickly as they turn from a main route, but still enough coming and going will occur to allow residents to feel secure.

Use topography

The natural topography of an area can form a distinctive quality that, in hilly areas in particular, will give a distinctive form and character to settlements. It can also help people to orientate themselves. It is important not to ignore topography, or build comprehensive schemes that flatten, and therefore make the form of an area indistinct. It is also cheaper to build along contours and this will help reinforce the form of hills, although clearly routes straight up hills will create a memorable drama that will reinforce the summits. Taller buildings on summits can also exploit valuable views and help to reinforce the topography (Figure 7.17), although in contrast, open spaces located at summits can

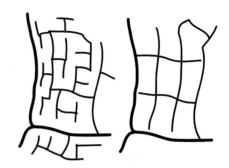

Figure 7.16 The scheme on the right is shallower than the scheme on the left as it requires people to turn less corners to reach their destination

Figure 7.17 In San Francisco the dramatic topography gives character to the grid whilst taller buildings form landmarks on summits

offer residents an important amenity where they can enjoy views out over the wider landscape as well as orientate themselves relative to other landmarks. It is also important to analyse the potential views across a landscape back to the housing so that the form of the settlement appears attractive in the landscape. Views backing the housing should also be considered so that the form of the settlement appears attractive in the landscape.

Create areas of character

The uncritical use of standard house types, and conformity to strict high-way and amenity standards, can create areas of residential development that are indistinguishable from other areas. When these areas are large, it is particularly difficult to distinguish one from another and so residents, and especially visitors, often lose their way (Figure 7.18).

Figure 7.18   Indistinguishable housing is disorientating and boring

When planning residential developments developers or builders have the chance to create distinctive forms of housing that will distinguish one residential neighbourhood from another. This can be achieved through the types of buildings that are erected. It may be desirable to echo some of the qualities of an existing location through the careful use of materials or the form of the buildings already there. In new areas, however, it might be desirable to establish a distinctive and new architectural style or character that helps distinguish one neighbourhood from the next (Figure 7.19).

Figure 7.19   Districts will be more memorable if the design of the area results in a distinctive character

Form and scale to suit the role of the street

The section and plan of the street should ensure that its form and scale reflect its position in the urban hierarchy. The more important routes should have a larger scale, possibly be wider and a little more formal. These urban streets should readily link together with main neighbourhoods, and form the principal routes though the area. In contrast, the smaller streets and spaces serving fewer houses can have a more intimate scale and a more informal form so that it is easy to understand that they serve a more local function (Figure 7.20).

Figure 7.20   In Malmo Sweden the streets and public spaces have a variety of forms and scales to suit their position within the urban hierarchy

Focal points

Creating focal points within a scheme will give it structure and variety, especially if they reflect the position of the feature in the urban hierarchy. For example, the larger urban parks and the larger scale squares and crescents are most appropriately used as memorable focal points (or areas) linking the main routes together (Figure 7.21), whilst the small-scale

Figure 7.21   Major focal points on the major streets

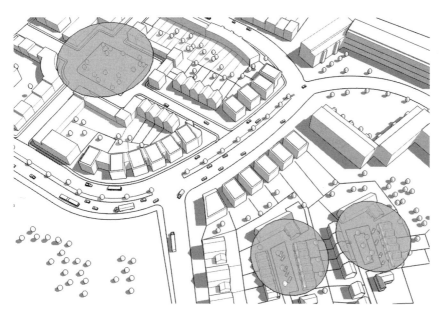

Figure 7.22   Minor focal points on the minor streets

squares, courtyards and informal play areas would be features of the smaller and quieter routes (Figure 7.22). These 'nodes' should be distinctive as they will help people to distinguish one area of a scheme or junction from another as they pass through.

Using local and new landmarks

Established urban areas often contain existing local landmarks that help people orientate themselves within a scheme. Features such as distinctive buildings or monuments can close views, and be located in the new focal points as landmarks integrated into the scheme (Figure 7.23). Views to distant landmarks can also be exploited to make connections across a

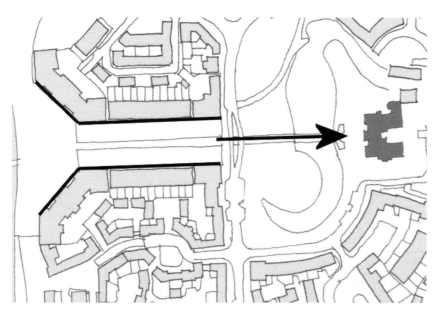

Figure 7.23   If possible use local landmarks at focal points to draw attention to them and help people orientate themselves

settlement. Alternatively, new land-marks, such as distinctive building types or pieces of art, might be used to mark a particular point in a scheme in the hope that they might be noticed and, through its distinctiveness, allow people to mark their location.

Using landscape

Key features of the hard and soft land-scape can also be used, not only to give distinction to areas of a scheme, but also to help give structure to a res-idential area. The retention of existing trees, for example, can help give a maturity to an area while, at the same time, making the area memorable and distinctive (Figure 7.24), while new trees can make specific routes distinctive by, for example, using boule-varding to highlight them (Figure 7.25). In a similar way, the integration of a stream or river into the public realm will make specific areas along the edge distinctive from neighbouring streets (Figure 7.26).

Figure 7.24   Retaining existing landscaping can make new schemes seem mature whilst also making them memorable

Figure 7.25   Boulevarding of trees can help to reinforce either major or minor routes

Figure 7.26   Integrating a river or stream into a scheme will help to make the area distinctive and popular

Coherent but permeable edges

Where a river or green open space forms an edge to a neighbourhood, it is possible to exploit the valuable views available by building the development along the frontage to form a clearly visible edge between one neighbourhood and the next. Such an edge, if its façades are given special attention, might reinforce the character of the open space or river, thus providing a sense of arrival in the neighbourhood (Figure 7.27). However, it is important to manage the accessibility into the neighbourhood so that the edge does not create an impermeable and, therefore, exclusive boundary between one area and the next, as social or economic polarisation may be the unfortunate consequence.

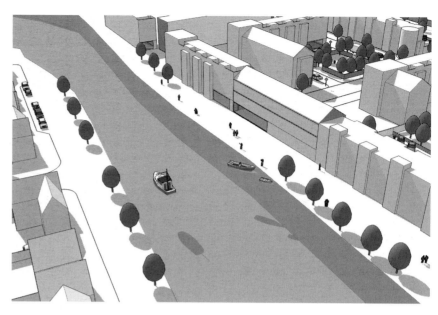

Figure 7.27   This riverside has coherent edges but the lack of a crossing means that the neighbouring communities could be isolated from each other

Similarly, where a busier route or railway line forms an edge to a neighbourhood, it is necessary to ensure that pedestrians and cyclists, in particular, have clear opportunities to make direct connections across the road or line to link with neighbouring areas and facilities. This way, the edge doesn't become a negative quality that isolates residents within a particular area (Figure 7.28).

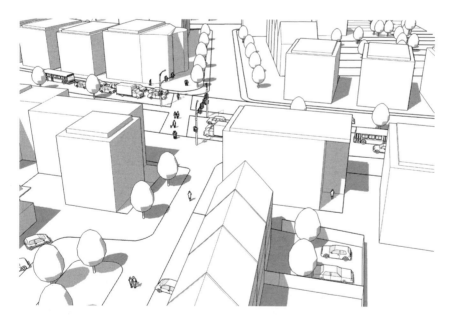

Figure 7.28   Pedestrians and cyclists need special facilities to help them cross busier routes between neighbourhoods

Pedestrians and vehicles together

Learning from the experiences of attempts to segregate pedestrians from vehicles, we now know that in general pedestrians feel safer and can orientate themselves better on traditional streets, even if this means mixing

Figure 7.29   We now know that pedestrians can orientate themselves better on traditional streets even if they have to mix with traffic

with traffic (Figure 7.29). This means that segregated deck access routes, underpasses and back alleys should be less common unless they serve a particular function within a small part of a scheme.

Locating key public uses

General activity and the sense of vitality associated with commercial activity, community buildings or schools, will allow certain areas of a scheme be distinctive and recognisable. These areas should be located along key routes and at key focal points of a scheme to make those points more memorable, whilst the more distinctive building forms might also help to form local landmarks (Figure 7.30).

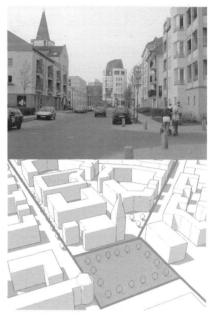

Figure 7.30   Locate key public uses along the main routes or at focal points to make these points more memorable whilst the different building forms will create useful landmarks

APPROACHES TO LAYOUT DESIGN TO ENHANCE FEELINGS OF SAFETY

Create connections to provide some vitality

The new community will need to connect with existing sources of pedestrian activity in order to facilitate movement between them. In particular, useful routes to local destinations, such as shops, open spaces or other community facilities, should be considered–this may not be easy, as existing residents may not want people from new housing schemes using what they might regard as 'their' streets. However, creating as much connectivity as possible should be the aspiration, particularly as the new residents will become the 'eyes of the street', thus providing extra surveillance of both streets and public space activity and ensuring more security within the neighbourhood.

Don't design roads without frontage

As a result of both previous design advice relating to safety *and* highways standards, it has been common practice for houses to face away from the distributor roads which serve a residential area. Generally, the backs of these properties abut important public spaces, often surrounded by high fences or walls, thus creating privacy for the residents (Figure 7.31). The

Figure 7.31   An example of access without frontage

impact of such an arrangement for the house owner is that the garden is directly adjacent to a road, and all the noise and pollution that might be associated with that. In addition, the garden is vulnerable, as a thief can quickly scale the fence at the rear of the property. For a pedestrian walking along such a road, the environment is equally poor as there is no surveillance of the space from neighbouring homes, whilst the extensive areas of back fences can be disorientating, as each fence looks like another. In general, therefore, it is important to make sure that the fronts of houses face the main public routes, whilst the backs are contained within the urban block where they are quiet and more secure.

Ensure that cul-de-sacs don't limit the choice of safe routes for pedestrians

A criticism of the use of cul-de-sacs is that they limit the route options available to pedestrians when they feel intimidated by other people using the same route. Essentially, the pedestrian has no opportunity to make a detour away from someone they would rather not meet. It is therefore important to judge whether pedestrians have a choice of safe routes to their destination. Traditional, regular, and deformed grids offer this choice as this allows for two routes around the block and, where they must be used, cul-de-sacs should be kept short and make only a limited contribution to the accessibility of an area (Figure 7.32). This design is ideal for the police in patrol cars as they readily drive

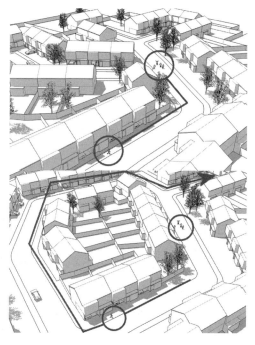

Figure 7.32   Cul-de-sacs can limit escape routes

through routes that connect together, whilst cul-de-sacs would require them to constantly retrace their route.

Don't design public spaces without frontage

Resulting from a theory that public spaces might be a focus for antisocial behaviour, you might find housing areas with public spaces that have no surveillance as the neighbouring houses face away from them. This is a self-fulfilling prophecy as if the houses have nothing to do with neighbouring spaces these spaces may become more vulnerable to antisocial behaviour. Although the more likely scenario would be that they will merely feel unsafe and become underused by the very people that they were put there to serve (Figure 7.33).

Figure 7.33   Resulting from the theory that public space might become a focus for antisocial behaviour homes face away from such spaces making them underused and therefore seem less safe

Avoid windowless elevations to footpaths and parking areas

Within the details of a scheme, it is important to ensure that blank elevations do not occur, particularly along footpaths or onto parking areas. People will feel safer using a footpath that is over-looked directly by neighbouring properties; whilst residents will want to be able to look out of their houses at the areas where their cars are parked (Figure 7.34).

Figure 7.34   Poor ground floor and limited first floor surveillance of this path makes it feel less secure

In the UK it is quite common to have small parking courts off the street, behind the urban block. Such courtyards often contain individual houses or flats above garages, thus ensuring some modicum of surveillance of the space, whilst the residents in these homes also have a relatively quiet corner in which they live (Figure 7.35). Alternatively, small courts of about six cars to the rear of properties, but without such surveillance, might be typically gated so that only residents have access (Figure 7.36).

Figure 7.35   Individual houses located within parking courts can provide some surveillance of the parking area whilst also being in a quiet location away from the street

Figure 7.36   Small parking courts to the rear of homes can be gated for additional security

Create a clear distinction between public and private areas

The notion of defensible space reminds us that people feel more secure where there is a clear distinction made between public and (semi) private spaces, and where the difference is reinforced by a sensible boundary. Where no clear distinction exists the result might be that the public wander into areas considered private; and the residents will feel that they have no, or little, control over this. The layout of residential areas should clearly distinguish between public streets and other types of public space, and the private land associated with housing or apartments. This should be clear from the pattern of development, from the sensible use of walls, gates or fences used to distinguish the relative areas, and the use of entrance control measures, such as intercom and security door systems, used to manage access more closely (Figure 7.37).

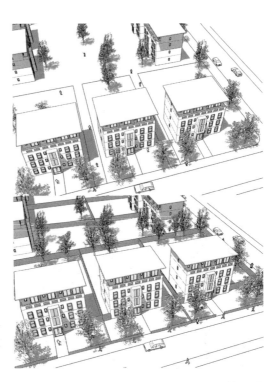

Figure 7.37   Create a clear distinction between public and private space

Think carefully about the long-term implications of gated communities

As a reaction to fear of crime, but also an aspiration to live in exclusive environments, gated communities are becoming a common feature of some urban areas. Such communities are developed either as exclusive residential areas with gated access and security built-in as part of the original design (Figure 7.38); or they may have previously

Figure 7.38   Think carefully about the long term implications of gated communities

been open neighbourhoods where existing routes have been closed off, with only a gated main entrance used for access. Both types of development appear to be typical of societies where there is a significant disparity of wealth between people. Apart from improving security, the gating can allow residents to manage the provision of some services, such as street lighting, as well as the maintenance of green open spaces. Typically, these communities create immediate auto-dependency as people have to come and go by car as routes between the communities and shops and services are significantly longer, whilst routes and spaces neighbouring these developments often have no surveillance and may feel intimidating to pedestrians. Such auto-dependency shifts the nature of shopping and community service provision to a coarse grain, suited to exclusive car travel and it is likely that smaller shops will not survive. Non-residents must also travel a long way in order to get around such communities. Such developments also force traffic onto a more limited number of routes, thus further reducing the quality of those routes and creating congestion at certain times of the day. Having to go through barriers can also be intimidating for non-residents, and incidental social contact becomes harder as all visits to the area must be planned and purposeful. Therefore, the provision of extensive areas of gated communities fundamentally alters the nature of urban areas and urban life and is an extreme example of the theory that all non-residents are treated as potential criminals often excluded from what were formally public areas.

Use back alleys and underpasses carefully

The desire to improve access for pedestrians in residential areas might result in the introduction of back alleys or underpasses to roads. Back alleys were a common feature of residential developments in the UK, for example, during the eighteen and nineteenth century. They provided rear access to gardens, stables and garages. More recently, it has been realised that the lack of surveillance in back alleys can make them feel unsafe, whilst they can also be used for dumping and other types of antisocial behaviour. The lack of investment to the backs of properties and their boundaries can mean that they look shabby over time. The police also view back alleys as potential escape routes for criminals and, where security is a particular problem, back alleys have been removed or gated. In this way, residents have a greater degree of control over who comes and goes within them. In general it is not recommended to require or encourage pedestrians to use back alleys (Figure 7.39).

Figure 7.39   Back alleys can be viewed as problematic although they provide useful rear access to homes and gardens

Underpasses might create a similarly poor quality of environment. Resulting from the generally good intention of separating pedestrians from vehicles, underpasses take pedestrians away from the normal surveillance of neighbouring buildings and passing traffic. Where underpasses are always busy they might be a success, but where their use is sporadic it is more than likely that they will be unpopular as they will feel less safe (Figure 7.40). In general, it is better to offer pedestrians crossing facilities at ground level, particularly in residential areas where most roads will not be that busy.

Use deck access carefully

The idea of separating pedestrians from vehicles was a dominant design idea during the 1960s and 1970s as it was thought that pedestrian routes would then be safer. Typically, however, pedestrians were put in deck environments above ground level. Such deck environments can be extensive, but lack distinctive features. They often have unattractive stairwells and lifts as well as poor surveillance from neighbouring homes, and limit pedestrian choice to prescribed routes. Neighbouring residents often feel they lack control over what goes on within them, whilst the decks and access ramps often form an unattractive feature. Such decks are also very expensive to provide. Away from the decks, the ground floor environment typically becomes dominated by roads and garage environments that can also feel unsafe, resulting in the lack of human contact (Figure 7.41). Deck access is not, therefore, a recommended form of access for large parts of a residential scheme, although it might be reasonable for smaller individual buildings.

Figure 7.40   When they are used a lot by pedestrians underpasses might be a success but where their use is sporadic they are more likely to be unpopular as they will feel less safe

Figure 7.41   Comprehensive deck access developments tend to create depressing, insecure and inconvenient pedestrian environments leaving the ground floor to become dominated by traffic

Don't create a dominating landscape

A common feature of some residential areas from the 1960s and 1970s in the UK was the provision of extensive natural landscaping strips along routes into urban areas and between residential neighbourhoods. Often, if the fronts of properties faced away from the principal access roads, then between the neighbourhoods the landscaping was the most dominant feature of the environment. These strips were typically dense 'buffers' used to reduce the visual impact of the road from neighbouring properties. The result, however, is particularly disorientating, as the landscape character of the route doesn't change, leaving one part of the environment to look exactly like another (Figure 7.42). Natural landscaping within urban areas is important, but it shouldn't replace surveillance of public spaces by people from neighbouring properties; whilst its character should also vary so that there is interest and to help people find their way around.

Don't design blind corners and bad lighting

Pedestrians are particularly affected by the detailed qualities of a layout, and small areas can feel less safe if they are not carefully designed. Blind corners can be particularly intimidating where a high wall or landscaping might make people feel isolated and unable to see what is around a corner (Figure 7.43). Areas with bad lighting will also feel intimidating, so it is necessary to light streets and pedestrian routes running through open spaces. These small areas are important. Whilst streets may generally feel safe, if small areas connecting the streets together feel intimidating, then pedestrians will avoid them, thereby missing the necessary connections between one neighbourhood and the next (Figure 7.44).

Locate utility meters within the public realm

Locating gas, electricity or water meters in the public realm reduces the likelihood of bogus callers. They are also easily accessible for meter readers. It is important to ensure, however, that such meters are attractively integrated into façades,

Figure 7.42 Principal access roads dominated by landscaping can be disorientating

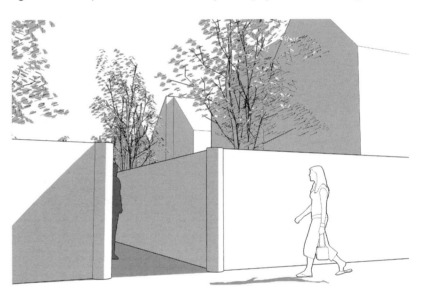

Figure 7.43 Blind corners shouldn't be introduced

Figure 7.44 Lighting should extend through important open spaces

or located at ground level, so that they don't dominate the view of the building (Figure 7.45).

Don't design features that will help thieves gain access to the upper floors of a property

It is important that outbuildings, porches, garages and flat-roofed extensions don't combine to form climbing aids for a would-be thief to easily gain access to the upper floors of a property (Figure 7.46)!

Figure 7.45   Meters should be located in the public realm to reduce the incidence of bogus callers but rather than dominating façades (above) they can be located and integrated more sensitively

Figure 7.46   Outbuildings, porches, garages and flat-roofed extensions should not combine to provide access to upper floors

FURTHER READING

Lynch (1961) introduced us to the concept of *imageability* and helped designers to start thinking about the qualities of an area that might help people find their way around. Bentley *et al.* (1985) elaborate on these points by reinforcing the concept of *legibility* in urban design jargon.

Writing about security and urban design is sometimes frustrating, as the analysis is often reductive, focusing exclusively on security issues and ignoring the whole range of other issues that might inform how you design a place. Crowe's (2000) book *Crime Prevention Through Environmental Design* is of this nature, although it usefully considers strategies for dealing with crime through design in a variety of contexts. Similarly, Coleman's (1985) *Utopia on Trial* explores why certain parts of housing schemes might be the target of vandalism and other forms of social malaise, and suggests remedial action. Writing that retains a more holistic view of planning and design includes Jane Jacob's (1961) *Death and Life of Great American Cities*, which introduces the notion of 'eyes on the street' and the idea that a well-used sidewalk is also likely to feel like a safe one. Also holistic in its view is Bill Hillier's (1996) work on space syntax, which also contains a strong concern for security. In *Space is the Machine* his chapter entitled 'Can architecture cause social malaise?' reviews important work on the relationship between urban grids, patterns of connectivity and integration and incidences of crime or feelings of safety. In *Defensible Space* Oscar Newman (1972) introduces the concept of the same name; a concept which has been influential, although Hillier is critical of it. Authors like Poyner and Webb (1991) (*Crime Free Housing*) and Stollard (1991) (*Crime Prevention Through Housing Design*) have turned concepts into more specific advice about how to layout housing, although they tend to focus on defending the home and, being written in the early 1990s, parts of it can be a little out of date. A more recent guide by the UK Government *Safer Places* (Office of the Deputy Prime Minister/Home Office, 2004) offers more up-to-date advice and includes reference to a range of environments including housing.

8 Contemporary residential townscape

INTRODUCTION

A townscape results from the conscious or unconscious bringing together of buildings and landscape to create the new urban scene. Attractive residential areas are always popular. Cullen (1961:7) argues both that planning a townscape is a distinctive art that should be consciously considered, and that it should be done so that the visual interplay between landscape, buildings and space can release a particular type of drama or distinctive residential character. As urban designers, therefore, we should be concerned about the quality of the urban scene resulting from our designs.

Compare the two sets of townscapes shown in Figures 8.1 and 8.2 to get some idea of what townscape might be about. The first residential area shows a standard house builder scheme (Figure 8.1). It could essentially be anywhere in the UK. The roads are standardised, the houses are standardised, the materials for fences and pavements are standardised and the elements of the scene are composed without any concern for how they might visually fit together. As you pass through the scheme, nothing varies. The result, visually, is a jumble of nothing. It is the same jumble of nothing that you might visit on the edge of Southampton, Swindon, Stoke-on-Trent, Stockport, Stockton or Stirling. It is what Relph (1976) calls a 'placeless' development.

The second image shows a housing scheme where the urban scene

Figure 8.1 Standardised house builder's scheme with no regard for designing place

Figure 8.2 Conscious place making in the design of a residential area

would appear to have been more consciously considered (Figure 8.2). As you pass through the scheme the houses are more original and composed with a unified, but varying form. Their layout defines a variety of distinctive spaces. The buildings and landscape are also carefully detailed while adding a richness to each emerging view. The result is a series of places. On one level, this is like no other housing scheme. On another level, the scheme contains many distinctive areas that the designers have tried to make unique and interesting–in other words, distinctive places within the scheme.

TRADITIONS IN TOWNSCAPE

Considering the form that townscapes have historically taken it is possible to identify two broad traditions, one is informal and the other is formal.

Informal townscape

The incremental growth and development of older villages and towns has often resulted in informal townscapes. They typically contain a wide range of space and building types and building materials. They have also developed a complex informal visual rhythm within the street scene into which these individual elements fit (Figure 8.3). Sharp (1968:13) tried to describe this quality as follows: '…variety that is not so much of contrast but variety within the same kind, variety within an established rhythm, variety (one might almost say) within similarity, within a broad unity of character.'

Often this variety emerged for functional, rather than aesthetic, reasons. The availability of narrow sites or local finance for building, the piecemeal nature of development, traditional building techniques and technologies, the availability of materials, building skills or building regulations might all be used to explain the characteristic townscapes that have emerged. Consequently, however, whilst these explanations have disappeared, the forms that resulted remain, and the concern for townscape has encouraged planners, developers and designers to seek ways to recreate these forms within newer schemes.

Figure 8.3   Traditional townscapes have often developed a complex informal visual rhythm within the street scene into which these individual elements fit

Formal townscape

Typically developed at a moment in time, the beauty of a formal townscape requires a different vocabulary and set of concerns for both its design and then subsequent appreciation. Moughtin (1992) celebrates the qualities of order, unity, proportion, scale, symmetry, balance, rhythm and contrast in his celebration of formal townscapes. Although informal townscapes might have some of these qualities within the individual buildings, it is at the scale of the larger set piece plan that the formal townscape comes into its own (Figure 8.4a–g).

If we want to discuss the qualities of a formal townscape then this language would provide us with a starting point, just as the concepts would provide us with direction in designing such a plan. The most formal townscapes require a tremendous amount of control in their planning and development, but historic precedents are still celebrated and can inform contemporary design thinking, even if they are not to be imitated (Figure 8.5).

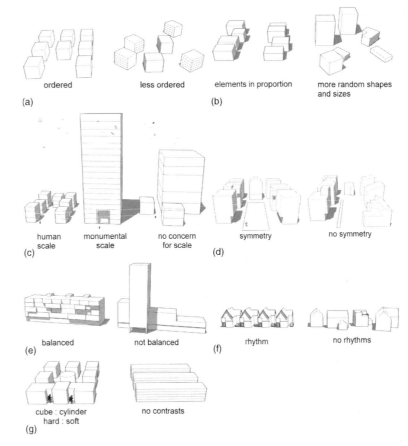

Figure 8.4   (a) order and unity (b) proportion (c) scale (d) symmetry (e) balance (f) rhythm (g) contrast

Figure 8.5   The formal townscape of Edinburgh New Town is evident in its plan

The contemporary townscape

Contemporary townscapes rarely mimic historic precedents, whilst they also rarely conform doggedly to either a formal or informal tradition. The use of planning documents such as design codes or master plans often tries to conceive ways in which the visual relationship between buildings might be shaped, whilst developers of larger schemes can certainly try and consciously manage the areas of the scheme to allow a variety of either formal or informal townscape characteristics to emerge. The layouts in Figure 8.6 show a range of both formal and informal contemporary forms of development that suggest that our new townscapes could and should take any number of forms.

Figure 8.6   Contemporary residential townscapes

TOWNSCAPE CONCEPTS

Townscape concepts have remained relatively stable since the original development of the theme during the 1950s and 1960s. Given that we are interested in design, it is, thankfully, a subjective area so the concepts suggest a direction for thinking, appreciation and practice, but they don't try to dictate how you should respond in any given situation, and they certainly don't dictate design solutions.

In formulating his approach, Cullen (1961) started from the principle that we can learn from an appreciation of townscape precedents by categorising repeating themes in the way that townscapes are composed. We will use three themes from townscape thinking that seem to be valuable: (1) specific approaches to composing a visual drama, (2) a concern for the content of a place, (3) and a conscious regard for what is called 'serial vision'. In addition, we may be interested in reflecting within our design something of the town–or even landscape qualities of the region, town or site. As such, we should also reflect on specific approaches to context character analysis that might shape our adopted designs.

LEARNING FROM TOWNSCAPE PRECEDENTS

As with many of the themes and issues considered in this book, it is extremely valuable to collect examples of precedents to inform your appreciation and thinking, as well as to allow you to reflect on what you want to realise within your designs. Precedents in townscape allow us to consider the various qualities that have been achieved in the past, so it is always useful to sketch or take pictures of impressive views created by the layout of buildings and spaces within the landscape so that something of these qualities might be pursued in future work. As important as the general perspective view, however, is the need to analyse the plans, sections and content to appreciate what it is about the forms of the three-dimensional solids and voids, as well as the materiality of the views, that gives them character (Figure 8.7). Themes for such an analysis are discussed in the following sections.

Figure 8.7   Studying townscape precedents can help generate an appreciation of how areas of character are composed

COMPOSING A VISUAL DRAMA

The notion of place in townscape thinking is relatively narrow, but still useful for a designer. The simple idea is that a place is created when a person can get within a distinctive space created between a group of buildings, and that townscape design should be about the creation of a multiplicity of such places within a scheme (Figure 8.8). The juxtaposition of built and natural elements should help to give a place an individual character so that a person can define their location in one part of a scheme relative to others. This is in some respects a similar notion to those offered in legibility analysis, although the balance of concern is shifted away from the rather functional notion of 'way finding' to embrace a richer (and particularly visual) aesthetic response which is derived from the drama, distinction or beauty of the townscape composition.

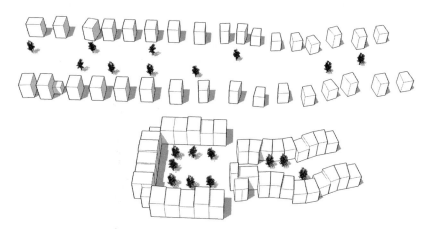

Figure 8.8   Places are formed when designers put the elements of the environment together to create distinctive spaces

Townscape theory has often sought to characterise and bring to our attention ways in which the composition of the built environment repeatedly achieves certain qualities within a place. They don't prescribe in any detail how such issues might be addressed in contemporary schemes, nor would it be reasonable to suggest that this is an exhaustive list, but they do draw our attention to ways in which we might both define and then sensitively design the townscape of a residential area.

Using landscape and natural features

A development site may have a distinctive position within the natural landscape that could lead to special urban design considerations. It is common, if sites can be viewed from a distance, to judge how the development might contribute to views of the broader urban environment within its natural setting. All local areas will have traditions for how housing is seen within its natural setting and these should be researched through the study of views. However, a number of general suggestions might be useful to show how the theme might be approached:

- Ridge lines are often protected so that the natural profile of the land remains visible (Figure 8.9)
- Urban areas tend to appear relatively compact and visually coherent, rather than sprawling into the open countryside (Figure 8.10)
- Contours can generally be followed so that the form of development reinforces the profile of the land (Figure 8.11)

Figure 8.9   Protect the views of ridge lines

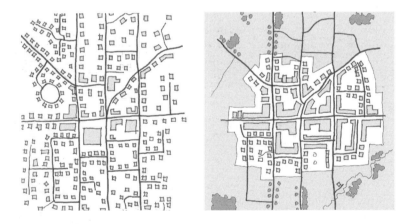

Figure 8.10   Urban areas should try to be compact

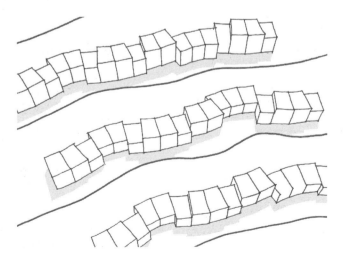

Figure 8.11   Contours can be followed so that development reinforces the profile of the land

- Natural features such as rivers and valleys can be reinforced by the form, scale and massing of development and remain visible, rather than views of them being broken up or built over (Figure 8.12)
- Development schemes can foreground mature hedges and tree planting so that the housing is seen within a natural setting, rather than appearing as a hard intrusion within the landscape (Figure 8.13)
- High points can be protected from development to allow people access to enjoy longer views (Figure 8.14), or they can be built up to a greater height to allow the profile of the urban area to be more dramatic and reinforce the topography (See Figure 7.17)
- Buildings and roof lines might step down slopes rather then appearing as singular and therefore more bulky units, whilst terracing along the contour could be broken or roof lines varied to allow the housing to echo the slope more closely (Figure 8.15).

In general, the aims of the approach adopted are: to maintain the topographical and natural character and integrity of the landscape; allow the housing to appear as a part of, or within that landscape; and to ensure that the housing shows a positive face to its wider context.

Figure 8.12   Respect and integrate natural features

Figure 8.13   Foregrounding natural elements might help a scheme to fit into its landscape when viewed from a distance

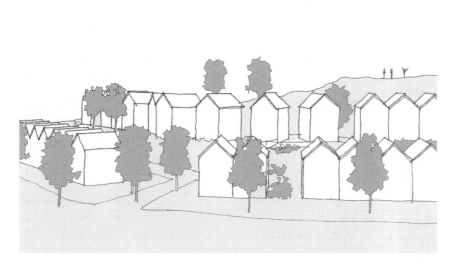

Figure 8.14   High points can be protected from development so that people have access to long views

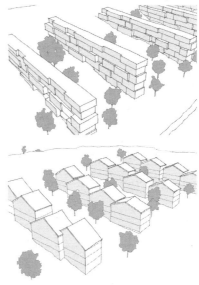

Figure 8.15   Buildings and rooflines can step down slopes to help reinforce topography (bottom)

Strategic views

Within certain locations, it might be possible to recognise strategic views across a landscape or within an urban environment. Such views might be towards landmark buildings such as churches or other civic buildings. It might be a view from within the town to the countryside beyond. It might be a view along a landscape corridor to open countryside or towards the sea. Such views will be important to local people generally and offer significant enjoyment. These should be protected from, or be framed by, developments that should contribute to, but not detract from, the view (Figure 8.16).

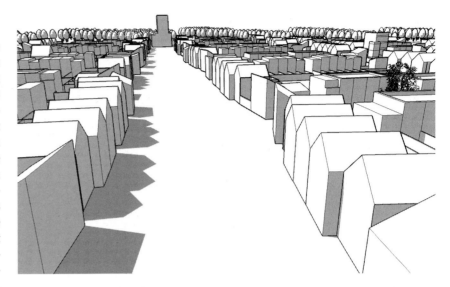

Figure 8.16   Protect and reinforce strategic views

Skylines and rooflines

Settlements can often have dramatic skylines in the distance (Figure 8.17) or a closer view of rooflines (Figure 8.18). Such features have commonly evolved over long periods but it would not take long for an insensitive development to destroy them. New housing should echo and contribute to the rhythm of both the skyline and eaves, and not detract from established and valued landmark buildings that might provide an established focus for a view. Where there is the potential to establish a new and interesting roofline, the opportunity should be viewed positively.

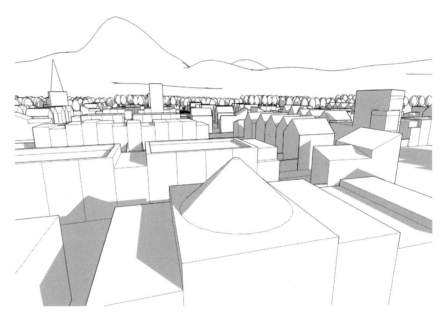

Figure 8.17   Skyline

Punctuation

Long, straight views down a street may be a deliberate feature of a scheme adopting quite a formal approach to the townscape, although such views can be monotonous and psychologically exhausting, providing people with none of the interest of a changing view and no sense of

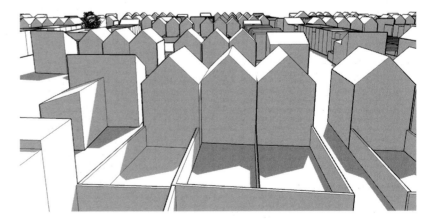

Figure 8.18   Roofline

progress for those walking within it (Figure 8.19). Looking at historic streets, it has been noted that often buildings within sections of a street appear to form groups, and that often individual buildings stand forward of the building line to close off one group from another. Such buildings are described as punctuating a view just as, for example, a comma punctuates a long sentence. The buildings are typically of a special type or design, giving them higher visibility within the street (Figure 8.20).

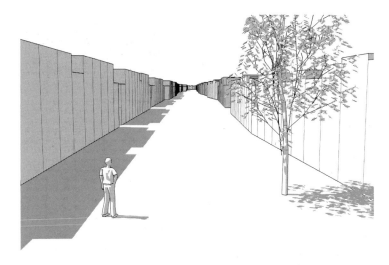

Figure 8.19 Long straight views can be monotonous and psychologically exhausting

Closed vistas

One of the most common townscape qualities is the idea of closing a vista (Figure 8.21). Long views through a scheme sometimes end in nothing; for example, the side of a house or a group of garages. To make a view more memorable, and to add a sense of purpose, coherence, and quality to a residential area, it may be possible to deliberately locate special house types to close an important view. On certain higher order junctions, this might include the careful design and location of apartment buildings. Whilst in quieter parts of a scheme, this might include simply varying the form of an otherwise standard house type in some way. At the most simple level it could mean making sure that no important views simply end in blank elevations, walls, or garages.

The engineering of the highway can also serve an important role here. Insensitive signage, poorly located lighting, or highway features like internally illuminated bollards, can undermine the quality of some important views by drawing attention away from more attractive buildings and landscapes.

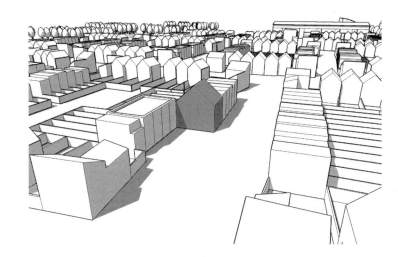

Figure 8.20 Punctuation can create a pause in an otherwise longer view down a street

Foils and incidents

In both the informal and formal townscape traditions the drama of a

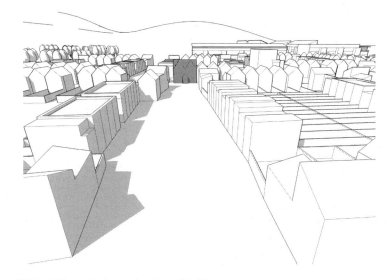

Figure 8.21 Deliberately designed or located buildings can close a vista

townscape is sometimes realised by a deliberate visual interplay between contrasting forms. This might result from judiciously locating a large tree within an otherwise highly urban setting. In this respect, both the 'urbanness' of the buildings and the 'naturalness' of the tree become highlighted. In townscape language, the tree is called a *foil* (Figure 8.22).

Other types of foil might include locating a round building in an otherwise rectilinear courtyard; locating a circus within a rigorously linear street pattern; an instance of contrasting architectural style or roof form within a view; a moment of contrasting colour within a scheme, or a dramatic change of scale, for example, from a human scale to the monumental. We might talk about how foils involve the complementary use of visual opposites, although this should not be seen as an excuse to throw discordant elements together. Foils typically contrast to a general visual theme, whilst both elements viewed individually would be considered as attractive or interesting in their own right.

Similar in effect to a foil is the townscape notion of an incident. A residential street can have a continuous form, but the view may have an outstanding feature, encouraging the eye to linger on a particular aspect of the view. This could be a taller building, or a building with complementary but contrasting massing. A building may have distinctive gables, or include a tower. An incident acts a little like a punctuating feature (see above) but it adds to or enriches a point in the view; rather than making a view of the street discontinuous (Figure 8.23).

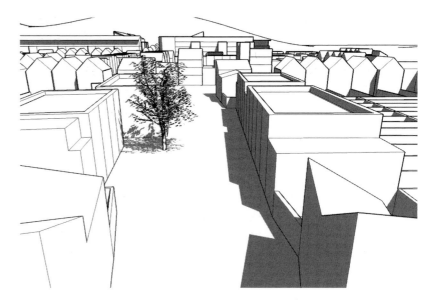

Figure 8.22   Natural elements can act as foils in an otherwise built environment

Figure 8.23   A change of scale and form can create a visually welcome incident in an otherwise monotonous street

Fluctuation

Traditional European towns do not typically have continuous building lines; instead, the buildings step back from the street to varying degrees. This gives the street space a fluctuating quality. The quality of fluctuation is at its most obvious where the street space isn't perceived as continuous, but as a series of clusters resulting from the widening and narrowing of the space created by the location of buildings (Figure 8.24).

Outdoor room

Planning housing into groups is an approach that can lead to the generation of a whole range of squares, circuses and courtyards that offer very distinctive place-making opportunities. To heighten their distinctiveness, these 'outdoor rooms' need a sense of enclosure, and careful planning of both the street cross-section and built form using appropriate building types. When they are successful, they can make particularly attractive domestic and communal settings (Figure 8.25).

Projection/recession

Although building lines might be continuous, it may be possible to compose the street view so that elements of the building (for example, bay or oriel windows) and roofline (for example, gables) project and recess slightly into the street. This creates added richness in the foreground and adds interest to the street scene. Selecting buildings and adding features to them does not mean merely creating random 'ups and downs' or 'ins and outs', as this randomness will be obvious. Instead, the variety should be carefully composed within the parameters of an established rhythm, as Sharp (1968) reminds us (Figure 8.26).

The authors of *A Design Guide for Residential Areas* (Essex County Council, 1973: 70) suggest similar concepts. They point out that groups of buildings can appear as either **passive** or **assertive**. A passive group would use a smaller range of house types, have limited variation in either the building or roof line, and use a

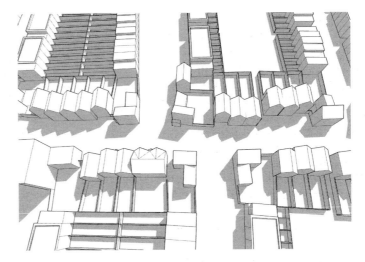

Figure 8.24   Building lines can deliberately fluctuate to create groupings within the street scene

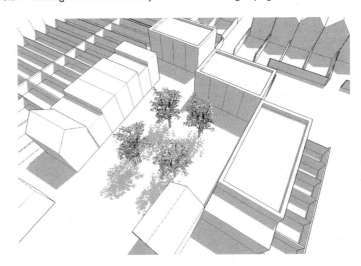

Figure 8.25   In contrast to a street, buildings can be grouped to form squares or courtyards that have the qualities of an outdoor room

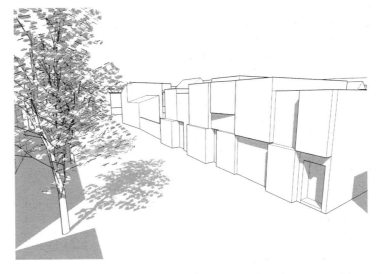

Figure 8.26   Elements of façades can be composed to project and recess to create a richer and more interesting view

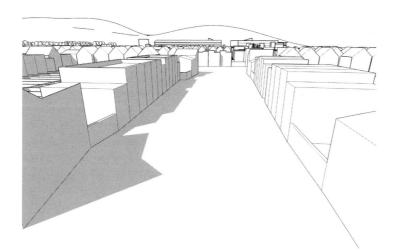

Figure 8.27   Passive townscape

limited palette of materials and colours (Figure 8.27). By contrast, more assertive buildings within a group would have a greater variety of narrow fronted building types, include complementary variation in materials or colours, and have variation in both building and roofline (Figure 8.28).

Narrowing/gateways

A common townscape trick is to narrow the environment, bring buildings closer together, or increase the scale of development at the entrance to an area in order to provide a sense of arrival. Gateways like this might reinforce the exclusivity of a scheme and therefore can appear excluding to non-residents. If this is considered undesirable, then the design may need to be made more subtle (Figure 8.29).

Corners and end elevations

Residential areas contain many outside corners where streets meet, and these corner sites are typically highly visible and can perform a positive townscape role. Built-up corners are memorable and distinctive, and they can be exploited by offering variation in building type, roof form, scale and massing or façade treatment. However, often at their worst, buildings on corners can ignore their

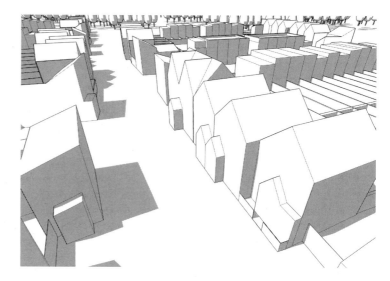

Figure 8.28   Assertive townscape

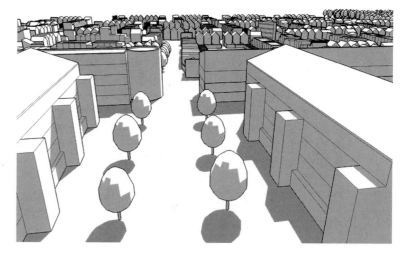

Figure 8.29   Buildings can change scale or be closer together to create the qualities of a gateway

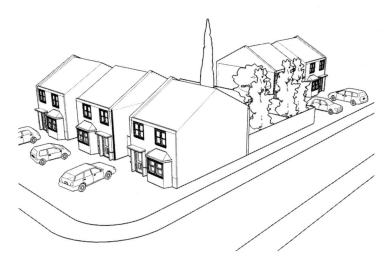

Figure 8.30   A bad corner

potential role. Standard buildings face in one direction offering blank façades to the other, whilst blank rear garden walls or fences border the entrance to the adjoining route (Figure 8.30). By adding extensions, bays, windows and other detailing to the end elevation, it is possible to make minor improvements to this situation (Figure 8.31), but the best solution would be to construct specially designed corner buildings to make proper use of the site (Figure 8.32).

It is important to remember that corner plots often have reduced garden sizes. To realise their townscape potential, therefore, plots may need to be larger; wide-fronted houses or apartments might be used, or standards for parking and amenity space could be reduced (Figure 8.33).

Figure 8.31   A better corner

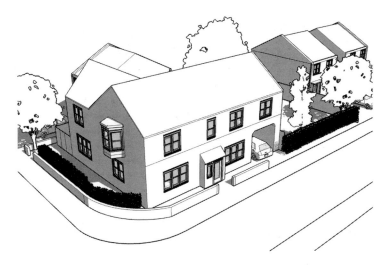

Figure 8.32   A good corner

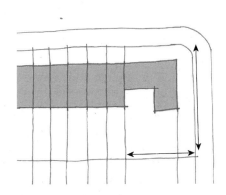

Figure 8.33   At corners plots may need to be larger or standards reduced to realise the townscape potential of the site

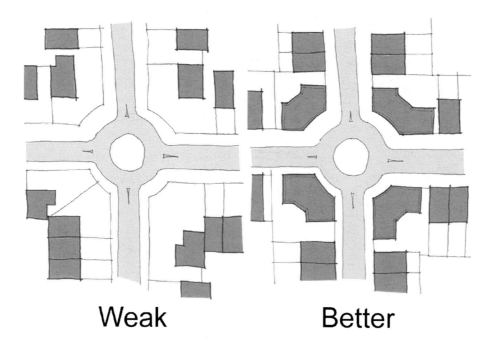

Figure 8.34 Roundabouts require special care to ensure that the road does not dominate the character of the space

Outside corners can be undermined by the use of highway management devices such as roundabouts, which force back the location of buildings due to the curvature of the road. Roundabouts require special care to ensure a positive townscape, although it might be useful to consider whether a roundabout within a residential area is necessary (Figure 8.34).

Inside corners are also a common feature of courtyards, squares and the tops of cul-de-sacs. Arranging housing on plots 'radially' can create poor triangular front garden plots and a dominance of driveways. However, it is possible to use build-

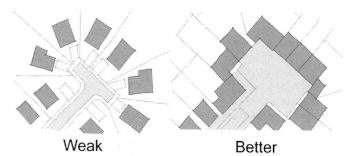

Figure 8.35 Arranging plots radially on inside corners does not create a satisfying form

ing forms or garages to reinforce the angularity of the corner and create a visually and functionally more pleasing solution (Figure 8.35).

Using natural features to define spaces

It is not necessary to use only buildings to define space within the urban environment; trees and shrubs can provide a distinctive townscape form and atmosphere. At the most general level, you may need to decide whether the character of a settlement will result from the buildings seen within a green setting, or whether any trees will be an addition to the urban spaces created between the buildings. It is possible, within a scheme, to vary its character by changing the role of the landscaping. At the urban edge, trees can make a visual link between the scheme and the wider landscape, whilst towards the centre of the neighbourhood they can be an addition to the urban spaces. Trees and other features can then be composed in either a formal or informal way to reflect, in many ways, some of the townscape functions performed by buildings. Through boulevarding trees can reinforce the formal linearity of the street, but at the same time define spatially; for example, the highway space from pedestrian areas. Trees and

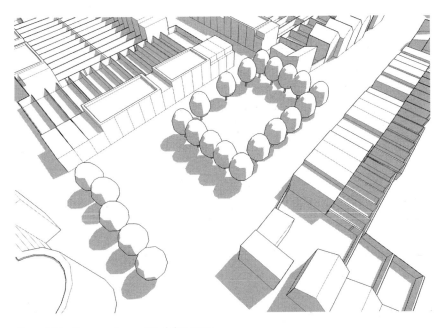

Figure 8.36   Trees can be used to define space

other landscaping can punctuate views, close a vista, create enclosure, form a gateway or offer shelter from sun, wind and rain (Figure 8.36).

It is necessary to select species carefully, and professional advice should be sought. Of particular importance is the need to understand both the dimensions of the fully grown tree, its necessary growing conditions, the impact of its roots, and any costs associated with its ongoing management.

Shadows cast by trees may help to keep buildings cool. Where this is undesirable, it is necessary to ensure that, at full growth, shadows tend to fall on the ground. Tree roots are also often a concern (Figure 8.37). In many trees 90% of roots occur in the top 60 cm of soil, and although they don't often go deep they can extend widthways to the height of the tree, unless root guards are used to contain the growth. Experts will inform you that tree roots don't grow into dry areas and it is extremely rare that they cause problems to solid building foundations (except in clay soils where the soil will contract as a result of the tree taking moisture out of the soil), so some trees can be planted quite close to buildings without negative impacts. It makes sense, however, to provide room for any anticipated tree canopy so that ongoing pruning or pollarding isn't necessary.

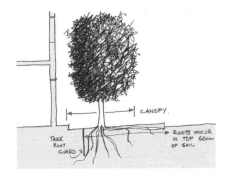

Figure 8.37   Make room for an anticipated tree canopy and consider how roots might be managed if they could affect a building

Phasing parcels

Townscape qualities such as those discussed above require some control over the design of the public realm (or street) environment, but often housing schemes are built out in phases by different developers. Therefore, to guarantee some control over the quality of the public realm, it may be sensible to make sure that developers are given phases that encompass both sides of a street so that they are encouraged to

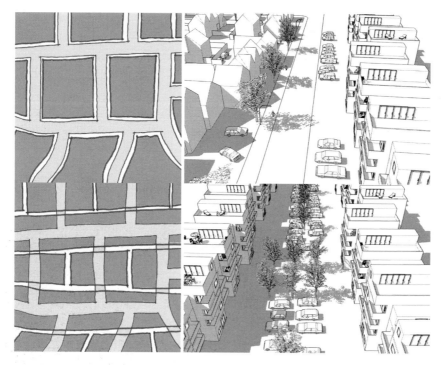

Figure 8.38   Creating two phases of development either side of a street will create an incoherent street scene so developments should be phased with streets in the centre to ensure that the scene can be controlled

have concern for its qualities, rather than phases being divided up, giving one developer one side of the street and one developer another. Most importantly, where possible this principle should apply to all types of environment within a residential area, including along the main estate roads that often suffer from lack of careful townscape treatment (Figure 8.38).

CONTENT

The content of a townscape refers to the styles, textures, patterns or colours that enrich and detail the urban scene. Whilst the configuration of both built and natural forms might help to spatially contain and define a particular place within a scheme, it is the content that enriches it. Aspects of the content requiring attention include the style of the housing, the materials used for building and hard surfaces, the nature of boundaries, the availability of front gardens, the use of street furniture, and the location of bins.

Housing style

In this book the debate about what a house or housing should look like has been relegated to quite a low position, even though for architects and residents it is a common theme for discussion. It is clear, however, that the style of the domestic architecture pursued will have a significant impact on the nature of the townscape, although there is no reason at all to suggest that very contemporary schemes don't need to think about townscape as much as more neotraditional schemes, even if the results will be visually quite different. The contrast merely highlights how important the style of architecture is to the townscape character. There are many examples of attractive contemporary townscapes, such as the courtyards of the Expo site, Malmo (Figure 8.39). By contrast, Chancellor Park in Chelmsford is based on coherent neotraditional approaches to townscape (Figure 8.40).

Figure 8.39   Contemporary architecture creates a contemporary townscape, but the traditional principles can still apply

Figure 8.40   Traditional architecture will create a traditional townscape although contemporary highway measures might make it original

Figure 8.41 It is possible to analyse the elements of a building and consider how they contribute to the character of a townscape

A useful shorthand for analysing the style of buildings is to consider it on two levels. Firstly, the *elements* of the buildings can be analysed. These would include the designs for characteristic entrances, windows or doors, as well as features like railings, gates or chimneys. The types of material used in construction. The patterns used in detailing or emerging from the construction techniques used, such as brick bonding patterns, or the deliberate use of colour to either help schemes fit in or stand out from their built or natural contexts (Figure 8.41). Secondly, the buildings can be analysed in terms of how the building mass and these various elements are used together to form the scale and massing, the roof form, the pattern of fenestration or the composition of elevations (Figure 8.42). Such an analysis may be helpful in understanding the context where new housing is being designed for a site within an historic area and you want to understand what constitutes, architecturally, the character of the context.

Hard surfaces

The materials used in creating the hard landscape make up a large proportion of any townscape view, and so they need to be considered carefully. The materials will add colour and texture to a place, whilst their selection and use can add to the character of a scheme.

Certain regions might have historically tended to use particular types of material because of their local availability whilst there are many functional and aesthetic paving traditions that can inspire a design. Hard surfaces are commonly varied to define areas of the public realm for particular types of activity or use, such as distinguishing a footpath from a cycle route, picking out a seating area, or highlighting a play area. Materials that will complement those used in the surrounding buildings should be selected; whilst lighter colours should be applied for larger areas,

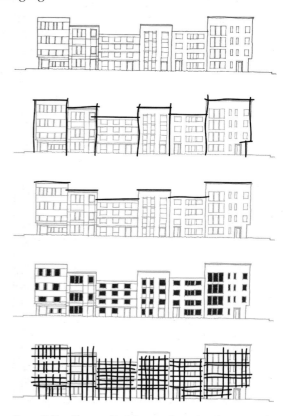

Figure 8.42 Groups of buildings can be analysed in terms of their scale and massing, roof form, pattern of fenestration or the composition of their façades

Figure 8.43   Paving materials should be selected to complement those used in the buildings, whilst colours, textures and patterns should be used sparingly so that the hard landscape remains relatively unfussy

and colours and textures should be used sparingly so that the hard land-scape remains comparatively unfussy (Figure 8.43).

Asphalt is the most common surface as it is cheap and can be readily coloured. Asphalt can also be imprinted with textures to create paving effects. Sometimes it is combined with other materials that are used for edging or to create a functional or aesthetic pattern, which gives it some character (Figure 8.44, top). Concrete paving slabs and blocks offer a diverse range of colours and textures, and tend to be relatively affordable, although over time they might break or become uneven if laid in heavily used areas (Figure 8.44, middle). Visually they mimic traditional stone pavers, slabs or cobbles, which tend to be more expensive but can last significantly longer (Figure 8.44, bottom). It is useful to note that if a local authority is to adopt the developed surfaces, they may have a preferred palette of materials that they can maintain and it may be necessary to consult with them to agree on what might be suitable.

Boundaries: walls, hedges, fences, railings

Different cultures have quite different approaches to the use of bound-aries within residential areas. For example, whilst low front walls are common in the UK, they are rare in the Netherlands. However, bound-aries can make up a large part of the townscape view within the public realm. There may be a tendency to cheapen the appearance of a scheme by relying on cheap timber fencing as opposed to spending money on brick or stone-walling and it would be advisable to judge the relative importance of particular boundaries for the townscape quality of a scheme and vary the materials accordingly (Figure 8.45).

Boundaries can also provide a significant level of richness and charac-ter to a scheme, and attention to their design should be given accordingly. This is seen in the use of white timber fencing in neotraditional housing schemes in the USA (Figure 8.46). The fencing can vary considerably in its design, but its use can create a significant degree of harmony within a scheme, and help to unify a street scene.

Figure 8.44   Paving materials make a significant contribution to the character of a place

Figure 8.45   Boundaries can cheapen the appearance of an otherwise good scheme or add a sense of quality so their form and materials should be selected carefully

Figure 8.46   White timber fencing used in Seaside varies considerably in its design but when seen together creates interest and a good degree of unity in the street scene

Gardens

Greenery is an incredibly popular feature of most residential streets, and the front garden, in particular, offers residents a wonderful opportunity to personalise their home environment whilst contributing to the collective view. However, it is sometimes difficult to control the use and quality of gardens. Trees, for example, initially planted in front gardens, bring mature greenery into a street view. Once they have moved in, however, residents may remove the trees, thus altering the desired character. Some restrictive covenants might stop this and can even indicate a necessary level of general upkeep.

In design terms, it is useful to note the popularity of even a small amount of semi-private space in front of a home, and that even a small planting strip can add a significant amount of colour to what could otherwise be a hard and lifeless environment. It may also be beneficial to group the gardens and entrances or drives of adjacent homes, as this visually extends the garden frontage within the street (Figure 8.47).

Street furniture

Street furniture refers to the lamp columns, planters, bollards, railings, cycle parking stands, pedestrian and traffic signage and signals, seating, public phone and post boxes and bins that occupy space within the street. Some of these pieces of furniture will have been purchased from supplying companies; although there may be scope to make them in some way original to a scheme or developer. Others, like phone boxes, might have a corporate form. Where finance exists, it may be possible to get original pieces designed for a scheme.

In planning the location of street furniture, a small number of principles are worth considering:

- Locate these important features so that they avoid creating conflict with activities which might occur within the street, such as putting planters where they do not get in the way of pedestrians
- Locate and sometimes combine them so that they avoid visual clutter, such as combining signage onto a single rather than multiple columns
- Group amenities like seating, telephone booths and post boxes in spaces created at well-used pedestrian junctions and where they are likely to be used
- Utilise features like bollards sparingly so that they don't create a cluttered appearance
- Carefully combine the location of street furniture with the patterns and designs used for the hard surfaces so that their relationship appears coherent (Figure 8.48).

Figure 8.47   Grouped gardens, paths and drives (bottom) might extend the garden frontage within the street

Figure 8.48   Street furniture should form a coherent part of the street scene where it is used

Figure 8.49   Bin stores should be designed as an integrated element of façades or shielded by planting or fencing

Bins

Bin stores should be designed into schemes; either as part of the façades or as separate, but well-designed, structures within the front garden where they can be shielded by planting (Figure 8.49).

SERIAL VISION

Although we experience some aspects of townscape when we stand still within a street or square, the richness of the environment isn't really revealed to us until we are on the move, and we can more fully experience the changing views that an urban area has to offer. An awareness of these changing views is what Cullen (1961) termed 'serial vision'. It reminds us that we should consider the environment as a series of places and emerging views, and reflect a little on how the environment will be experienced by its users who rarely stand still.

The concept is a little like comparing a photograph to a film. For example, architects often photograph their buildings as if they are the main focal point of attention and only experienced as static objects located firmly in space. Serial vision, by contrast, would consider the role that many individual buildings play in the constantly changing view of a town as we pass through it. The emphasis is most firmly on the qualities of the space created between the buildings, and the contribution to that space that individual buildings or other elements of the landscape might make (Figure 8.50).

Everyone experiences the urban environment in different ways and from very different perspectives. But the concept of serial vision might encourage a designer to get down into the streets and other public spaces that they are designing and try and compose together some of the various elements discussed above in order to build a set of contrasting, but

Figure 8.50   Serial vision

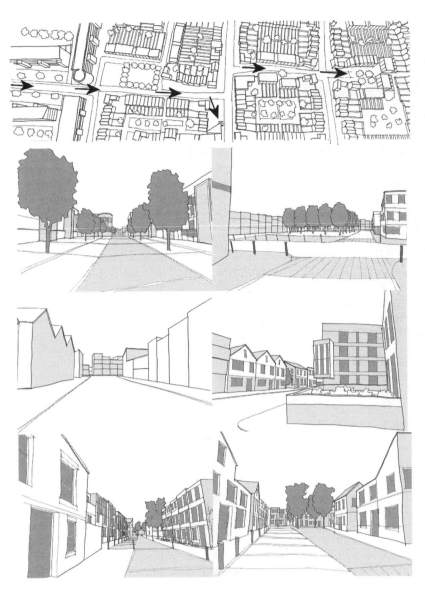

also complementary, places. This would be better than common streets of constant visual monotony or, by contrast, a townscape of random, unrelated and visually contrasting projects where the quality of the space between the buildings is actually an afterthought.

CONTEXT CHARACTER ANALYSIS

So far in this chapter we have considered how we can learn from townscape precedents and specific approaches to composing a visual drama. In addition, the concept of the content of place has been introduced as has the suggestion that designers might have a conscious regard for serial vision. New townscapes can also emerge, however, from an appreciation of the site within its wider context.

A townscape created within a scheme could be utterly original if it is built in an area without any particularly distinctive or valued urban or suburban qualities, with designers working hard to create an attractive scheme that bears little relationship visually to what has gone before. By contrast, however, a sense of place might be created, or an existing sense of place reinforced, by using aspects of the existing context to inform the design. In this way, the scheme can be seen to respond very specifically to the qualities of the site, the local context, or even the wider region.

The discussion in previous sections provides many of the themes that you might like to go and explore in relation to a context, but, to summarise, if the context is good then consider:

- retaining distinctive qualities of the site, such as water features, trees, buildings, existing field and plot patterns, and/or boundaries
- exploiting attractive views and turning the scheme away from poor views or 'bad neighbours'
- enhancing existing townscape qualities, such as any existing vistas, punctuation, a sense of progression and recession, or distinctive roof, ridge or tree lines
- reflecting the general dimensional features that characterise a place such as: the levels of plot coverage and plot development ratios, the characteristic location of buildings on their plots, the scale and massing of buildings, a characteristic storey height, building line or the sectional dimensions of typical streets and public spaces
- local domestic traditions which might shape the form of architecture or urban space that emerge. For example, the common and popular use of verandas in the south east USA, or
- the adoption of characteristic building forms or materials which are distinctive to a region, such as using a particular roof form, a distinctive type of chimney, a unique boundary treatment or type of stone previously used as a traditional building material within an area.

Creating places in this way means that designers need to spend some time within an area recording the features of the site within its context, as well as the building traditions that might be relevant from the wider region. This should be done by observation. These observations would give added weight if local people were to be invited to contribute their view as to what features make their local area distinctive, and which features they might like to see echoed or reinterpreted within a scheme.

In creating townscapes, designers respond to such an analysis in many ways. Some would argue that planners of contemporary townscapes should have control over general features like building lines, plot coverage and the general scale and massing of buildings along the street, leaving other matters to the discretion of architects working on individual phases. Writers of stringent design codes, or people working on new schemes in very high quality contexts, however, argue that a coherent townscape will only emerge if different phases used common elements in common relationships–especially if there are local building traditions that might be echoed in new schemes. The code writers of the new development of New Point in South Carolina (Figure 8.51 bottom) required that plot buyers design and build houses that echo the form and character of nearby Beaufort (Figure 8.51 top) with considerable success, although it would be hard to argue that New Point is an original contemporary environment.

Figure 8.51   The code writers of New Point (bottom) have required house builders to recreate the townscape of Beaufort (top) in South Carolina

TOWNSCAPE AND WAY FINDING

Features of the urban scene make a contribution to way finding as well as having a townscape role. However, it might be useful to consider the two themes separately within design, as a complex townscape might make an area illegible to its users. Lozano (1974) makes a useful distinction when he argues that different parts of an urban hierarchy of spaces should be assigned different visual roles. Streets that are the main connections within and between neighbourhoods, whilst having a coherent townscape, should certainly convey through their form a clear role as *paths* (see Chapter 7). Streets that serve a more local purpose can accommodate variety and richness within both the built form and townscape content. This echoes Lynch's (1961:6) quote from the previous chapter, where he said 'the surprise must occur in an over-all framework; the confusions must be small regions in a visible whole'. In other words, we enjoy getting lost in the richness of a complex townscape so long as we know how to find our way back to a main street that reminds us where we are and where we are going.

FURTHER READING

Camillo Sitte considered the visual relationship between buildings in *City Planning According to Artistic Principles* back in 1889, and in *Town Planning in Practice* Raymond Unwin (1909) reflected quite extensively on 'formal and informal beauty' and how it might be realised. In 1955, Ian Nairn wrote *Outrage* and discussed the destruction of regional distinctiveness and the spread of urban sprawl. Gordon Cullen's (1961) *Concise Townscape* remains a good introduction to his thinking, whilst Gosling's (1996) *Gordon Cullen: Visions of urban design* looks at his wider body of work. Sharp (1968) explored British townscapes in *Town and Townscape*, DeWolfe (1963) considered the Italian townscape, whilst McWilliam (1975) recorded Scottish townscapes. Stressing the important relationship between highway design and townscape quality is McCluskey's *Road Form and Townscape* (1979) whilst Appleyard *et al.* (1964) considered how townscape might be reinterpreted if seen from the perspective of a driver in *The View From the Road*. In *Urban Design: Street and square* Moughtin (1992) outlines concepts for, and explores examples of, formal townscape composition, and in *Making Townscape* Tugnutt and Robertson (1987) present their thinking as to how new buildings should be added to sites in areas of high townscape value. In *The Aesthetic Townscape* Yoshinobu Ashihara (1983) takes a more international perspective in exploring how people experience urban space exploring situations from across the globe. In a more academic vein Relph (1976) provides a conceptualisation of place and identity and reflects on trends shaping the contemporary landscape in *Place and Placelessness*. Whilst Lozano (1974) provides a critique of modernist townscapes in his paper 'Visual Needs in the Urban Environment', where he argues that we enjoy a degree of complexity and variety within our urban environments.

Unwin (1909) applies his early townscape thinking to neighbourhood planning. More recent works applied to housing layout include the original *A Design Guide for Residential Areas* produced by Essex County Council (1973), *An Introduction to Housing Layout* produced by the Greater London Council (1978) and the more recent *Essex Design Guide* produced by the Essex Planning Officer's Association (2005). Townscape also features strongly in Bosselmann's (1998) *Representation of Places: Reality and realism in city design* where he considers the role of new visual technologies in helping us understand, design and then represent places.

Finally, it is useful to review Jarvis' (1980) paper 'Urban Environments as Visual Art or as Social Setting?' Jarvis locates a concern for townscape within the wider urban design field and argues that the traditional picturesque approach to urban design can tend towards the exclusive and esoteric, focusing on the environment as an object to be merely appreciated. He argues that urban designers should also be looking for design concepts that promote involvement and respond to user experiences and needs; concepts considered elsewhere in this book.

9 Social life in outdoor residential spaces

SOCIAL LIFE AND TRAFFIC

A dominant theme in the design of housing areas during the twentieth century was the desire to make provision for the car. Within existing areas, this usually meant using previously open street spaces or even paving over gardens for parking. In new residential areas, increased usage of cars has brought the need to accommodate traffic to the forefront of street design, whilst layouts and housing forms have evolved to encompass this. This is an historic, but not inevitable, process and it is worthwhile considering the changing nature of street life and how the form of our streets and public spaces quite closely reflect the values and priorities of our societies. Streets have become a means for general thoroughfare, rather than destinations or places useful and used by the local residents. Domestic life and activity has therefore tended to withdraw from the street and other public spaces, becoming, instead, focused within domestic interiors and in private gardens. It would be nice to think that during the twenty-first century one of the dominant themes in the design of areas might be the reintroduction of socialising space into residential streets.

Hans Monderman, a Dutch highway engineer, has been working for a number of decades on creating people-friendly streets. He likes to draw a distinction between the *traffic world and social world* (Engwicht, 2005: 41–56). He suggests that drivers are now used to occupying the *traffic world* and that urban space has been appropriated to ensure that not only drivers, but other users of the built environment, conform to the types of behaviour that everyone expects. Within the *traffic world* the environment and the activities of people are constrained to be uniform, anonymous and predictable. Monderman argues, however, that drivers within the built environment should be required to enter and become subservient to the *social world* of residents and public space users who also inhabit urban streets and spaces. The actions and experiences of these people should be diverse, unpredictable, spontaneous, personal and voluntary. Rather than relying on strict and anonymous rules–usually created for vehicle users–about how people should act, streets should be designed to reinforce social relationships between all people. Designs and traffic management measures should make the environment a little less predictable for a driver so that they have to drive more carefully. For Monderman this means getting rid of the distinction between roads and sidewalks, and removing signs and road markings. Instead, streets should have shared surfaces, and people should mediate their way through the space by communicating directly with each other, particularly by using direct eye contact (Figure 9.1).

Figure 9.1   Streets should be designed so that people mediate their way through the space by using direct eye contact with each other

Over the last 40 years urban design has started to tackle the 'stranglehold' that vehicles have had over activities within the streets of residential areas. This is because in some areas the only communal spaces you will see are streets and the only human life you will see within these spaces are people coming and going in cars. This chapter therefore partly focuses on approaches to designs that might encourage social life and activities within street environments.

SOCIAL LIFE AND URBAN FORM

Although traffic has had a significant impact on the nature of activities occurring in residential streets, this can also be influenced by the forms of housing that have been developed and how they have been configured. Housing developed over the latter part of the twentieth century hasn't always created a positive relationship between the home and neighbouring street. Houses can be hidden behind walls, face away or be physically remote from neighbouring spaces, or even located behind garages (Figure 9.2). Bentley *et al.* (1985) makes much of the need to provide *active*

Figure 9.2   Housing behind high walls and located at a distance from a street will never encourage life in the public space

frontages to buildings along streets, and create scope for personalisation. If a home has no entrance to its neighbouring space, for example, then it would be difficult to support any form of activity–so often associated with entrances. Following this, it is important to ensure that the façades of buildings and front gardens provide an obvious visual link between the homes and their neighbouring spaces. In this way, residents will have a sense of involvement with the street, and hopefully, some sense of responsibility for it. Along this interface, it is also important to make sure that the threshold between the inside and outside is interesting and attractive. It is possible to make sure that streets within a neighbourhood have rich, interesting and active frontages, but it does need to be consciously considered–the result should be a street that is more active, visually rich and interesting and hopefully more cared for.

QUALITY VS. QUANTITY IN RESIDENTIAL OPEN SPACE

At the turn of the twentieth century, open space in residential areas was thought to make people healthier and meet a perceived need that had not been met in the streets of the industrialised cities of the previous century. The consequence of this good intention has been the provision of large areas of underused and sometimes badly maintained open spaces (Figure 9.3). More recently it has been accepted that, while recognising a need for open spaces–and not merely being concerned with the amount of open space–we should pay as much, if not more, attention to its quality and how it might be used. Such a concern should not, however, only be confined to the large parks that people might use once a week, but also to the smaller spaces provided within the vicinity of people's homes, often visited and used for daily recreation. While parks are really important, it is these smaller spaces, or 'pocket parks' that should also concern us.

Figure 9.3   It is not the quantity of open space within residential areas that is important, but the quality and ideas about how it might be used

BUCHANAN'S ENVIRONMENTAL AREAS

Buchanan's *Traffic in Towns* (Ministry of Transport, 1963) offers an early insight into attempts to manage the impact of vehicles on residential environments through the recommended implementation of *environmental areas*. Buchanan suggested that in these areas there should be no extraneous traffic, and consideration for the environment should dominate over the use of vehicles. This would be achieved by using a road hierarchy and traffic management measures so that through traffic passed by residential areas. Buchanan's own priorities shifted in practice away from concern for the *environmental areas* themselves and more towards the nature of the roads along which the traffic was to be channelled. An early review of two environmental areas in London also pointed out that, in an attempt to quieten some areas, the management measures implemented displaced heavier and faster moving traffic into other areas. In this respect, they made it easier to drive through the city, whilst degrading immediately adjacent housing. Environmental areas became islands of calm in a sea of fast moving traffic–a process that isolated residents within these areas from other parts of the urban environment (Figure 9.4).

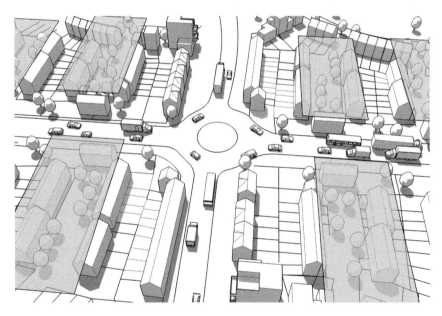

Figure 9.4   Environmental areas became islands of calm in a sea of fast moving traffic, a process that isolates residents from other parts of the urban environment

LIVEABLE STREETS

During the 1980s, Appleyard (1981) and Francis (1987) respectively argued that streets should be more *liveable*. Appleyard refers, in particular, to his often quoted research with Mark Lintell into resident satisfaction in three San Francisco streets where traffic volumes and speeds varied. The streets with less traffic were regarded by residents in a far more positive light, with evidence of both wider ranging social interaction and wider ranging home territories. In contrast, the heavily trafficked street resulted in both stress and withdrawal. In these areas, people tended to move home more quickly and seldom interacted with their neighbours. The disadvantaged or the old suffered most in such areas, as they were less mobile or able to move home. This work highlights the nature of the impact that traffic has on urban life and people's responses to their environment, and draws attention to the benefits of reducing the impact of traffic in residential areas.

Appleyard (1981) is clear that streets should have a variety of functions. They should be the setting for comfortable and safe urban living, where children can grow up and where the street mediates between the home and the outside world. As such, a street should be a place that children can safely explore and use for a range of activities. Streets can have both social and personal meaning for residents, whilst offering a setting for potential neighbourliness and street life, which should be acknowledged and protected. He argues that all street life is not positive but that the environment should allow residents to work out their relationships without having them suppressed by passing strangers in motorised vehicles.

Francis (1987: 28–33) also argues that, in contrast to the rather one-dimensional highway dominated street, designers should actively seek to promote a wider range of qualities:

1. **Use and user diversity**–allow wide ranging ages and social classes to be involved in the social life of a street
2. **Accessibility**–respect the access needs of all potential street space users
3. **Participation/modification**–involve residents in design and management, but also provide scope for personalisation and adaptation over time
4. **Real and symbolic control**–create a regime in which residents feel some responsibility for, and control of, the quality of the street environment, rather than the view that the street is the responsibility of a remote authority
5. **Traffic management**–slow traffic and limit through traffic to create the space and ambience for other activity to occur
6. **Safety and security**–provide a sense of security that results from having active building frontages, views of the street from people's homes and also a degree of coming and going of people in the street
7. **Ground floor–street relationship**–ensure that the street space links directly to the life inside the buildings fronting the street
8. **Comfort**–provide settings in which people feel able to relax, sit, stay-a-while and socialise during the right weather
9. **Ecological quality**–ensure that streets can contribute to environmental health. Greenery is a common request from residents, whilst street trees reduce noise, improve air quality and create visual relief
10. **Economic health**–a good quality street is likely to be popular, helping to maintain demand for housing in the street in particular, and within the built up area in general
11. **Environmental learning**–the street is an important context for the young in particular to learn about the everyday environment and social life, although it also provides an important setting for other people–i.e. the less mobile–to become familiar with neighbours or more actively socialise
12. **Love**–streets should become rich with positive associations and meanings leading to a high degree of attachment and care.

Such an attitude towards street design, and the issues that we should consider, is certainly at odds with professional preoccupations about carriageway widths, corner radii dimensions and counting the number of parking spaces.

TYPES OF ACTIVITY THAT COULD BE ENCOURAGED

Gehl (1996) provides a useful starting point for considering the types of activity that we might be seeking to encourage within streets. He argues that there are three types of activities that we might observe:

1. **Necessary activities**–things that we have to do
2. **Optional activities**–things that we choose to do, and
3. **Resultant (or social) activities**.

Previous studies have shown that the levels of necessary activity that occur in a street remain relatively constant whatever the quality of the environment. By contrast, however, improvements to the environment tend to lead to significant increases in the levels of optional activity, and that this in turn will result in evidence of more socialising between people.

Carr *et al.* (1992) spell out in more detail the range of activities with which different people engage and these might be usefully categorised in the same terms as those used by Gehl (see Figure 9.5). Using these ideas it becomes possible to widen our concern in street design beyond thinking about the efficient comings and goings of vehicles and pedestrians whilst also aspiring to accommodate a wider range of optional and resulting social activities. This in turn might encourage engineers to be interested in not only data relating to how many vehicles are passing through a place per hour, but also how many pedestrians and cyclists pass by in an hour; the time spent playing; sitting on a bench; or even measurements of the incidence of conversations observed in the street!

It is possible to think in general terms about how residential areas might be used in this way, but it is also important to consider in more detail the needs of specific groups. In particular, young and elderly people have specific needs that should be acknowledged.

From Gehl (1996) Life Between Buildings	From Carr *et al* (1992) Public Space
Necessary	Going to work/shops Deliveries Working on a property/car
Optional	Hanging out Sitting Lying Playing Gardening
Resultant Social	Talking and listening Observing

Figure 9.5   The types of activity that we might observe in a street

DESIGNING FOR YOUNG PEOPLE

The public spaces of a housing scheme are used most extensively by children and teenagers coming and going, playing and, as they get older, hanging out. This active use of space is important for physiological and psychological development. The neutrality of a public space is particularly important to young people who are developing their own identities and are seeking a space away from the direct gaze of adults and where they can start to be themselves.

Clare Cooper Marcus and Wendy Sarkissian (1986: 138–184) write extensively about designing for young people in housing schemes and point out that it is probably wise to think about and provide for the needs of young people by considering them in three age bands: preschool children, young children aged 5–12 and teenagers.

The preschool children need space close to home under the direct gaze of parents where they can play safely. Children at this age will tend to play within view of or audible range of homes. They will enjoy play equipment that allows them to practise their motor skills like swinging, sliding, balancing or climbing. They will also enjoy experimenting and manipulation of features like water or sand.

Cooper Marcus and Sarkissian (1986) also argue that you are most likely to see young children between the ages of 5 and 12 playing outside. These children socialise more. They are drawn to creative play and mastering their developed motor skills, which allow more elaborate types of activities like skipping, cycling or skateboarding. They become interested in rule-based and skill-based team games like football or basketball. They are keen to be creative, manipulate their environment and engage in fantasy, role playing and simple experiments like building a den or damming a stream. The commonly expressed adult thought that these children should play in either gardens or parks represents more a view of where adults think children should play, rather than a view of where children themselves want to go and what they want to do. A good design will try to acknowledge this.

Teenagers will engage in formal sports and socialising, but they will also want to 'hang out' in groups, either in visible locations where they can be seen by their peer group, or secluded locations where they are removed from the adult gaze.

The inventiveness of children in particular means that play will occur anywhere in housing areas, even using features of the environment that were not designed for play, and this secondary use of features should be anticipated. Most play will not occur in anticipated ways, and so don't expect that if you provide play equipment that it will become the focus of all play, as it is likely that it will only be used for a short while before other activities become preferred. In this respect, the child's quest to play can result in territorial conflicts with adults frustrated by the inconvenience that they perceive children create. For example, children often lay claim to pavement areas, bounce balls off walls or generate noise. Design might help to overcome some of these tensions, but it must be acknowledged that such tension often results partly from a socio-cultural trend. Ward (1978: p. 73), for example, quotes Joe Benjamin who states that: '[o]ur problem is not to design streets… that lend themselves to play, but to educate society to accept children on a participating basis.'

Residential streets and local spaces are a common site for play, and this is thought to be for four reasons. Firstly, because hard street surfaces don't get muddy and are good for wheeled toys, and activities like cycling or skateboarding. Secondly, they are accessible, being close enough to be used everyday and within the severe time restrictions imposed by parents. Thirdly, they can allow more expansive play over a wider area than back gardens where activities are severely restricted and more closely monitored by adults. Finally, they are preferred because children travel by foot and journeys will allow play between destinations.

The fear of a child being hit by a car is the main reason why, despite their value, streets have become undermined as play spaces. Studies in the UK have revealed that children tend to have accidents near their homes on residential roads; those aged between 12 and 15 years old are most at risk; accidents peak at the times when children are making journeys to school; and that seasonally accidents peak during the summer when children are outside playing without supervision (Department of the Environment, Transport and the Regions 1999b; Department for Transport 2002a).

In general, the accident rate in Britain has continually improved. This, on face value, would appear to be a good thing, but it is argued that the statistic merely hides a sad process; fewer children are injured by vehicles because parents have removed their children from streets fearing that the environment has become too dangerous. Engwicht (2005) refers to this as the process of residents psychologically withdrawing from their streets; a process that could be reversed.

DESIGNING FOR PEOPLE WHO ARE ELDERLY

Burton and Mitchell (2006) have written a much-needed publication about the design needs of people who are elderly or disabled. They highlight how elderly people have less strength and stamina and therefore become less mobile. In addition their vision, hearing and memory can become weaker, and they can suffer from incontinence. Burton and Mitchell argue that local streets are particularly important for elderly people who wish to maintain a degree of independence and self worth. Good streets offer very important opportunities for meeting physical and social needs, like seeing people, chatting, physical exercise and access to local amenities and facilities. They also allow people the enjoyment of being out in the fresh air and sunshine while experiencing nature and the changing seasons.

Their research highlights how elderly people are not always purposeful in using streets. Many trips are to the shops, post office, doctors or church, whilst a large number of people also use streets to visit friends or family. Many trips out are, however, merely about being outside, with no particular purpose or destination in mind. Where streets are poorly designed or managed, this can easily result in elderly residents becoming 'effectively trapped in their own homes' (Burton and Mitchell, 2006, p. 31) especially if, when out and about, they feel anxious, fearful, bored, confused, embarrassed or lonely.

APPROACHES TO LAYOUT DESIGN

Car-free schemes

A number of schemes exist where parking occurs at the edge of the neighbourhood so that public spaces within a scheme remain essentially car free. The Vauban in Freiburg (see Figure 5.1) and Französisches Viertel in Tübingen (Figure 9.6), Germany are successful residential areas where cars are parked in the secure community multi-storey garage at the entrances to the schemes. This leaves all other spaces in the scheme relatively free of traffic, although street spaces are still available for delivery vans and emergency vehicles. Keeping most traffic at the edge of the schemes liberates the public spaces within the rest of the residential areas for use in other ways.

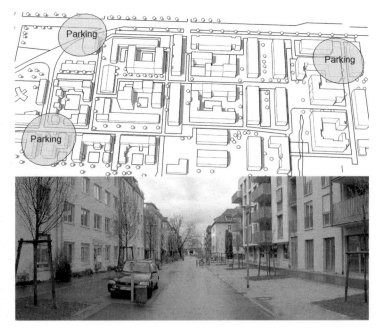

Figure 9.6   The car-free scheme of Französisches Viertel in Tubingen, Germany

Locate local communal spaces so that they are used

Some authors have suggested that in order for homes to be secure, all communal spaces should be located at the edge of neighbourhoods (Figure 9.7). This is because of the very unfortunate view that such spaces become the focus of antisocial behaviour. It is more likely, however, that where such a space is located away from the surveillance of homes it will become, not only misused, but also not used by those neighbouring residents who should regard the space as part of their 'home patch'. More recently, therefore, there has been a return to the tendency to locate local communal spaces at the centre of a relevant group of streets with houses and, more specifically, home entrances and living space windows, facing directly onto them (Figure 9.8),

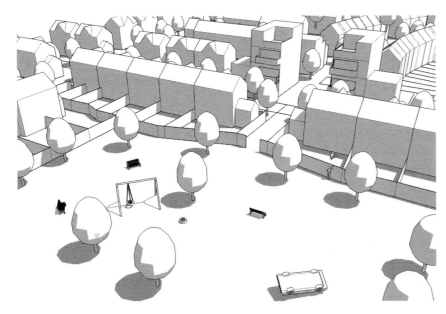

Figure 9.7   Some authors have suggested that in order for homes to be secure that all communal spaces should be located at the edge of neighbourhoods

Figure 9.8   Locating communal spaces should be done so that neighbouring residents come to regard it as part of their home patch

Sunny outdoor spaces

In temperate climates, people will use outdoor spaces where they get access to the sun. Thus, it is important to ensure that open spaces–or elements of an open space like seating–are not overshadowed by neighbouring buildings. In hotter climates, open spaces are more likely to be populated where shade is available, say from buildings or planting (Figure 9.9).

Activity is associated with entrances

Both necessary and optional activities within a residential environment are most commonly associated with the entrances to homes. If you have a high number of entrances occurring within a street, you will have a higher amount of activity taking place. If entrances are elsewhere then the environment will lack the incidental activity needed to create any sense of vitality or security. If you intend that a space should become an active place within a scheme, then it is important to ensure that homes have their main entrances onto the space. If entrances face onto another environment, such as a back street, it is unlikely that your 'active place' will be embraced by the residents (Figure 9.10).

Consciously consider how to animate a threshold between home and street and create space for personalisation

The threshold between home and street is sometimes designed so that residents can use it or personalise it (Figure 9.11). People often deliberately put carefully chosen objects in front windows.

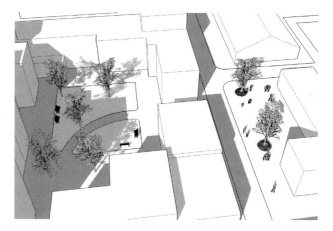

Figure 9.9   In temperate climates ensure that outdoor spaces get access to the sun

Figure 9.10   Face entrances onto spaces to create a degree of vitality

Figure 9.11   The threshold between home and street can be designed for use or personalisation

Homes can have front porches used for seating and socialising. Front steps can be used for formal or informal seating or as a location for children to play. People may choose to paint their front doors different colours, or even change their doors completely. They may put their own trees or plants into a front garden. They might add a seat. Porches and seating allow people a way of relaxing in or on the edge of the street. Other small, optional changes to the environment decorate and enrich the space and allow residents to convey something of their own identities and values into a street. Such personalisation needs space and front gardens are needed to allow it to happen, although these gardens do not need to be particularly large.

Sometimes such personalisation is kept to a minimum by restrictive covenants that limit how streets and front gardens or yards might be used. It is important to judge the extent to which such covenants restrict positive changes that people might wish to introduce, as well as some of the more negative changes that might be predicted.

Balconies and animated façades

Blank façades often result in a rather depressing environment between homes (Figure 9.12). For users of a street a degree of life can be observed through windows and from balconies. These glimpses

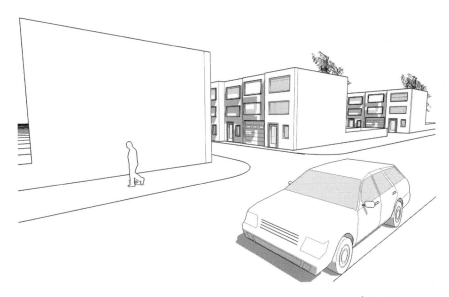

Figure 9.12   Blank façades anywhere in a scheme create depressing environments between homes, but they are most common on end elevations

become a part of the public space, as passers-by can learn something of the lifestyle of the people who live there. Residents can, however, control the extent to which their lives are visible by using curtains and blinds (Figure 9.13).

Blank façades might result from the inflexible use of standard house types or just an unconsidered layout, or from the desire to face homes

Figure 9.13   Windows and balconies create more animated façades and provide views of life within buildings

towards the sun, whilst insulating a north-facing façade (Figure 9.14). This results in an instant trade-off where the northern façade faces a street, and some form of compromise might need to be sought between the need to reduce energy consumption and a desire to provide signs of life.

Figure 9.14   An apartment building making the most of solar gain but with a less interesting façade within the public realm undermining the qualities of the street

Ground floor living

It may be desirable to allow residents of apartments on the ground level to have access to the spaces directly adjacent to their living areas (Figure 9.15). Access to this outdoor space would be a marketable feature of ground floor life. Residents would have a greater degree of control over the space just beyond their home, and they might personalise and care for it. Rather than becoming a sterile environment around the base of apartments, the same space may become a richer and more interesting part of the street, whilst the residents would feel more able to actively use these areas.

Create interconnected and generous sidewalks

Sidewalks or pavements are important, interconnected, traffic-free spaces, often used for a large amount of play and socialisation by children. Unlike gardens, these spaces can be used for more expansive games

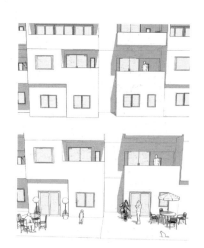

Figure 9.15   Give residents on the ground floor of apartments access to the space directly outside their living areas

Figure 9.16   On busier streets create interconnected and generous sidewalks

and less programmed forms of socialisation, whilst also being close to home or, for example, on the way to school. It is harder to play on them when they are narrow or always dominated by parking. If residential areas are going to have a reasonable amount of traffic going through them, then ensure that streets have generous sidewalks (Figure 9.16).

Design space for preschool children

Formal play facilities for preschool children should ideally be within sight and calling distance of their homes. Thus, adults should not need to give up other activities in order to allow their children to play there (Figure 9.17). Alternatively, all play facilities should have seating for

Figure 9.17   Locate play facilities for pre-school children within sight and calling distance of home

Figure 9.18   Play facilities should have seating for parents so that they can watch their children, but also meet and casually chat to other parents

parents so they can watch their children, while possibly meeting and casually chatting with other parents (Figure 9.18).

Play areas should be designed to be hazard free. The strong tendency in some societies is to build fences around play areas and equipment even if an immediate hazard, such as traffic, is not obvious (Figure 9.19). In this situation, it is the requirement of the children to alter their behaviour. In other societies, however, the view that children should have access to the entire environment for play is given more attention.

Figure 9.19   The tendency is to build fences around play areas and equipment even if an immediate hazard is not obvious

Figure 9.20   This play area is protected by bollards, but children are free to play more widely within this traffic calmed environment

In situations where traffic is calmed, play areas will be protected by bollards, but young children will be allowed to drift into other areas. This creates the conditions for social traffic calming where drivers realise that they must anticipate children anywhere within a scheme and that it is they, the creators of the hazard, who should drive more responsibly (Figure 9.20).

Play equipment should acknowledge the desire of the youngest children to master physical skills and explore the environment using their senses. Equipment should allow these young children to slide, swing, climb, balance, run and jump. Additionally, water is popular with children and the best schemes often have innovative, low maintenance water features for children to play with (Figure 9.21).

Figure 9.21   The best schemes have innovative, low maintenance water features for children to play with

Design for young children between 5 and 12 years of age

The fact that these children will want to use the whole environment puts pressure on designers to ensure that, within limits, it is safe to do so, and there is no greater case that can be made for introducing rigorous forms of traffic calming within the vicinity of homes. Often this means introducing road humps or chicanes, although in other contexts the evidence of children playing within the environment is enough to slow traffic down on shared surface routes (Figure 9.22).

Children of this age group develop a greater degree of independence, and start to play beyond the gaze of their parents or guardians. The liberty of children is more secure, therefore, where there are safe walking and cycling routes to specific sites of play within 5 minutes of home as well as between homes and schools or local shops and other amenities (Figure 9.23).

If possible, it might be desirable to leave a part of a site undeveloped, but manage it in the expectation that it will be used by young children for

Figure 9.22   Evidence of children playing on shared surfaces would be enough to slow traffic down

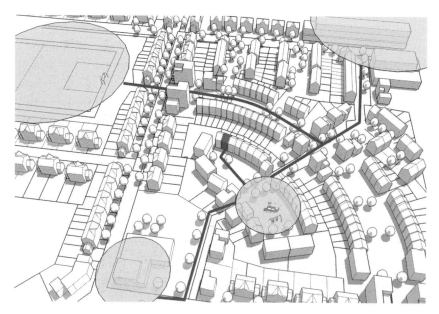

Figure 9.23   There should be safe routes for children between home and school, shops, play and sports areas, as well as any other locations which they might like to use

play involving contact with nature such as exploration, tree-climbing or the building of dens (Figure 9.24).

It is beyond the scope of this book to start discussing how to design the details of play spaces, but links to other sources are provided in *Further reading* at the end of the chapter.

Figure 9.24 Leaving part of a site undeveloped allows young children scope for more expansive play and contact with nature

Design for teenagers

The needs of teenagers are often least considered in the design of residential areas although, as a group, their needs might be regarded as the least demanding. They can travel further, but they are also very sensitive to territories that are not always visible to other adults. Wider neighbourhoods or larger schemes, however, should accommodate their needs.

Teenagers require 'hang out' spaces, including seating and shelter either on visible street corners or in secluded locations away from the gaze of adults. Such secluded locations might allow for outdoor fires and barbeques (Figure 9.25).

Figure 9.25 A hang out space in Rieselfeld provides good views and exposure on the top, seclusion and shelter underneath, along with a climbing wall and informal seating

Teenagers need hard surfaces for informally kicking or throwing a ball around (Figure 9.26), bmx biking, skateboarding or, for example, hoops for playing basketball (Figure 9.27). Seating around such spaces would allow observation and socialising as well as participation. These spaces need to be robust. They don't need to be beautiful, and probably wouldn't stay so–this should be accepted. Such spaces should be at a distance from homes so that conflicts over amenity do not occur.

Uninterrupted areas of grass are also popular and often used for informal team ball games or sitting and socialising in the sun.

Teenagers also need access to a wider range of more formal facilities like youth clubs, leisure centres, larger urban parks, malls and cinemas, and so access to either good cycle or bus routes become particularly important.

Figure 9.26   Fenced off, hard surface areas are used for informal ball games

Look for evidence of play

Analysis of a site should consider the value of existing features for the future young people living in the area. This might include looking for evidence of how existing children or teenagers in an area make use of the site. Where possible, consider protecting existing valued features such as open spaces, ponds or streams, and ensure that access to them by young people would remain both physically possible and socially acceptable following a new development.

Figure 9.27   Basketball hoops

Ensure that street furniture and surfaces are designed to acknowledge the needs of elderly people or people with physical disabilities

Surfaces need to be well-maintained whilst continuous, smooth but non-slippery 2-metre wide routes should be provided for wheelchair users, prams or the less secure footed, especially where rougher surfaces like cobbles might also be being considered (Figure 9.28). Crossing points should be kerb free. Some would argue that kerbs should drop to the road surface but it might be more appropriate to bring the road surface to the height of the sidewalk so that pedestrians are not inconvenienced, and vehicles have to slow down where people might cross. Features like trees, planters or bollards and arrangements for parking should not create difficult routes for the partially sighted (Figure 9.29). Changes of level should be kept to a minimum and always ramped with a gentle incline (1 in 20) if they are necessary. Wooden, rather than metal, seating is popular and should be provided with back and arm rests for comfortable use by people requiring support.

Figure 9.28   Maintain a smooth route through rougher surfaces

Figure 9.29   Features like parked cars, trees, planters or bollards should not create difficult routes for the partially sighted

Protect sidewalks or pedestrian areas from encroachment by vehicles

Use of streets is inhibited when parked vehicles encroach onto spaces that should be available to pedestrians. It may be necessary to protect certain areas from vehicles using them for parking by using kerbs, planters, bollards or other physical features (Figure 9.30). In addition, elderly people would feel safer where they don't have to share sidewalks with cyclists (Figure 9.31).

Figure 9.30   Protect sidewalks or pedestrian areas from encroachment by vehicles

Figure 9.31   Elderly people will feel safer where they don't have to share a sidewalk with cyclists

Public art in residential schemes

Public art might be a feature of a residential area but its inclusion should be carefully considered. Art used to reinforce a particular focal point within a scheme, could positively reinforce local resident identities and cultures. It might be used to reinforce a sense of ownership, care and concern for a space, and encourage people to derive new meanings from a scheme. Its use could acknowledge site histories, while creating some 'cultural distinction' within an area (Figure 9.32). It is important to remember, however, that any such art will need to be maintained by either residents, a housing association, agency or a local authority, and it might be worth contacting a specialist agency to help you commission and then maintain the work. Such organisations are aware of the pleasures and pitfalls of what might be involved.

Figure 9.32   Public art might be introduced, and specialist agencies can help with the commissioning and maintenance of works

HOME ZONES

Homes zones offer an approach to residential areas that bring together many of the design features discussed above into one design approach for residential streets. A home zone is a shared surface in a residential area where the design of the spaces between the homes provides maximum freedom of movement for pedestrians whilst also meeting the access needs of vehicles (Figure 9.33). The home zone is a direct translation of the _woonerf_ concept introduced in the Netherlands during the 1970s. A home zone should improve the attractiveness and safety of residential areas, promote greater use of public spaces for socialising and play, and encourage people to walk and cycle within their local area. A home zone should be a legal designation where, within the scheme designated by relevant signage, it is recognised that both pedestrians and vehicles share the use of the spaces between homes, and where, if an accident occurs, it is the driver who would be liable.

Figure 9.33   Examples of home zones

Home zone features are typically introduced into the quietest residential streets and require a distinct design treatment, which would require vehicles to proceed at roughly walking pace. Publications listed in *Further reading* at the end of this chapter provide detailed advice about how they should be designed, but the main principles for the design of a home zone are as follows:

Figure 9.34   The home zone should be overlooked by front doors and windows so that residents come to regard the street as an extension of their living space

- Home zones should not be considered in isolation, but should be linked together into a network connecting homes with relevant open spaces, play areas, schools, shops and other facilities and amenities. This allows people maximum freedom to come and go safely on foot or by bike
- Home zones should definitely be considered where there is a low volume of through traffic. This is because quiet streets are unused by vehicles for long periods of the day and so the space can be used for a greater diversity of activities
- The home zone should be bordered by entrances to people's homes and front windows overlooking the streets (Figure 9.34). This is because people who live on a home zone should consider the street space as an extension of their living space
- Home zones should not have sidewalks; instead make sure that shared surfaces are used which would encourage pedestrians to use the centre as well as the edge of the street space (Figure 9.35)

Figure 9.35   Home zones should use shared surfaces

- Make the entrances to the home zone clear. Buildings could be closer together as this will narrow the environment and change the character of the street from neighbouring areas. The highway could include a ramp onto the shared surface and possibly include other gateway elements like trees or planters (Figure 9.36)
- The entrance to a home zone should include a home zone sign indicating the status of the area (Figure 9.37)

Figure 9.36   Home zone entrance

Figure 9.37   Home zone sign

- Vehicles should not be able to drive or park too close to residential properties (Figure 9.38). This is because the shared surface is there to create greater freedom for non-vehicle uses and without this control cars might be parked too close to people's homes
- Traffic calming techniques discussed in Chapter 5 can be composed to slow down traffic, and measures should be less than 50 metres apart so that vehicles are required to maintain a slow speed. It is important to ensure, however, that the streets do not appear 'over-engineered' and so materials and calming features should be selected and composed to create an attractive street scene
- Parking, trees and other features of the environment should be used to limit significant views for drivers along a street. Longer views down a street only encourage drivers to drive faster, whilst a narrower or a closed view will encourage them to slow down and be more aware of things directly in front of them (Figure 9.39)

Figure 9.38   Vehicles should not be able to drive too close to people's homes

Figure 9.39   Parking, trees and other features might be used to limit significant views to encourage a slower driving speed

- Public lighting should be located to illuminate speed-reducing measures at night
- There should be adequate parking for both existing and potential new residents within the direct vicinity of people's homes. Home zones are not anti-car, and parked cars can make a positive contribution to the use of a street as people come and go from vehicles. Spaces can also be used for play when cars are not parked there. Parking arrangements can take a number of forms (Figure 9.40). Where views of parking are obvious within a street they might be shielded by planting to create a green character (Figure 9.41)
- Front gardens should be included or retained where possible so that residents can personalise the space in front of their homes and help 'green' the street.

Figure 9.40   Parking arrangements can take a number of forms

Figure 9.41   Where views of parking are obvious they might be shielded by planting

- Formal seating can be controversial so plan and locate it with care. If a home zone is attractive, residents would probably place temporary seating in a street (Figure 9.42), although more permanent features that can be used as seating might encourage people to linger for a while.
- Paving, instead of asphalt, could be used across the whole of the environment or in key locations to create a feeling that the home zone is a special place used by residents and not just a street dominated by people passing through it (Figure 9.43). Patterns of paving can highlight focal points for activities other than parking.
- The whole environment should offer the potential for play and related activities that do not disturb the peace of other residents. Where play

Figure 9.42   If a home zone is attractive residents will probably bring temporary seating into the street, although features might also be included that can be sat on

Figure 9.43   Paving can be used in key locations to help indicate focal points

areas are provided for younger children within the street they should be protected from incursion by traffic by using bollards, planting or other robust items of street furniture (Figure 9.44).

Figure 9.44   The environment should offer the potential for play and related activities that do not disturb the peace of other residents

FURTHER READING

Probably the most valuable book for considering the issues in this chapter further is *Housing as if People Mattered* by Clare Cooper Marcus and Wendy Sarkissian (1986). It has a wealth of design advice based on empirical studies into how spaces in residential areas are used. The images might appear a little dated by the advice is still very sound. Appleyard's book *Livable Streets* (1981) might be difficult to find but also offers an excellent introduction to this theme, examining the impacts of traffic on the urban environment, and early attempts to deal with the problem through traffic management and street design. Similarly, Anne Vernez Moudon's edited book *Public Streets for Public Use* (1987) examines the range of ways that streets have been designed to accommodate the needs of people. Although its focus is not exclusively residential, the book includes some very relevant papers including Mark Francis' 'The Making of Democratic Streets' (1987) which was referred to in this chapter. Jane Jacobs (1961) reminds us of the importance of the sidewalk, and how to knit neighbourhood parks into the urban fabric, both physically and functionally. Gehl (1996) and Carr *et al.* (1992) bring some conceptual clarity to how we might think about street life, a theme that could be taken further in other academic writing. More specific writing on children includes Ward's (1978) *The Child in the City* or the book *One False Move* by Hillman, Adams and Whitelegg (1990) which discusses declining child mobility. The needs of the elderly are considered by Burton and Mitchell (2006). In the UK, technical standards relating to the provision of pedestrian infrastructure for people with physical disabilities are provided in *Inclusive Mobility* (Department for Transport, 2002b) and readers should research if similar publications exist for other contexts. Many positive design ideas for creating an active interface between homes and streets can be found in Bentley *et al.* (1985), whilst a more specific discussion about how people might reclaim street space from vehicles, and how it might then otherwise be used, can be found in the works of Engwicht (1993, 1999 and 2005). More detailed discussions about the design of home zones can be found in Biddulph (2001), Institute of Highway and Incorporated Engineers (2002) and Department for Transport (2005). More specific thinking about formal planning and designing for children's play can be found in publications by the National Children's Bureau (2002), Ouvry (2003), Norman (2004), Bilton *et al.* (2005), Clark and Moss (2005), Rojals (2005) or Broto (2006). Some of these publications focus on how to involve children in planning and designing for play, some reflect on where and how children play and some are concerned more specifically with the provision of formal play spaces. *Housing as if People Mattered* (Cooper Marcus and Sarkissian, 1986) also contains a wealth of insight into how to accommodate space for young people within a scheme. Finally, the ongoing management of streets to keep them clean, safe and attractive is a particular problem which the publication *Paving the Way* by CABE and the Office of the Deputy Prime Minister (2002) addresses. It has a specifically British focus, but it does give an insight into relevant issues that influence street designs and how public authorities might then care for them.

Bibliography

Addenbrooke, P., Bruce, D., Courtney, I., Hellewell, S., Nisbet, A. and Young, T. (1981) *Urban Planning and Design of Road Public Transport*, London: Confederation of British Passenger Transport.

AEA Technology Environment (2005) *The Validity of Food Miles as an Indicator of Sustainable Development*, London: DEFRA.

Aldous, T. (1992) *Urban Villages: A concept for creating mixed-use urban developments on a sustainable scale*, London: Urban Villages Group.

Appleyard, D., Lynch, K. and Meyer, J. (1964) *The View From the Road*, Cambridge MASS: MIT Press.

Appleyard, D. (1981) *Livable Streets*, Berkeley: University of California Press.

Arnold, H. F. (1980) *Trees in Urban Design*, New York: Van Nostrand Reinhold.

Ashihara, Y. (1983) *The Aesthetic Townscape*, Cambridge, MASS: MIT Press.

Balcombe, R. (ed) (2004) *The Demand for Public Transport: A practical guide*, TRL Report TRL593, Crowthorne: Transport Research Laboratory.

Barton, H., Davis, G. and Guide, R. (1995) *Sustainable Settlements: A guide for planners, designers and developers*, Luton: Local Government Management Board.

Barton, H., Grant, M. and Guise, R. (2003) *Shaping Neighbourhoods: A guide for health, sustainability and vitality*, London: Spon Press.

Bedford, T., Jones, P. and Walker, H. (2004) *Every Little Helps: Overcoming the challenges to researching, promoting and implementing sustainable lifestyles*, London: University of Westminster.

Bentley, I., Alcock, A., Murrain, P., McGlynn, S. and Smith, G.P. (1985) *Responsive Environments: A manual for designers*, Oxford: Architectural Press.

Biddulph, M.J. (2000) Villages Don't Make a City, *Journal of Urban Design*, 5(1), 65–82.

Biddulph, M. (2001) *Home Zones: A planning and design handbook*, Bristol: Policy Press.

Biddulph, M.J., Franklin, B. and Tait, M. (2003) From Concept to Completion: A Critical Analysis of the Urban Village, *Town Planning Review*, 74(2), 165–193.

Bilton, H., James, K., Marsh, J., Wilson, A. and Woonton, M. (2005) *Learning Outdoors: Improving the quality of young children's play outdoors*, London: David Fulton Publishers.

Bosselmann, P. (1998) *Representation of Places: Reality and realism in city design*, Berkeley: University of California Press.

Broto, C. (2006) *Great Kids' Spaces*, Barcelona: Links International.

Burton, E. and Mitchell, L. (2006) *Inclusive Urban Design: Streets for life*, Oxford: Architectural Press.

CABE (2002) *Bungalows are Still People's Choice, According to MORI Poll*, CABE Press Release, 25 June.

CABE and Office of the Deputy Prime Minister (2002) *Paving the Way: How we achieve clean, safe and attractive streets*, London: Thomas Telford.

CABE (2003) *The value of housing design and layout*, London: Thomas Telford.

CABE (2005) *What home buyers want: Attitudes and decision making among consumers*, London: CABE.

Cadman, D. and Topping, R. (1995) *Property Development*, London: E and FN Spon.

Calthorpe, P. (1993) *The Next American Metropolis: Ecology, community, and the American dream*, New York: Princeton Architectural Press.

Carmona, M., Carmona, S. and Gallent, N. (2003) *Delivering New Homes: Processes, planners and providers*, London: Routledge.

Carmona, M., Heath, T., Oc, T. and Tiesdell, S. (2003) *Public Places Urban Spaces: The dimensions of urban design*, Oxford: Architectural Press.

Carr, S., Francis, M., Rivlin, L. and Stone, A. (1992) *Public Space*, Cambridge: Cambridge University Press.

Clark, A. and Moss, P. (2005) *Spaces to Play: More listening to young children using the Mosaic approach*, London: National Children's Bureau.

Coleman, A. (1985) *Utopia on Trial: Vision and reality in planned housing*, London: Shipman.

Colquhoun, I. (1991) *Housing Design: An international perspective*, London: BT Batsford.

Colquhoun, I. (1999) *RIBA Book of 20th Century British Housing*, Oxford: Architectural Press.

Cooper Marcus, C. (1982), The Aesthetics of Family Housing: the Residents' Viewpoint, *Landscape Research* 7(3), 9–13.

Cooper Marcus, C. and Sarkissian, W. (1986) *Housing as if People Mattered: Site design guidelines for medium-density family housing*, Berkeley: University of California Press.

County Surveyors' Society (1994) *Traffic Calming In Practice*, London: Landor Publishing.

Coupland, A. (1997) *Reclaiming the city: Mixed use development*, London: E and FN Spon.

Crawford, J.H. (2002) *Car Free Cities*, Utrecht: International Books.

CROW (1993) *Sign Up For The Bike: Design manual for a cycle-friendly infrastructure*, Ede: CROW (www.crow.nl).

CROW (1998) *ASVV: Recommendations for traffic provisions in built-up areas*, Ede: CROW (www.crow.nl).

Crowe, T.D. (2000) *Crime Prevention Through Environmental Design*, Boston: Butterworth-Heinemann.

Cullen, G. (1961) *The Concise Townscape*, London: Architectural Press.

Darlow, C. (1988) *Valuation and Development Appraisal*, 2nd Edition, London: Estates Gazette Ltd.

Del Mistro, R.F. (1998) The Compact City: Implications for Transport, in Freeman, P. and Jamet, C. (eds) *Urban Transport Policy: A sustainable development tool*, Rotterdam: Balkema.

Department of the Environment and Department of Transport (DoE/DoT) (1992) *Design Bulletin 32: Residential roads and footpaths layout considerations*, London: HMSO.

Department for Environment, Food and Rural Affairs (DEFRA) (2006a) *Municipal Waste Management Statistics 2004/05*, London: DEFRA.

Department for Environment, Food and Rural Affairs (DEFRA) (2006b) *Municipal Waste Management in the European Union*, London: DEFRA.

Department for the Environment, Transport and the Regions (DETR) (1998a) *Places, Streets and Movement: A companion guide to Design Bulletin 32, Residential roads and footpaths*, London: DETR.

Department for the Environment, Transport and the Regions (DETR) (1998b) *Planning for Sustainable Development: Towards better practice*, London: DETR.

Department for the Environment, Transport and the Regions (1999a) *20 mph Speed Limits*, Circular 05/09, London: DETR.

Department for the Environment, Transport and the Regions (1999b) *Child Road Safety Campaign*, London: DETR.

Department of Land Management of the University of Reading (1998) *Planning Mixed Use Development: Issues and practice*, London RICS.

Department of Transport (DoT) (1996) *Cycle-friendly Infrastructure Guidelines for Planning and Design*, Godalming, UK: Cyclists Touring Club.

Department for Transport (DfT) (2002a) *Child Road Safety: Achieving the 2010 target*, London: DfT.

Department for Transport (DfT) (2002b) *Inclusive Mobility: A guide to best practice on access to pedestrian and transport infrastructure*, London: DfT.

Department for Transport (DfT) (2005) *Home Zones: Challenging the future of our streets*, London: DfT.

Department of Transport, Local Government and the Regions (DTLR) (2002) *Green Spaces, Better Places*, London: DTLR.

DeWolfe, I. (1963) *The Italian Townscape*, London: The Architectural Press.

Dodd, T., Nicholas, S., Povey, D. and Walker, A. (2004) *Crime in England and Wales 2003/2004*, London: Home Office.

Duany, A., Plater-Zyberk, E. and Alminana, R. (2003) *The New Civic Art: Elements of town planning*, New York: Rizzoli.

Edwards, A.M. (1981) *The Design of Suburbia: A critical study in environmental history*, London: Pembridge Press.

Edwards, B. (2000) Sustainable housing, society and professionalism, in Edwards, B. and Turrent, D. *Sustainable Housing: Principles and practice*, London: E and FN Spon.

Edwards, B. and Turrent, D. (2000) *Sustainable Housing: Principles and practice*, London: E and FN Spon.

Edwards, B. (2001) *Rough Guide to Sustainability*, London: RIBA Publications.

Ely, A. (2004) *The Home Buyer's Guide: What to look and ask for when buying a new home*, London: Black Dog Publishing.

English Nature (2003) *Accessible Natural Green Space Standards in Towns and Cities: A review and toolkit for their implementation, Report 526*, Peterborough: English Nature.

English Partnerships and Urban Village Forum (1998) *Making Places: A guide to good practice in undertaking mixed development schemes*, London, Urban Village Forum and English Partnerships.

Engwicht, D. (1993) *Reclaiming Our Cities and Towns: Better living with less traffic*, Philadelphia: New Society Publishers.

Engwicht, D. (1999) *Street Reclaiming: Creating livable streets and vibrant communities*, Gabriola Island: New Society Publishers.

Engwicht, D. (2005) *Metal Speed Bumps: The smarter way to tame traffic*, Annandale: Envirobook.

Environment Agency (2001) *Water Resources for the Future: A strategy for England and Wales*, London: EA.

Essex County Council (1973) *A Design Guide for Residential Areas*, Chelmsford: Essex County Council.

Essex County Council (2006) *Designing for Cyclists: A guide to good practice*, Watford: BRE Press.

Essex Planning Officers' Association (2005) *The Essex Design Guide*, Chelmsford: Essex County Council and EPOA.

Ewing, R.H. (1999) *Traffic Calming: State of the practice*, Washington: Institute of Transportation Engineers.

Farthing, S., Winter, J. and Coombes, T. (1996) Travel Behaviour and Local Accessibility to Services and Facilities, in Jenks, M., Burton, E. and Williams, K. (eds) *The Compact City: A sustainable urban form*, London: E and FN Spon.

Finbow, M. (1988) *Energy Saving Through Landscape Design*, Volume 3, The Contribution of Shelter Planting, Croydon: Property Services Agency.

Francis, M. (1987) 'The Making of Democratic Streets', in Vernez Moudon, A (ed) *Public Streets for Public Use*, New York: Columbia University Press.

Gehl, J. (1996) *Life Between Buildings: Using public space*, Copenhagen: Arckitektens Forlag, 1987. English version republished by Danish Architectural Press, Copenhagen.

Girling, C. and Kellett, R. (2005) *Skinny Streets and Green Neighborhoods: Design for environment and community*, Washington: Island Press.

Golland, A. and Blake, R. (eds) (2004) *Housing Development: Theory, process and practice*, London: Routledge.

Gosling, D. (1996) *Gordon Cullen: Visions of urban design*, London: Academy Editions.

Greater London Council (1978) *An Introduction to Housing Layout*, London: Architectural Press.

Harris, C. and Borer, P. (2005) *The Whole House Book: Ecological building design and materials*, Second Edition, Machynlleth: Centre for Alternative Technology.

Hillier, B. and Hanson, J. (1984) *The Social Logic of Space*, Cambridge: Cambridge University Press.

Hillier, B. (1996) *Space is the Machine*, Cambridge: Cambridge University Press.

Hillman, M., Adams, J. and Whitelegg J. (1990) *One False Move... a study of children's independent mobility*, London: Policy Studies Institute.

Hough, M. (1984) *City Form and Natural Process*, London: Routledge.

Howarth, D. (2000) Water conservation and housing, in Edward, B. and Turrent, D. (eds) *Sustainable Housing Principles and Practice*, London: E F and N Spon.

Hudson, P. (2000) *Managing Your Community Building*, 3rd Edition, London: Community Matters.

Institute of Highway and Incorporated Engineers (2002) *Home Zones: Design guidelines*, London: IHIE.

Isaac, D. (1996) *Property Development: Appraisal and finance*, Basingstoke: Macmillan.

Jacobs, J. (1961) *The Death and Life of Great American Cities: The failure of town planning*, Harmondsworth: Penguin.

Jarvis, R.K. (1980) Urban Environments as Visual Art or as Social Setting? *Town Planning Review*, 51, 50–66.

Kelbaugh, D. (1989) *The Pedestrian Pocket Book: A new suburban design strategy*, New York: Princeton Architectural Press.

Kennedy, M. (1997) Water: Use and Value, in *European Academy of the Urban Environment, Designing Ecological Settlements*, Berlin: Dietrich Reimer Verlag.

Kent Design Initiative/Kent County Council (2006) *The Kent Design Guide*, Maidstone: KDI/KCC (www.kent.gov.uk; www.the-edi.co.uk).

Kulash, W.M. (2002) *Residential Roads*, Third Edition, Washington: Urban Land Institute.

Land Use Consultants (1993) *Trees in Towns*, London: HMSO.

Laurie, I.C. (1979) *Nature in Cities: The natural environment in the design and development of urban green space*, Chichester: Wiley.

Lewis, S. (2005) *Front to Back: A design agenda for urban housing*, Oxford: Architectural Press.

Littlefair, P.J. (1991) *Site Layout Planning for Daylight and Sunlight: A guide to good practice*, Watford: Building Research Establishment.

Llewelyn-Davies (2000) *Sustainable Residential Quality: Exploring the housing potential of large cities*, London: LPAC.

Lovell, A. (2005) *Traffic Calming Techniques*, London: Institution of Highways and Transportation.

Lozano, E. (1974) Visual Needs in the Urban Environment, *Town Planning Review*, 45(4), 351–374.

Lynch, K. (1961) *The Image of the City*, Cambridge MASS: MIT Press.

Madanipour, A. (2001) How relevant is 'planning by neighbourhoods' today? *Town Planning Review*, 72(2), 171–191.

Madanipour, A. (2003) *Public and Private Space of the City*, London: Routledge.

Marriott, P. (1997) *Forgotten Resources? The role of community buildings in strengthening local communities*, York: York Publishing Services Ltd.

Marshall, S. (2005) *Streets and Patterns*, London: Spon Press.

Martin, P., Turner, B. and Waddington, K. (2000) *Sustainable Urban Drainage Systems –Design Manual for England and Wales*, London: Construction Industry Research and Information Association.

McCluskey, J. (1979) *Road Form and Townscape*, London: Architectural Press.

McWilliam, C. (1975) *Scottish Townscape*, London: Collins.

Ministry of Transport (1963) *Traffic in Towns: A study of the long-term problems of traffic in urban areas*, London: HMSO.

Moughtin, C. (1992) *Urban Design: Street and square*, Oxford: Butterworth Architecture.

Mulholland Research Associates (1995) *Towns or Leafier Environments: A survey of family home buying choices*, London: MRA.

Nairn, I. (1955) *Outrage*, London: The Architectural Press.

National Children's Bureau (2002) *More Than Swings and Roundabouts: Planning for outdoor play*, London: NCB.

National Urban Forestry Unit (1999) *Trees and Woods in Towns and Cities: How to develop local strategies for urban forestry*, Wolverhampton: National Urban Forestry Unit.

Neal, P. (2003) *Urban Villages and the Making of Communities*, London: Spon Press.

New Urban News (2001–2002 edition) *New Urbanism: Comprehensive report and best practices guide*, Ithaca NY: New Urban Publications.

Newman, O. (1972) *Defensible Space: People and design in the violent city*, London: Architectural Press.

Newton, J. and Westaway, N. (1999) *Sustainable Homes: Embodied energy in residential property development: A guide for registered social landlords*, Teddington: Sustainable Homes, Hastoe Housing Association.

Norman, N. (2004) *An Architecture of Play: A survey of London's adventure playgrounds*, New York: Four Corners.

North West Environment Watch (2004) *The Portland Exception: A comparison of sprawl, smart growth and rural land loss in 15 US cities*, Seattle: North West Land Watch.

Office of the Deputy Prime Minister (ODPM) (2000) *Planning Policy Guidance Note 3: Housing*, London: ODPM.

Office of the Deputy Prime Minister (ODPM) (2001a) *Planning Policy Guidance Note 25: Development and Flood Risk*, London: ODPM.

Office of the Deputy Prime Minister (ODPM) (2001b) *Mixed Use Development, Practice and Potential*, London: ODPM.

Office of the Deputy Prime Minister/Home Office (2004) *Safer Places: The planning system and crime prevention*, Tonbridge: Thomas Telford.

Ouvry, M. (2003) *Exercising Muscles and Minds*, London: National Children's Bureau.

Panerai, P., Castex, J., Depaule, J.C. and Samuels, I. (2004) *Urban Forms: The death and life of the urban block*, Oxford: Architectural Press.

Perry, C.A. (1929) The neighbourhood unit, in: Lewis, H.M. (ed) *Regional Plan of New York and its Environs*, Volume 7, Neighbourhood and Community Planning (New York, Regional Plan of New York and its Environs).

Pharoah, T. and Devon County Council (1991) *Traffic Calming Guidelines*, Exeter: DCC.

Pitt, D., Soergell, K. and Zube, E. (1979) Trees in the city, in Laurie, I.C. (ed) *Nature in Cities: The natural environment in the design and development of urban green space*, Chichester: John Wiley.

Popular Housing Forum (1998) *Kerb Appeal: The external appearance and site layout of new houses*, Winchester: PHF.

Poyner, B. and Webb, B. (1991) *Crime Free Housing*, Oxford: Butterworth Architecture.

PRP (2002) *High Density Housing in Europe: Lessons for London*, London: East Thames Housing Group.

Relph, E. (1976) *Place and Placelessness*, London: Pion.

Roaf, S., Fuentes, M. and Thomas, S. (2001) *Ecohouse: A design guide*, Oxford: Architectural Press.

Rojals, M. (2005) *Design for Fun Playgrounds*, Barcelona: Links International.

Roseland, M. (1998) *Towards Sustainable Communities: Resources for citizens and their Governments*, Gabriola Island: New Society Publishers.

Rowley, A. (1996) Mixed-use development: ambiguous concept, simplistic analysis and wishful thinking? *Planning Practice and Research*, 11(1), 85–97.

Rudlin, R. and Falk, N. (1999) *Building the 21st Century Home: The sustainable urban neighbourhood*, Oxford: Architectural Press.

Schmitz, A. (ed) (2004) *Residential Development Handbook*, Third Edition, Washington: Urban Land Institute.

Shankland Cox (1994) *Mixed Uses in Buildings, Blocks and quarters*, Luxembourg: Office for Official Publications of the European Communities.

Sharp, T. (1968) *Town and Townscape*, London: John Murray.

Sitte, C. (1889) *City Planning According to Artistic Principles*, translated in Collins, G.R. and Crasemann Collins, C. (1986) *Camillo Sitte: The Birth of Modern City Planning*, New York: Rizzoli.

Southworth, M. (1996) Walkable Suburbs? An Evaluation of Neotraditional Communities at the Urban Edge, *Journal of the American Planning Association*, Winter, 28.

Southworth, M. and Ben-Joseph, E. (2003) *Streets and the Shaping of Towns and Cities*, New York: McGraw-Hill.

Spon's *Architects' and Builders' Price Book* (2005) London: Spon Press.

State Government of Victoria (2005) *Melbourne 2030*, Melbourne: SGV, Department of Sustainability and Environment.

State of Western Australia (2000) *Liveable Neighbourhoods: A Western Australian government sustainable cities initiative*, Perth: Western Australia Planning Commission.

Steventon, G. (1996) Defensible space: a critical review of the theory and practice of a crime prevention strategy, *Urban Design International*, 1(3), 235–245.

Stollard, P. (1991) *Crime Pevention Through Housing Design*, London: Chapman and Hall.

Taylor, D. (2000) Renewable energy in housing, in Edwards, B. and Turrent, D. (eds) *Sustainable Housing Principles and Practice*, London: E F and N Spon.

Towers, G. (2005) *At Home in the City: An introduction to urban housing design*, Oxford: Architectural Press.

Town and Country Planning Association (TCPA) (2004) *Biodiversity by Design: A guide for sustainable communities*, London: TCPA.

Trancik, R. (1986) *Finding Lost Space: Theories of urban design*, Chichester: John Wiley and Sons.

Tugnutt, A. and Robertson, M. (1987) *Making Townscape: A contextual approach to building in an urban setting*, London: Mitchell.

UK Government (1994) *Biodiversity: The UK action plan*, London HMSO.

United Nations Conference on the Environment and Development (UNCED) (1992) *Agenda 21: Programme of action for sustainable development*. Rio Declaration on Environment and Development, New York: United Nations Department of Public Information.

Unwin, R. (1909) *Town Planning in Practice: An introduction to the art of designing cities and suburbs*, London: T. Fisher Unwin.

Urban Task Force (1999) *Towards and Urban Renaissance*, London: E F and N Spon.

URBED (1999) *But Would You Live There? Shaping attitudes to urban living*, London: Urban Task Force.

Vernez Moudon, A (ed) (1987) *Public Streets for Public Use*, New York: Columbia University Press.

Ward, C. (1978) *The Child in the City*, London: Architectural Press.

White, P. (2002) *Public Transport: Its planning, management and operation*, Fourth Edition, London: Spon Press.

Zhou, J. (2005) *Urban Housing Forms*, Oxford: Architectural Press.

Index